Country Pork

Editor: Julie Schnittka
Food Editor: Mary Beth Jung
Assistant Food Editor: Coleen Martin
Senior Home Economist: Mary Fullmer
Assistant Editor: Kristine Krueger
Art Director: Stephanie Marchese
Production: Ellen Lloyd
Test Kitchen Home Economists: Karla Spies, Julie Seguin, Rochelle Schmidt
Test Kitchen Assistants: Suzi Hampton, Judith Scholovich
Photography: Scott Anderson, Glenn Thiesenhusen
Photo Studio Coordinator: Anne Schimmel

©1996, Reiman Publications, L.P.
5400 S. 60th St., Greendale WI 53129
International Standard Book Number: 0-89821-194-8
Library of Congress Catalog Card Number: 96-71401

PICTURED ABOVE. Tangy Glazed Ham (page 76) and Stuffed Pork Chops (page 77).

PICTURED ON THE COVER. Clockwise from top: Rosemary Pork Roast with Vegetables (page 68), Tender Pork Sandwiches (page 22), Ginger Pork Chops with Caramelized Onions (page 47) and Apple-Topped Ham Steak (page 46).

Folks Are Lickin' Their Chops

(over our chops, roasts, ribs and tenderloins!)

SUCCULENT FLAVOR and pure versatility have made pork a mealtime mainstay for generations of cooks. But there's never been a single source like this for hundreds of practical pork preparation ideas…until now.

Country Pork puts over 280 family-approved and kitchen-tested recipes right at your fingertips.

The savory selections you'll find in this unique cookbook will help you make marvelous meals out of ribs, roasts, tenderloins, bacon, ham, sausage…and (of course) those ever-popular chops! No matter what cut of pork you plan to prepare, you're sure to find a recipe to create unforgettable fare.

Readers of *Country Woman* and *Taste of Home* magazines eagerly shared these family-favorite recipes, and you'll come to rely on them again and again for simple dinners at home or special occasions.

Inviting the gang over to watch the game? In West Springfield, Pennsylvania, Gena Kuntz's "Hawaiian Pizza" (page 68) always scores big with hungry fans.

Gwen Goss of Garden City, Kansas hears cheers when she turns ordinary ground pork into saucy "Barbecued Meatballs" (page 70).

Planning a more formal gathering? Pat Panopoulos' "Stuffed Crown Roast of Pork" (page 69) showcases tart cranberries and a sweet orange glaze. Try this dish and you'll see why it makes continuing appearances on her dining room table in Spring Hill, Florida.

These examples provide just a taste of the many Meaty Oven Meals included in this full-color cookbook. In addition, you'll find many more recipes for Skillet Main Dishes, Slow-Cooked Specialties, Comforting Casseroles…even Ribs & Grilled Favorites.

But don't limit your use of pork to main courses alone! *Country Pork* will show you plenty of innovative ways to include it in Hearty Starters & Snacks, Salads & Side Dishes, Sandwiches for All Seasons, and Country Soups & Stews.

Busy folks have always depended on pork because it cooks up in no time. Within the colorful pages of this unique collection, there are 35 "Quick & Easy" recipes that have especially *short* ingredient lists and *fast* preparation times.

Today's pork is leaner—and more delicious—than ever before, so people on restricted diets can also enjoy its country-style taste. Just look for the 38 recipes marked with this ✓ to alert you to dishes that are prepared with less salt, sugar and fat and that include Diabetic Exchanges.

So, go ahead and dig into this one-of-a-kind cookbook. Bringing home the bacon—and all the other full-of-flavor cuts of pork featured on the following pages—has never been more tasty.

Country Pork

Hearty Starters & Snacks...6

Salads & Side Dishes...10

Sandwiches for All Seasons...20

Country Soups & Stews...32

Skillet Main Dishes...44

Slow-Cooked Specialties...62

Meaty Oven Meals...66

Comforting Casseroles...84

Ribs & Grilled Favorites...96

Index...110

FOR ADDITIONAL COPIES of *Country Pork* or information on other books, write: *Taste of Home* Books, P.O. Box 990, Greendale WI 53129. **Credit card orders call toll-free 1-800/558-1013.**

Hearty Starters & Snacks

Ham Balls

Janet Zeager, Middletown, Pennsylvania
(PICTURED AT LEFT)

These mouth-watering meatballs are a Pennsylvania Dutch specialty, so I enjoy offering them to folks who come to visit. The combination of ham and pork makes these a hearty snack.

    1 pound fully cooked ham, finely ground
    1 pound ground pork
    1 cup milk
    1 cup crushed cornflakes
    1 egg, lightly beaten
    1/4 cup packed brown sugar
    1 tablespoon ground mustard
    1/2 teaspoon salt
GLAZE:
    1 cup packed brown sugar
    1/4 cup vinegar
    1 tablespoon ground mustard

In a large bowl, combine the first eight ingredients; blend just until mixed. Shape into 1-in. balls; place in a single layer in a greased 15-in. x 10-in. x 1-in. baking pan. In a saucepan over medium heat, combine glaze ingredients; cook and stir until sugar is dissolved. Spoon over ham balls. Cover and bake at 350° for 15-20 minutes. Uncover and bake 15-20 minutes more or until ham balls are just beginning to brown. Gently toss in glaze. Serve warm. **Yield:** about 8 dozen.

Super Ham Spread

Paula Pelis, Rocky Point, New York
(PICTURED AT LEFT)

I reach for this recipe whenever I need a simple yet special snack for guests. As a matter of fact, I've been serving it for over 20 years, and it's always met with rave reviews.

    1 container (8 ounces) cold pack cheddar cheese
        spread, softened
    1 package (3 ounces) cream cheese, softened
1-1/2 cups minced fully cooked ham
    1/3 cup ground pecans
    1/4 cup finely chopped green onions
    1 tablespoon Dijon-mayonnaise blend
    1 teaspoon Worcestershire sauce

FESTIVE FINGER FOOD. *Pictured at left, top to bottom: Ham Balls, Super Ham Spread and Cajun Pork Sandwiches (all recipes on this page).*

---

    1 teaspoon prepared horseradish
Party bread, crackers *or* pretzels

In a bowl, combine cheese spread and cream cheese; mix well. Stir in the next six ingredients. Cover and chill at least 1 hour. Let stand at room temperature 30 minutes before serving. Serve with party bread, crackers or pretzels. **Yield:** 2-1/2 cups.

SUPER SERVING SUGGESTION. Instead of serving the Ham Balls with toothpicks, use pretzel sticks! Everyone will love the creative touch, and you'll appreciate the reduced waste and mess.

Cajun Pork Sandwiches

Mae Kruse, Monee, Illinois
(PICTURED AT LEFT)

This recipe's specially seasoned rub gives tender juicy pork a slightly spicy flavor. You'll watch in delight as these delicious sandwiches disappear from your buffet table! I also like to prepare these for weekend lunches.

✓ This tasty dish uses less sugar, salt and fat. Recipe includes *Diabetic Exchanges.*

    2 pork tenderloins (1 pound *each*), trimmed
    2 teaspoons vegetable oil
    3 tablespoons paprika
    2 teaspoons dried oregano
    2 teaspoons dried thyme
1-1/2 teaspoons garlic powder
    1/2 teaspoon pepper
    1/2 teaspoon salt, optional
    1/2 teaspoon ground cumin
    1/4 teaspoon ground nutmeg
    1/4 teaspoon cayenne pepper
    36 French bread slices *or* mini buns
Butter *or* mayonnaise
Lettuce leaves
Thin slivers of green and sweet red pepper

Place tenderloins in a greased 13-in. x 9-in. x 2-in. baking pan. Rub each with 1 teaspoon oil. In a bowl, combine paprika, oregano, thyme, garlic powder, pepper, salt if desired, cumin, nutmeg and cayenne; pat over tenderloins. Cover and refrigerate overnight. Bake at 425° for 25-30 minutes or until a meat thermometer reads 160°-170°. Let stand for 10 minutes; thinly slice. Spread bread or buns with butter or mayonnaise; top with lettuce, pork and green and red pepper. **Yield:** 3 dozen. **Diabetic Exchanges:** One sandwich (prepared without salt and served on a mini bun with 1 teaspoon fat-free mayonnaise) equals 1 starch, 1 lean meat; also, 124 calories, 194 mg sodium, 15 mg cholesterol, 16 gm carbohydrate, 8 gm protein, 3 gm fat.

Tasty Pork Nuggets

Katie Koziolek, Hartland, Minnesota

Through my 30 years of being married to a pork producer, I've come across quite a few wonderful recipes. These nuggets are fabulous finger food for snacks, lunches and dinners.

✓ This tasty dish uses less sugar, salt and fat. Recipe includes *Diabetic Exchanges*.

    1 cup cornflake crumbs
    1/3 cup toasted wheat germ
    3 tablespoons sesame seeds
1-1/2 teaspoons dried parsley flakes
    1/2 teaspoon paprika
    1/2 teaspoon ground mustard
    1/2 teaspoon celery salt
    1/2 teaspoon onion powder
    1/4 teaspoon lemon-pepper seasoning
    1/4 teaspoon salt, optional
    1 pound lean boneless pork, cut into 1-inch x
        1-1/2-inch cubes
    1 cup plain nonfat yogurt

Combine the cornflake crumbs, wheat germ, sesame seeds, parsley, paprika, mustard, celery salt, onion powder, lemon pepper and salt if desired; set aside. Dip pork cubes in yogurt, then roll in crumb mixture. Arrange pork in a single layer on a baking pan coated with nonstick cooking spray. Bake at 400° for 15-18 minutes or until juices run clear. For a crispier coating, broil for 2-3 minutes after baking. **Yield:** 2-1/2 dozen. **Diabetic Exchanges:** Three nuggets (prepared without salt) equals 2 lean meat, 1/2 starch; also, 128 calories, 135 mg sodium, 27 mg cholesterol, 8 gm carbohydrate, 13 gm protein, 5 gm fat.

Sausage Dip

Susie Wingert, Panama, Iowa

This warm sausage dip is a family-favorite snack on cool fall days. The men in your family will especially love this country-style appetizer.

1-1/2 pounds bulk pork sausage
2-1/2 cups chopped fresh mushrooms
    2 medium green peppers, chopped
    1 large tomato, seeded and chopped
    1 medium red onion, chopped
1-1/2 teaspoons salt
    1 teaspoon pepper
    1 teaspoon garlic powder
    1/2 teaspoon onion powder
    2 packages (8 ounces *each*) cream cheese, cubed
    1 cup (8 ounces) sour cream
Tortilla chips

In a large skillet over medium heat, cook the sausage until no longer pink; drain. Add the next eight ingredients; cook until the vegetables are tender. Reduce heat to low; add cream cheese and sour cream. Cook and stir until cheese is

melted and well blended (do not boil). Serve warm with tortilla chips. **Yield:** 6 cups.

Bacon-Wrapped Water Chestnuts

Debi Jellison, Jacksonville, Florida

Whenever I attend a potluck, folks always ask me to bring these snacks—they've become my trademark. I especially like to prepare them for holiday gatherings.

    1 pound sliced bacon
    2 cans (8 ounces *each*) whole water chestnuts,
        rinsed and drained
    1 cup ketchup
    3/4 cup packed brown sugar

Cut bacon strips into thirds; wrap a strip around each water chestnut and secure with wooden picks. Place in an ungreased 15-in. x 10-in. x 1-in. baking pan. Bake at 375° for 25 minutes or until bacon is crisp. Meanwhile, in a small saucepan, combine ketchup and brown sugar; cook and stir over medium heat until sugar dissolves. Remove chestnuts to paper towels; drain. Dip in ketchup mixture; place in a lightly greased 13-in. x 9-in. x 2-in. baking pan. Spoon remaining sauce over chestnuts. Return to the oven for 10 minutes. **Yield:** about 5 dozen.

Smokehouse Quesadillas

Sherri Winters, Trenton, Texas

Quesadillas are a nice alternative to traditional finger sandwiches. But our teenage children have also been known to eat them for breakfast!

✓ This tasty dish uses less sugar, salt and fat. Recipe includes *Diabetic Exchanges*.

    1/4 cup ranch salad dressing
    6 flour tortillas (7 inches)
    6 thin slices (1 ounce *each*) fully cooked ham
    6 thin slices (1 ounce *each*) Monterey Jack cheese
Salsa

Spread about 2 teaspoons of dressing on each tortilla. Top each with a slice of ham and a slice of cheese. Roll up jelly-roll style. In a lightly greased skillet, cook quesadillas over medium heat, turning constantly, until cheese is melted. Cut each quesadilla into four pieces. Serve with salsa for dipping. **Microwave Directions:** Assemble quesadillas as directed. Wrap each quesadilla in paper towel and microwave on high for 1 minute or until cheese is melted. This recipe was tested in a 700-watt microwave. **Yield:** 2 dozen. **Diabetic Exchanges:** One serving of two pieces with 1 tablespoon salsa (prepared in the microwave with fat-free ranch dressing and low-fat ham) equals 1 starch, 1 meat; also, 139 calories, 568 mg sodium, 22 mg cholesterol, 13 gm carbohydrate, 7 gm protein, 6 gm fat.

Party Pitas

Janette Root, Ellensburg, Washington

Whenever the ladies of our church host a bridal shower, these pita sandwiches appear on the menu. Not only are they easy and delicious, they add color to the table.

✓ This tasty dish uses less sugar, salt and fat. Recipe includes *Diabetic Exchanges*.

    1 package (8 ounces) cream cheese, softened
1/2 cup mayonnaise
1/2 teaspoon dill weed
1/4 teaspoon garlic salt
    8 mini pita breads (4 inches)
  16 fresh spinach leaves
3/4 pound shaved fully cooked ham
1/2 pound thinly sliced Monterey Jack cheese

Combine cream cheese, mayonnaise, dill and garlic salt. Cut each pita in half horizontally; spread 1 tablespoon cream cheese mixture on each cut surface. On eight pita halves, layer spinach, ham and cheese. Top with remaining pita halves. Cut each pita into four wedges; secure with a toothpick. **Yield:** 32 pieces. **Diabetic Exchanges:** One serving of two pieces (prepared with fat-free cream cheese and mayonnaise and low-fat ham) equals 1 meat, 1 vegetable, 1/2 starch; also, 133 calories, 598 mg sodium, 26 mg cholesterol, 10 gm carbohydrate, 11 gm protein, 5 gm fat.

Braunschweiger Vegetable Dip

Barbara Fleming, Kingston Springs, Tennessee

I like to serve this spread around the holidays. But my family likes it so much that they often request it year-round.

    1 package (8 ounces) braunschweiger sausage
    1 cup (8 ounces) sour cream
    2 tablespoons dry onion soup mix
    1 teaspoon Worcestershire sauce
    3 to 6 drops hot pepper sauce
Raw vegetables for dipping

In a mixing bowl, combine the first five ingredients; mix well. Cover and chill for at least 1 hour. Serve with vegetables. **Yield:** 2 cups.

Ham 'n' Cheese Puffs

Joyce Schotten, Renner, South Dakota

A full-time job, farm life and our kids' activities keep me on my toes, so I don't have time to prepare fancy dishes. These puffs are a real down-home delight and appeal to everyone.

    1 cup water
1/2 cup butter *or* margarine
    1 cup all-purpose flour
1/2 teaspoon ground mustard
    4 eggs

    1 cup finely chopped fully cooked ham
1/2 cup shredded sharp cheddar cheese
Warm prepared cheese sauce, optional

In a heavy saucepan over medium heat, bring water and butter to a boil. Add flour and mustard all at once; stir until a smooth ball forms. Remove from the heat; let stand for 5 minutes. Add eggs, one at a time, beating well after each addition. Beat until smooth. Stir in the ham and cheese (cheese does not have to melt). Drop batter by tablespoonfuls 2 in. apart onto greased baking sheets. Bake at 400° for 30-35 minutes or until golden. Serve warm or cold with cheese sauce for dipping if desired. **Yield:** about 4-1/2 dozen.

Deviled Ham and Egg Appetizer

Neva Schnauber, Fort Collins, Colorado

My mother would make this recipe as a way of using leftover ham and hard-cooked eggs...they always made the holidays extra special. Childhood memories are made of tasty treats like these.

    6 hard-cooked eggs
3/4 cup finely chopped fully cooked ham
1/4 cup mayonnaise
    1 tablespoon sweet pickle relish
    2 teaspoons prepared mustard
1/8 teaspoon salt
Dash pepper

Slice eggs in half lengthwise. Remove yolks to a small bowl; set whites aside. Mash yolks; stir in ham, mayonnaise, relish, mustard, salt and pepper. Spoon into the egg whites. Cover and chill until ready to serve. **Yield:** 1 dozen.

Sausage-Stuffed Mushrooms

Kathy Deezik, Hartstown, Pennsylvania

A few years back, I was looking for a snack that would suit my family's tastes. I combined three different recipes and came up with this one. They love the rich Parmesan flavor.

  20 to 24 large fresh mushrooms
    2 tablespoons finely chopped onion
    2 to 3 garlic cloves, minced
    1 tablespoon butter *or* margarine
1/4 pound bulk pork sausage, cooked, crumbled
        and drained
    3 tablespoons Italian-seasoned dry bread crumbs
    3 tablespoons grated Parmesan cheese
    1 tablespoon dried parsley flakes
    1 egg white

Remove mushroom stems from caps. Set caps aside (discard stems or save for another use). In a skillet, saute onion and garlic in butter until tender. Combine sausage, bread crumbs, cheese, parsley and egg white in a medium bowl. Stir in onion mixture. Fill the mushroom caps; place in a lightly greased 15-in. x 10-in. x 1-in. baking pan. Bake at 350° for 10-15 minutes or until mushrooms are tender and tops are browned. **Yield:** about 2 dozen.

Salads & Side Dishes

 Quick & Easy

Sausage Bean Delight

Julie Arndt, Indian Head, Pennsylvania

(PICTURED AT LEFT)

One of our children recently declared she doesn't like green beans. But she eagerly digs into this tempting dish.

    3/4 pound bulk pork sausage
    1 large onion, sliced
    1 garlic clove, minced
    2 tablespoons olive *or* vegetable oil
    1 pound fresh green beans, cut into 2-inch pieces

In a large saucepan, cook and crumble sausage until no longer pink; drain and set aside. In the same pan, saute onion and garlic in oil until tender. Stir in beans; cover and cook over medium heat until beans are tender. Add sausage; heat through. **Yield:** 4 servings.

Basil Pasta and Ham Salad

Pauline Piggott, Northville, Michigan

(PICTURED AT LEFT)

With fresh basil and tomatoes in the dressing, this refreshing salad delightfully captures the flavor of summer.

✓ This tasty dish uses less sugar, salt and fat. Recipe includes *Diabetic Exchanges.*

TOMATO BASIL DRESSING:
    1 cup chopped fresh tomatoes
    1/4 cup chopped fresh basil
    2 tablespoons chopped green onions
    2 tablespoons olive *or* vegetable oil
    2 tablespoons lemon juice
    1 garlic clove, minced
    1/2 teaspoon sugar
    1/4 teaspoon salt, optional
    1/4 teaspoon pepper
SALAD:
    2-1/2 cups (10 ounces) uncooked spiral pasta
    1 cup cubed fully cooked ham
    1 can (2-1/4 ounces) sliced ripe olives, drained
    1/3 cup chopped fresh basil

Combine tomatoes, basil, onions, oil, lemon juice, garlic, sugar, salt and pepper if desired. Chill for at least 15 minutes. Cook pasta according to package directions until firm to the bite; drain and rinse with cold water. Transfer to a salad bowl. Add ham, olives and basil; toss. Add dressing; toss to coat. **Yield:** 8 servings. **Diabetic Exchanges:** One 3/4-cup serving (prepared with low-fat ham and without salt) equals

---

SUMMERTIME SPECIALTIES. *Pictured at left, top to bottom: Sausage Bean Delight, Basil Pasta and Ham Salad and Smoked Tenderloin Salad (all recipes on this page).*

1-1/2 starch, 1 meat; also, 186 calories, 333 mg sodium, 8 mg cholesterol, 26 gm carbohydrate, 8 gm protein, 6 gm fat.

Smoked Tenderloin Salad

Roberta Whitesell, Phoenix, Arizona

(PICTURED AT LEFT)

During our hot summers, I rely on salads. In this recipe, the pork is grilled so I can stay out of the kitchen.

✓ This tasty dish uses less sugar, salt and fat. Recipe includes *Diabetic Exchanges.*

DRESSING:
    1/2 cup orange juice
    2 tablespoons olive *or* vegetable oil
    2 tablespoons cider vinegar
    1 tablespoon grated orange peel
    2 teaspoons honey
    2 teaspoons Dijon mustard
    1/2 teaspoon coarsely ground pepper
SALAD:
    1 pork tenderloin (1 pound), trimmed
    10 cups torn salad greens
    2 seedless oranges, peeled and sliced
    1/4 cup chopped pistachios *or* cashews, optional

In a small bowl, combine all dressing ingredients; cover and chill. Grill pork, covered, over medium coals for 15-20 minutes or until meat thermometer reads 160°-170°, turning occasionally. Let stand for 5 minutes; thinly slice tenderloin. To serve, line large platter with greens; top with orange sections and tenderloin. Sprinkle with nuts if desired. Drizzle with dressing. **Yield:** 5 servings. **Diabetic Exchanges:** One serving (prepared without nuts) equals 2-1/2 lean meat, 1 vegetable, 1/2 fruit, 1/2 fat; also, 223 calories, 99 mg sodium, 54 mg cholesterol, 14 gm carbohydrate, 21 gm protein, 9 gm fat.

Crunchy Ham Salad

Lucille Schreiber, Gleason, Wisconsin

Whenever I have to bring a dish to pass for a large gathering, I'm asked to bring this salad. I always get many compliments.

    1 cup shredded carrots
    1 cup diced celery
    1/4 cup finely chopped onion
    1/2 cup mayonnaise
    1 teaspoon milk
    1 teaspoon prepared mustard
    2 cups shoestring potato sticks
    1 cup diced fully cooked ham

In a large bowl, combine carrots, celery and onion. Combine mayonnaise, milk and mustard. Pour over vegetable mixture and toss to coat. Cover and chill until ready to serve. Just before serving, toss in the potato sticks and ham. **Yield:** 4-6 servings.

Ham and Spaghetti Salad

Marsha Murray, Niverville, Manitoba

My husband and I have three children, so budget-minded meals are the order of the day. This delicious dish provides plenty of hearty ingredients without breaking the bank.

```
1/2 cup broken uncooked spaghetti (2-inch pieces)
  2 tablespoons vegetable oil
  5 teaspoons soy sauce
  1 tablespoon vinegar
1/4 teaspoon salt
  1 cup diced fully cooked ham
  2 green onions, chopped
1/2 head lettuce, torn
  1 tablespoon sesame seeds, toasted
```

Cook spaghetti until tender; drain, rinse and set aside. In a large bowl, combine oil, soy sauce, vinegar and salt. Add spaghetti, ham and onions; toss to coat. Cover and chill for 1-3 hours. Just before serving, add lettuce and sesame seeds; toss gently. **Yield:** 4 servings.

Bacon Broccoli Salad

Mrs. Alan Alspaugh, Melbourne, Florida

Here in the hot Florida sun, we appreciate refreshing no-fuss salads like this. It's a popular side dish at church potlucks and picnics.

```
 10 bacon strips, cooked and crumbled
  1 cup fresh broccoli florets
1/2 cup raisins
1/2 cup sunflower seeds
1/2 cup mayonnaise
1/4 cup sugar
  2 tablespoons vinegar
```

In a medium bowl, combine bacon, broccoli, raisins and sunflower seeds; set aside. Mix together mayonnaise, sugar and vinegar; pour over broccoli mixture and toss to coat. Cover and chill for 1 hour. Stir before serving. **Yield:** 4 servings.

Curried Ham and Fruit Salad

Anne Frederick, New Hartford, New York

This good-for-you salad is a quick and convenient way to use up leftover ham. Plus, I've found that it's perfect to serve as a special salad at luncheons.

✓ **This tasty dish uses less sugar, salt and fat. Recipe includes *Diabetic Exchanges*.**

```
1-1/2 cups cubed fully cooked ham
    2 medium red apples, cut into 1/2-inch cubes
```

```
1/2 cup sliced celery
1/2 cup mayonnaise
  1 tablespoon milk
1/2 teaspoon curry powder
  1 small cantaloupe or honeydew melon, cut into wedges
1/4 cup chopped pecans, toasted, optional
```

In a large bowl, combine ham, apples and celery. In a small bowl, combine mayonnaise, milk and curry powder; pour over ham mixture and toss to coat. Cover and chill for 1 hour. Serve over melon wedges; sprinkle with pecans if desired. **Yield:** 4 servings. **Diabetic Exchanges:** One 1-1/2-cup serving (prepared with low-fat ham, fat-free mayonnaise, skim milk and cantaloupe and without pecans) equals 1-1/2 lean meat, 1-1/2 fruit; also, 181 calories, 987 mg sodium, 25 mg cholesterol, 27 gm carbohydrate, 12 gm protein, 3 gm fat.

Spinach Salad with Avocado Dressing

Lucille Schreiber, Gleason, Wisconsin

I love trying new recipes, adding my own touch with a little of this and a pinch of that. This fresh salad nicely combines vegetables, flavors, textures and colors.

```
 12 cups torn fresh spinach
1-1/2 cups diced fully cooked ham
 10 cherry tomatoes, quartered
  6 small fresh mushrooms, sliced
  1 small cucumber, sliced
  1 ripe avocado, peeled and pitted
  2 tablespoons fresh lime or lemon juice
1/2 cup plain yogurt
  1 teaspoon finely chopped onion
1/2 teaspoon sugar
1/4 teaspoon salt
```

Arrange spinach, ham, tomatoes, mushrooms and cucumber in individual salad bowls. In blender container or food processor, puree avocado, lime juice, yogurt, onion, sugar and salt; drizzle over salads. **Yield:** 6 servings.

Baked Chimichanga Salad

Katie Koziolek, Hartland, Minnesota

I frequently prepare a large pork roast so I can have leftovers for these chimichangas. My family prefers this salad version to the deep-fried variety.

SALSA:

```
  3 to 4 cups chopped fresh tomatoes
  1 can (4 ounces) chopped green chilies
  1 to 2 jalapeno peppers, seeded and finely chopped
```

1 teaspoon vinegar
1 garlic clove, minced
1/2 teaspoon ground cumin
GUACAMOLE:
2 ripe avocados, peeled and pitted
1/2 cup chopped seeded tomato
1-1/2 teaspoons lemon juice
1/2 teaspoon seasoned salt
6 to 8 drops hot pepper sauce
FILLING:
1 cup chopped onion
1/2 cup chopped green pepper
1/2 cup finely chopped celery
1 medium carrot, shredded
1 garlic clove, minced
2 tablespoons chili powder
1 teaspoon salt
1/2 teaspoon dried oregano
1/2 teaspoon ground cumin
4 tablespoons vegetable oil, *divided*
5 cups shredded *or* chopped cooked pork
1/2 cup water
20 flour tortillas (7 inches)
Shredded lettuce
Sliced ripe olives
2 cups (8 ounces) shredded Colby, Monterey Jack *or* cheddar cheese
1 cup (8 ounces) sour cream

Combine all salsa ingredients; cover and chill for at least 2 hours. In a bowl, mash the avocados. Add remaining guacamole ingredients; mix well. Cover with plastic wrap touching surface of guacamole; chill. For filling, in a skillet over medium heat, saute vegetables and seasonings in 2 tablespoons oil until tender. Add pork and water; reduce heat to low and cook until water is absorbed and mixture is heated through. Heat tortillas according to package directions. Place about 1/4 cup filling in center of each tortilla. Fold ends and sides over filling, then roll up. Place, seam side down, on a lightly oiled baking sheet. Brush each chimichanga with remaining oil. Bake at 450° for 5 minutes or until crisp and lightly browned. To serve, arrange lettuce on 10 individual plates. Top each with two hot chimichangas. Sprinkle with olives and cheese. Serve with salsa, guacamole and sour cream. **Yield:** 10 servings. **Editor's Note:** Chimichangas may be assembled in advance and frozen before brushing with oil. To heat, thaw slightly, brush with oil and bake on a lightly oiled baking sheet at 400° for 10-15 minutes or until heated through.

Quick & Easy

Spicy Southern-Style Tomato Cups

Gwilia Lightle, Kansas City, Kansas

I'm retired and enjoy collecting recipes...I only wish I had time to try every one of them! I found this recipe in a local newspaper. My family loves the combination of flavors.

2 medium tomatoes, cored
4 tablespoons sliced green onions, *divided*

1 garlic clove, minced
2 tablespoons olive *or* vegetable oil, *divided*
1 tablespoon red wine or cider vinegar
1/8 teaspoon sugar
1/8 teaspoon salt
Pinch pepper
1/2 cup diced fully cooked ham *or* Canadian bacon
1/3 cup canned whole kernel corn, drained
2 cups shredded salad greens

Cut a thin slice off tops of tomatoes. Scoop out pulp, leaving a 1/4-in. shell; invert shells on paper towel to drain. Chop tops, pulp, and seeds; set aside. In a small skillet, saute 2 tablespoons onions and garlic in 1 teaspoon oil for about 2 minutes or until slightly softened. Remove from the heat. Add 1 tablespoon oil, vinegar, sugar, salt, pepper and 3 tablespoons chopped pulp; mix well. Pour into a small bowl; set aside. In the same skillet, cook ham, corn, remaining onions and remaining pulp in remaining oil for 4 minutes or until most of the liquid has evaporated, stirring occasionally. Spoon into tomato shells. Serve on a bed of lettuce; drizzle with the reserved tomato-vinegar mixture. **Yield:** 2 servings.

Turnips, Taters and Ham

Evelyn Thompson, Middlesboro, Kentucky

Every year, my husband clears space in the garden to plant turnips. He likes to eat them right out of the garden or in a variety of dishes, including this one I created just for him.

✓ This tasty dish uses less sugar, salt and fat. Recipe includes *Diabetic Exchanges*.

1 small onion, chopped
2 tablespoons butter *or* margarine
2 tablespoons all-purpose flour
1/2 teaspoon salt, optional
1/4 teaspoon dried basil
Dash pepper
1 cup water
1/4 cup milk
4 medium potatoes, peeled and sliced 1/4 inch thick
3 small turnips, peeled and sliced 1/8 inch thick
1 cup cubed fully cooked ham
3 tablespoons minced fresh parsley

In a saucepan, saute onion in butter until tender. Stir in flour, salt if desired, basil and pepper. Gradually stir in water and milk. Bring to a boil over medium heat; boil for 2 minutes, stirring constantly. Remove from the heat. In a greased 11-in. x 7-in. x 2-in. baking dish, layer potatoes, turnips and ham; pour sauce over all. Cover and bake at 350° for 1-1/4 hours or until potatoes are tender. Garnish with parsley. **Yield:** 6 servings. **Diabetic Exchanges:** One 3/4-cup serving (prepared with margarine, skim milk and low-fat ham and without salt) equals 1-1/2 starch, 1 fat, 1/2 lean meat; also, 176 calories, 420 mg sodium, 11 mg cholesterol, 26 gm carbohydrate, 8 gm protein, 5 gm fat.

GARDEN HARVEST. *Clockwise from lower right: Warm Fajita Salad, Pork 'n' Sweet Potato Salad, Lima Bean Casserole, Potluck Potatoes and Sausage 'n' Apple Baked Squash (all recipes on pages 16 and 17).*

Potluck Potatoes

Lori Smith, Newark, Ohio
(PICTURED ON PAGE 14)

This casserole goes over well whenever I take it to a gathering. Even though I have to double the recipe, it's still an inexpensive side dish for our large family of 10.

    4 medium potatoes, peeled and cooked
    2 tablespoons butter *or* margarine, melted
1/8 teaspoon salt
1/8 teaspoon pepper
    2 to 4 tablespoons milk
    1 cup (4 ounces) shredded cheddar cheese, *divided*
3/4 cup diced fully cooked ham
1/4 cup finely chopped onion
1/4 cup finely chopped green pepper

In a large bowl, mash potatoes until smooth. Add butter, salt, pepper and enough milk to make a soft mashed potato consistency. Stir in 2/3 cup cheese, ham, onion and green pepper. Transfer to a greased 1-1/2-qt. baking dish. Bake, uncovered, at 350° for 20-25 minutes or until heated through. Sprinkle with remaining cheese. **Yield:** 4-6 servings.

Quick & Easy

Lima Bean Casserole

Faith Porter, Hagerstown, Maryland
(PICTURED ON PAGE 14)

An abundance of homegrown lima beans and leftover sausage inspired me to create this dish more than 20 years ago. It's proven to be a timeless classic.

1/2 pound bulk sage pork sausage
    2 packages (10 ounces *each*) frozen lima beans
    2 medium carrots, thinly sliced
1/2 cup water
1/2 teaspoon sugar
1/4 teaspoon salt
Pinch pepper

In a saucepan, cook and crumble sausage until no longer pink; drain. Add lima beans, carrots, water, sugar, salt and pepper. Cook, uncovered, for 20-25 minutes or until vegetables are tender; drain. **Yield:** 10 servings.

Pork 'n' Sweet Potato Salad

June Gerlach, St. Petersburg, Florida
(PICTURED ON PAGE 14)

Instead of traditional salads that are tossed together, this is layered with somewhat tropical ingredients for a beautiful presentation. It's wonderful for special occasions.

✓ This tasty dish uses less sugar, salt and fat. Recipe includes *Diabetic Exchanges.*

    1 can (20 ounces) pineapple chunks, undrained
    1 cup mayonnaise

    2 teaspoons curry powder
1/4 teaspoon paprika
    1 small bunch romaine
    3 pounds sweet potatoes, cooked, peeled and sliced
    2 cups cubed cooked pork
    1 medium green pepper, cut into chunks
    1 small onion, minced
1/4 cup slivered almonds, toasted, optional

Drain pineapple, reserving 3 tablespoons juice; set pineapple aside. Combine the juice, mayonnaise, curry powder and paprika. Line a large serving platter with romaine. Arrange potatoes, pork, pineapple, green pepper and onion on top. Sprinkle with almonds if desired. Top with curry dressing. **Yield:** 6 servings. **Diabetic Exchanges:** One serving of 2 cups salad with 2 tablespoons dressing (prepared with unsweetened pineapple, fat-free mayonnaise and lean pork and without almonds) equals 2 starch, 2 vegetable, 1-1/2 lean meat, 1 fruit; also, 329 calories, 329 mg sodium, 44 mg cholesterol, 57 gm carbohydrate, 18 gm protein, 3 gm fat.

Warm Fajita Salad

Bobbie Jo Yokley, Franklin, Kentucky
(PICTURED ON PAGE 15)

A friend shared this recipe with me after picking it up at a pork producers convention. Since then, I've prepared it for customers of my catering business with rave reviews.

✓ This tasty dish uses less sugar, salt and fat. Recipe includes *Diabetic Exchanges.*

    1 cup lime juice
1/4 cup chicken broth
1/4 cup soy sauce
    2 garlic cloves, minced
    1 tablespoon vegetable oil
    1 teaspoon sugar
    1 teaspoon liquid smoke
3/4 teaspoon ground cumin
1/2 teaspoon dried oregano
1/4 teaspoon ground ginger
1/4 teaspoon hot pepper sauce
    1 pound boneless pork loin, trimmed and cut into thin strips
    1 large onion, sliced
    1 medium green pepper, cut into strips
    1 medium sweet yellow pepper, cut into strips
    1 tablespoon lemon juice
    6 cups torn romaine
    12 cherry tomatoes, quartered

In a large resealable plastic bag, combine the first 11 ingredients. Remove 2 tablespoons; cover and chill. Add pork to remaining marinade; toss to coat. Cover and chill for 30 minutes to 3 hours, turning occasionally. Drain pork, discarding marinade. Heat reserved marinade in a large skillet over medium-high heat. Add pork, onion and peppers; stir fry for 3-4 minutes or until pork is no longer pink. Drizzle with lemon juice. Remove from the heat. Arrange lettuce on four individual plates; top with meat mixture and tomatoes. **Yield:** 4 servings. **Diabetic Exchanges:** One 1-1/4-cup serving (prepared with low-sodium chicken broth and light soy sauce) equals 3 lean meat, 3 vegetable, 1/2 starch, 1/2 fat; also, 298 calories, 584 mg sodium, 68 mg cholesterol, 22 gm carbohydrate, 28 gm protein, 12 gm fat.

Sausage 'n' Apple Baked Squash

Sandra Bedggood, Thorndale, Ontario

(PICTURED ON PAGE 15)

This hearty side dish is perfect for winter evening meals and complements an assortment of meats. I clipped it from a newspaper years ago and it soon became a family favorite.

    1/2 cup chopped apple
    1/4 cup chopped onion
      2 tablespoons dry bread crumbs
    1/4 teaspoon ground sage
    1/8 teaspoon pepper
    1/2 pound bulk pork sausage
      2 small acorn squash, halved and seeded

In a medium bowl, combine apple, onion, bread crumbs, sage and pepper. Add sausage; mix well. Spoon into squash halves; place in a greased 13-in. x 9-in. x 2-in. baking dish. Cover and bake at 375° for 45 minutes. Uncover and bake 10 minutes more or until sausage is no longer pink and squash is tender. **Yield:** 4 servings.

Fantastic Potatoes

Janice Smelser, Silver Point, Tennessee

A common combination of potatoes, bacon and cheese is made extra special with the unique addition of olives. This old-fashioned comforting dish is great with all kinds of meats.

      4 medium potatoes, peeled and diced
    1/2 pound sliced bacon, cooked and crumbled
      1 cup diced process American cheese
    3/4 cup mayonnaise
    1/4 cup sliced stuffed olives
      2 tablespoons chopped onion
      2 tablespoons chopped green pepper

In a saucepan, cook potatoes in water until tender; drain. Stir in remaining ingredients. Spoon into an ungreased 8-in. square baking dish. Bake, uncovered, at 350° for 30 minutes or until bubbly and heated through. **Yield:** 6-8 servings.

Italian Ham and Cheese Salad

Brenda Trainer, Austin, Minnesota

I came up with this recipe when I was asked to prepare a main-dish salad for a ladies group on a limited budget. Everyone agreed it tasted like a million bucks!

      1 package (12 ounces) spiral pasta, cooked, drained and cooled
    1-1/2 cups cubed fully cooked ham
      1 cup cubed cheddar cheese

      1 medium green pepper, diced
      1 cup diced red onion
      1 can (2-1/4 ounces) sliced ripe olives, drained
    3/4 cup creamy Italian salad dressing
    1/2 cup ranch salad dressing
    1/2 teaspoon dried basil
    1/2 teaspoon pepper
    1/4 teaspoon garlic powder
    1/4 teaspoon salt

In a large bowl, combine the first six ingredients. Combine remaining ingredients and pour over salad; toss to coat. **Yield:** 8-10 servings.

Sweet-and-Sour Baked Beans

Barbara Nielsen, Chula Vista, California

This recipe has proven to be a great standby for parties, barbecues and potlucks. I especially like it because I can keep all the ingredients on hand for last-minute preparation.

      1 pound sliced bacon
      4 large onions, sliced
      1 cup packed brown sugar
    1/2 cup cider vinegar
    1-1/2 teaspoons ground mustard
      2 cans (15 ounces *each*) butter beans, rinsed and drained
      2 cans (16 ounces *each*) New England-style baked beans, undrained
      1 can (15-1/4 ounces) lima beans, rinsed and drained
      1 can (16 ounces) kidney beans, rinsed and drained

In a skillet, cook bacon until crisp; crumble and set aside. Discard all but 2 tablespoons drippings. Add onions, brown sugar, vinegar and mustard to drippings; simmer for 10 minutes, stirring frequently. Stir in beans and bacon. Pour into an ungreased 3-qt. baking dish. Bake, uncovered, at 350° for 1-1/2 hours. **Yield:** 18-20 servings.

Bacon, Cabbage and Noodles

Jeanie Castor, Decatur, Illinois

I received this recipe from a friend of Hungarian descent. Some folks turn up their noses when this is presented, but after one taste, they always come back for seconds...and thirds!

    3/4 pound sliced bacon, diced
    1/2 medium head cabbage, thinly sliced
    1/4 teaspoon salt
Dash pepper
      2 cups (8 ounces) thin egg noodles, cooked and drained

In a large skillet, cook bacon until crisp; set aside. Discard all but 3 tablespoons drippings. Add cabbage to drippings; cover and cook on low for 20 minutes or until cabbage is tender, stirring occasionally. Stir in salt, pepper, noodles and bacon. Heat through. **Yield:** 12-14 servings.

Luncheon Pasta Salad

Julie Heitsch, St. Louis, Michigan

I first tasted this salad at a ladies luncheon at church. My husband and children ask for this dish regularly. Freshly baked breadsticks are a tasty accompaniment.

✓ **This tasty dish uses less sugar, salt and fat. Recipe includes *Diabetic Exchanges*.**

- 1 cup spiral pasta, cooked, drained and cooled
- 1 cup cubed fully cooked ham
- 1 small cucumber, diced
- 1 small tomato, seeded and diced
- 5 radishes, sliced
- 2 tablespoons diced onion
- 1 bottle (8 ounces) cucumber ranch salad dressing, *divided*
- 1/4 teaspoon salt, optional
- 1/4 teaspoon pepper
- 4 cups torn lettuce
- 3/4 cup cubed Colby *or* cheddar cheese

In a large bowl, combine the first six ingredients. Add 1/2 cup dressing, salt if desired and pepper; toss to coat. Cover and chill for at least 2 hours. Just before serving, add lettuce, cheese and remaining dressing; toss. **Yield:** 8 servings. **Diabetic Exchanges:** One 1-cup serving (prepared with low-fat ham, reduced-fat dressing and low-fat cheddar cheese and without salt) equals 1 starch, 1 meat, 1 fat, 1/2 vegetable; also, 215 calories, 495 mg sodium, 21 mg cholesterol, 17 gm carbohydrate, 9 gm protein, 12 gm fat.

Quick & Easy

Pork Sausage Hominy

Pearl Baggett, Oklahoma City, Oklahoma

The first time I prepared this recipe, it won first place in a cooking contest sponsored by a local sausage company. It's a very lovely, inexpensive and tasty dish to offer guests.

- 1 pound bulk pork sausage
- 1 cup chopped onion
- 1 can (15-1/2 ounces) hominy, drained
- 1 can (14-1/2 ounces) stewed tomatoes
- 1 envelope taco seasoning mix
- 1 teaspoon dried oregano
- 1 teaspoon dried basil
- 1/2 teaspoon ground cumin

Dash hot pepper sauce
- 2 cups (8 ounces) shredded cheddar cheese, *divided*
- 1 small head lettuce, shredded
- 1 package (10-1/2 ounces) corn chips, broken
- 1 small green pepper, sliced
- 1 small sweet red pepper, sliced
- 2 medium tomatoes, sliced

In a skillet, cook sausage and onion until sausage is no longer pink and onion is tender; drain. Add hominy; cook and stir over low heat for 5 minutes. Add stewed tomatoes, seasonings and 1 cup cheese. Simmer for 2-3 minutes or until cheese is melted. To serve, arrange lettuce on a large serving platter; sprinkle with corn chips. Top with meat mixture. Garnish with pepper, tomatoes and remaining cheese. **Yield:** 6-7 servings.

Sausage-Stuffed Baked Apples

Bertha Carver, Gravois Mill, Missouri

With hearty sausage, crisp apples and a subtle sweet flavor, this is almost a meal in itself. My family especially enjoys this dish on a chilly evening.

- 1 pound bulk pork sausage
- 1/4 cup chopped onion
- 6 medium tart baking apples
- 1 egg
- 1/3 cup packed brown sugar
- 1/2 cup maple syrup

In a skillet, cook sausage and onion until sausage is no longer pink and onion is tender; drain and cool slightly. Core apples; cut in half horizontally. Place in an ungreased 13-in. x 9-in. x 2-in. baking pan. In a bowl, combine egg and brown sugar; stir in sausage mixture. Spoon into the apples. Cover and bake at 350° for 15 minutes. Uncover and bake 15 minutes more or until apples are tender. Serve with syrup. **Yield:** 12 servings.

Salsa Potatoes and Pork

Margaret Pache, Mesa, Arizona

Pork and salsa delightfully dress up ordinary fried potatoes. With just five ingredients, this recipe is one you'll likely reach for whenever you need a side dish in a hurry.

- 1/4 pound boneless pork, trimmed and cut into thin strips
- 1 tablespoon cooking oil
- 4 medium potatoes, cooked, peeled and thinly sliced
- 1/3 cup salsa
- 2 tablespoons plain yogurt, optional

In a large skillet, cook pork in oil for about 3 minutes or until no longer pink. Remove pork and set aside. In the same skillet, fry potatoes for 4 minutes or until browned. Add pork and salsa; toss. Heat through. Serve with yogurt if desired. **Yield:** 4 servings.

Dirty Rice

Mrs. Lum Day, Bastrop, Louisiana

This is an old Louisiana recipe that I've had longer than I can remember. It's a very popular Southern dish. To turn this into a main meal, simply add more sausage and chicken livers.

- 1/2 pound bulk pork sausage
- 1/2 pound chicken livers, chopped
- 1 cup chopped onion

1/2 cup chopped celery
1/3 cup sliced green onions
2 tablespoons minced fresh parsley
1 garlic clove, minced
3 tablespoons butter *or* margarine
1 can (10-1/2 ounces) chicken broth
1/2 teaspoon dried basil
1/2 teaspoon dried thyme
1/2 teaspoon salt
1/4 teaspoon pepper
1/4 teaspoon hot pepper sauce
3 cups cooked rice

In a skillet, cook sausage for 2-3 minutes; stir in chicken livers. Cook 5-7 minutes more or until sausage and chicken livers are no longer pink; drain and set aside. In the same skillet, saute onion, celery, green onions, parsley and garlic in butter until the vegetables are tender. Add broth, basil, thyme, salt, pepper and hot pepper sauce; mix well. Stir in rice, sausage and chicken livers. Heat through, stirring constantly. **Yield:** 10-12 servings.

Sausage and Creamed Corn Casserole

Lauretta Throm, Toledo, Ohio

Now that I'm retired, I have more time for cooking delightful dishes like this country-style casserole. It always disappears whenever I take it to a potluck.

1/2 pound bulk pork sausage
1/4 cup chopped onion
1/3 cup chopped green *or* sweet red pepper
1-1/4 cups herb-seasoned crumb stuffing mix, *divided*
1 can (14-3/4 ounces) cream-style corn
2 teaspoons chopped fresh parsley *or* 1 teaspoon dried parsley flakes
1 tablespoon butter *or* margarine, melted

In a skillet, cook sausage, onion and green pepper until sausage is no longer pink; drain. Add 1 cup stuffing mix, corn and parsley. Spoon into a greased 1-qt. baking dish. Combine butter and remaining stuffing mix; sprinkle over casserole. Bake, uncovered, at 375° for 30-35 minutes or until golden brown. **Yield:** 4-6 servings.

Sesame Pork with Cabbage

Sarah Smith, Morganton, North Carolina

I created this recipe after sampling a similar version while living in Korea. People always comment on the nice combination of crunchy cabbage and tender pork.

1/2 pound boneless pork, trimmed and cut into thin strips
2 tablespoons cooking oil
4 cups shredded cabbage
1 tablespoon sesame seeds, toasted
1/4 teaspoon salt
1/8 to 1/4 teaspoon cayenne pepper

In a large skillet over medium-high heat, cook pork in oil until no longer pink. Add remaining ingredients. Cover; reduce heat to medium and cook for 5 minutes or until cabbage is crisp-tender, stirring occasionally. **Yield:** 8 servings.

Maple Ham Peaches

Helen Davis, Waterbury, Vermont

Back when my husband and I owned a dairy farm, we also produced maple syrup and used it often in baking and cooking. This recipe splendidly stars that sweet confection.

✓ This tasty dish uses less sugar, salt and fat. Recipe includes *Diabetic Exchanges.*

1 egg *or* egg substitute equivalent
1/2 pound fully cooked ham, ground
1/3 cup soft bread crumbs
1/4 cup maple syrup
Dash ground cloves
3 cans (16 ounces *each*) peach halves, well drained

In a medium bowl, beat egg. Add ham, crumbs, syrup and cloves; mix well. Shape into 12 balls. Place peaches, hollow side up, in a greased 13-in. x 9-in. x 2-in. baking pan. Nest a ham ball in each peach. Bake, uncovered, at 350° for 20 minutes or until heated through. **Yield:** 6 servings. **Diabetic Exchanges:** One serving of two peach halves (prepared with egg substitute equivalent, low-fat ham, sugar-free maple-flavored syrup and unsweetened peaches) equals 1 starch, 1 fruit, 1/2 lean meat; also, 155 calories, 531 mg sodium, 18 mg cholesterol, 30 gm carbohydrate, 9 gm protein, 1 gm fat.

Sausage Pilaf

Kelly Morrissey, Overland Park, Kansas

I received this recipe from my mother years ago, and it's been a family favorite ever since. Pork sausage really bulks up ordinary rice pilaf for fantastic flavor.

1/2 pound bulk pork sausage
1 cup chopped celery
1/2 cup chopped onion
1/2 cup chopped green pepper
1 can (10-3/4 ounces) condensed cream of mushroom soup, undiluted
1-1/4 cups milk
1 jar (2 ounces) diced pimientos, drained
1/2 cup uncooked long grain rice
1/2 teaspoon poultry seasoning
1/4 teaspoon salt
1 cup soft bread crumbs
2 tablespoons butter *or* margarine, melted

In a skillet, cook sausage, celery, onion and green pepper until sausage is no longer pink and vegetables are tender; drain. Stir in soup, milk, pimientos, rice, poultry seasoning and salt. Pour into an ungreased 1-1/2-qt. baking dish. Cover and bake at 350° for 50 minutes, stirring occasionally. Combine bread crumbs and butter; sprinkle on top. Bake, uncovered, 20 minutes more. **Yield:** 6-8 servings.

Sandwiches for All Seasons

Nutty Ham and Apple Sandwiches

Dorothy Kirkonij, South San Francisco, California
(PICTURED AT LEFT)

Almonds and apple add a pleasant crunch to these out-of-the-ordinary sandwiches. For a little variety, try substituting a different kind of bread or cheese.

8 teaspoons spicy brown mustard
8 slices rye bread
4 lettuce leaves
1 large tomato, thinly sliced
4 slices cheddar cheese
1/2 pound fully cooked ham, thinly sliced
1 tart apple, thinly sliced
1/4 cup sliced almonds

Spread mustard on each slice of bread. On four slices, layer lettuce, tomato, cheese, ham and apple. Top with almonds and remaining bread. **Yield:** 4 servings.

Greek Pitas

Lisa Hockersmith, Bakersfield, California
(PICTURED AT LEFT)

I like to serve these when the gang's over for football games—they taste like gyros and the guys love them! You can prepare the meat and sauce ahead of time for added convenience.

1 carton (8 ounces) plain yogurt
1 cup diced peeled cucumber
1 teaspoon dill weed
1/4 teaspoon seasoned salt
1/4 cup olive *or* vegetable oil
1/4 cup lemon juice
2 tablespoons Dijon mustard
2 garlic cloves, minced
1-1/2 teaspoons dried oregano
1 teaspoon dried thyme
1-1/4 pounds lean boneless pork, thinly sliced
6 pita breads, halved
1 medium tomato, chopped
2 tablespoons chopped onion

In a small bowl, combine yogurt, cucumber, dill and seasoned salt; cover and chill for 6 hours or overnight. In a large resealable plastic bag, combine oil, lemon juice, mustard, garlic, oregano and thyme; add pork. Seal bag and

> **LAZY-DAY LUNCHES.** *Pictured at left, top to bottom: Nutty Ham and Apple Sandwiches, Greek Pitas and BLT Tortillas (all recipes on this page).*

turn to coat; chill for 6 hours or overnight, turning occasionally. Drain and discard marinade. In a skillet over medium heat, stir-fry pork for about 4 minutes or until no longer pink. Stuff into pita breads; top with cucumber sauce, tomato and onion. **Yield:** 6 servings.

BLT Tortillas

Darla Wester, Meriden, Iowa
(PICTURED AT LEFT)

I used to do catering, and these BLT's were always a hit. Because they're so simple, they're great when time is short.

✓ This tasty dish uses less sugar, salt and fat. Recipe includes *Diabetic Exchanges*.

1/2 cup mayonnaise
1/2 cup sour cream
2 tablespoons original ranch salad dressing mix
1/4 teaspoon crushed red pepper flakes
8 flour tortillas (7 inches), warmed
16 bacon strips, cooked and drained
2 to 3 cups shredded lettuce
2 cups chopped tomato
Green and sweet red pepper strips, optional

In a bowl, combine mayonnaise, sour cream, salad dressing mix and red pepper flakes; spread on tortillas. Layer with bacon, lettuce and tomato. Top with peppers if desired. Roll up tortillas. **Yield:** 8 servings. **Diabetic Exchanges:** One tortilla (prepared with fat-free mayonnaise and sour cream and three strips of green pepper) equals 1-1/2 starch, 1 vegetable, 1 fat, 1/2 meat; also, 232 calories, 511 mg sodium, 12 mg cholesterol, 28 gm carbohydrate, 9 gm protein, 9 gm fat.

Pineapple Ham Sandwiches

Kathy Krug, Hinsdale, Illinois

I first sampled these at a bridal luncheon years ago. Now I frequently make them for our weekly neighborhood dinners.

1 can (29 ounces) tomato sauce
1 can (8 ounces) crushed pineapple in juice, undrained
1 cup water
2/3 cup packed brown sugar
1 teaspoon prepared mustard
5 whole cloves
1 pound fully cooked ham, thinly sliced
8 to 10 onion rolls, split

In a saucepan over medium heat, combine tomato sauce, pineapple, water, brown sugar, mustard and cloves. Bring to a boil; reduce heat and simmer, uncovered, for 1 hour or until reduced by about one-third. Remove cloves. Add ham; simmer for 20 minutes or until heated through. Serve on rolls. **Yield:** 8-10 servings.

Tender Pork Sandwiches

Shanna Roper, Kimberly, Idaho
(PICTURED ON THE FRONT COVER)

As a mother of five, I'm busy to say the least, so fast yet flavorful dishes like this are a real plus for me. The creamy sauce makes these sandwiches simply delicious.

✓ **This tasty dish uses less sugar, salt and fat. Recipe includes *Diabetic Exchanges*.**

        6 lean boneless pork cutlets (1-1/2 pounds and
           1/4 inch thick)
        1 teaspoon lemon-pepper seasoning
        4 teaspoons butter *or* margarine
      1/4 teaspoon salt, optional
      1/2 cup mayonnaise
    1-1/2 teaspoons lemon juice
      1/2 teaspoon yellow *or* Dijon mustard
        6 kaiser *or* hamburger buns, split and toasted
        6 lettuce leaves
        6 tomato slices

Sprinkle pork with lemon pepper. In a large skillet, melt butter; cook pork for about 2 minutes per side or until browned and no longer pink. Sprinkle with salt if desired. Combine mayonnaise, lemon juice and mustard; spread on inside of buns. Layer pork, lettuce and tomatoes on buns. **Yield:** 6 servings. **Diabetic Exchanges:** One sandwich (prepared with no-salt lemon-pepper seasoning, margarine and fat-free mayonnaise and without salt and served on a hamburger bun) equals 2 starch, 2 meat; also, 287 calories, 454 mg sodium, 45 mg cholesterol, 26 gm carbohydrate, 20 gm protein, 10 gm fat.

Wiener Wraps

Sadie Stoltzfus, Kinzers, Pennsylvania

A homemade wheat dough makes these "pigs in a blanket" stand out from all other varieties. They go great with a cup of soup or are a nice snack by themselves.

        1 package (1/4 ounce) active dry yeast
    1-1/4 cups warm water (110° to 115°)
        2 cups whole wheat flour
      1/4 cup packed brown sugar
        1 teaspoon salt
        1 teaspoon vanilla extract
    1-1/2 to 2 cups all-purpose flour
        8 slices process American cheese
        3 tablespoons ketchup
        8 hot dogs

In a large mixing bowl, dissolve yeast in warm water. Add whole wheat flour, brown sugar, salt and vanilla; beat until smooth. Add enough all-purpose flour to form a soft dough. Turn onto a floured board; knead for 6-8 minutes or until smooth and elastic. Cover and let rest 10 minutes. Roll into a 20-in. x 14-in. rectangle; cut into eight 7-in. x 5-in. pieces. On each piece of dough, place a slice of cheese, 1 teaspoon ketchup and a hot dog. Fold edges of dough over and press

---

tightly to seal. Place on a greased baking sheet. Bake at 350° for 30 minutes or until golden brown. **Yield:** 8 servings.

Canadian Bacon and Cheese Biscuits

Susanne Bastable, Eagle River, Ontario

My husband and I own and operate a fishing lodge here in northwestern Ontario. We're always looking for new sandwiches to serve our guests. These have met with raves for years.

        2 cups all-purpose flour
        4 teaspoons baking powder
        1 teaspoon Italian seasoning
      1/2 teaspoon salt
      1/4 cup shortening
      3/4 cup milk
        2 tablespoons prepared mustard
        5 slices Swiss cheese (1/8 inch thick)
        5 thin slices red onion (3 inches around)
        5 round slices fully cooked Canadian bacon

In a medium bowl, combine the flour, baking powder, Italian seasoning and salt. Cut in shortening until mixture resembles coarse crumbs. Add milk; stir only until combined. Turn dough onto a floured surface; knead just until smooth, about 8 times. Roll to 1/4-in. thickness. Cut 10 biscuits with a 3-in. round cutter. Spread each with about 1/2 teaspoon mustard. Cut cheese with a 3-in. round cutter and place a slice on five of the biscuits. Top with onion and bacon. Cover with remaining biscuits, mustard side down. Place on a greased baking sheet. Bake at 425° for 15-18 minutes or until lightly browned. Serve hot. **Yield:** 5 servings.

Marinated Spiedis

Phyllis House, Averill Park, New York

Marinating the tenderloin overnight makes it moist and flavorful. Plus, this recipe is easy on the cook. Just broil or grill when you're ready and serve dinner in a matter of minutes!

        1 cup olive *or* vegetable oil
      1/3 cup fresh lemon juice
        4 garlic cloves, minced
        2 to 3 bay leaves, crushed
        1 teaspoon dried oregano
        1 teaspoon ground cumin
      1/2 teaspoon salt
      1/2 teaspoon pepper
        3 medium onions, chopped
        4 pounds pork tenderloin, trimmed and cut into
           1-inch pieces
       12 hot dog buns, split and buttered

In a large bowl, combine the first 10 ingredients. Cover and refrigerate for at least 8 hours. Drain, discarding marinade. Thread pork on small skewers (soaked if using bamboo). Broil 6 in. from the heat, turning frequently, for 15-20 minutes or until the meat is no longer pink and pulls away easily from the skewers. Wrap a bun around meat and pull off

---

skewer. **Yield:** 12 servings. **Editor's Note:** Spiedis can also be grilled over hot coals for 10-12 minutes or until the meat is no longer pink.

Pork and Cabbage Pockets

Jan Smith, Kalispell, Montana

I like to welcome my family home on fall days to the aroma of these hearty pockets. I sometimes double the recipe so I can have leftovers for busy-day dinners.

        1 package (1/4 ounce) active dry yeast
        1 cup warm water (110° to 115°)
    1/4 cup shortening
    1/4 cup sugar
        1 egg
        1 teaspoon salt, *divided*
        3 to 3-1/2 cups all-purpose flour, *divided*
        1 pound bulk pork sausage
        3 cups shredded cabbage
        1 medium onion, chopped
    1/4 cup water
    1-1/2 teaspoons dried oregano
    1-1/2 teaspoons ground cumin
    1/4 teaspoon pepper
        1 tablespoon butter *or* margarine, melted

In a large mixing bowl, dissolve yeast in water. Add shortening, sugar, egg, 1/2 teaspoon salt and 2 cups flour; beat until smooth. Add enough remaining flour to form a soft dough. Turn onto a floured board; knead for 6-8 minutes or until smooth and elastic. Place in a greased bowl, turning once to grease top. Cover and let rise in a warm place for 1 hour or until doubled. Meanwhile, in a skillet, cook sausage until no longer pink; drain. Add cabbage, onion, water, oregano, cumin, pepper and remaining salt. Cook, uncovered, for 15 minutes or until vegetables are tender and no liquid remains. Cool to room temperature. Punch dough down. Roll into a 24-in. x 12-in. rectangle; cut into eight 6-in. squares. Spoon 1/3 cup filling into the center of each square. Bring corners to the center and pinch to seal; pinch seams together. Place on a greased baking sheet. Cover and let rise for 30 minutes. Brush with melted butter. Bake at 375° for 25-30 minutes or until golden brown. **Yield:** 8 servings.

Ham 'n' Swiss Muffins

Susan Webber, Lansing, Michigan

Whenever the entire family gathers at our cabin for a weekend excursion, I greet them with these mouth-watering muffins. The fresh and lively flavor is unbeatable.

        2 cups (8 ounces) shredded Swiss cheese
        1 cup diced fully cooked ham
    1/2 cup finely chopped green pepper
        1 small onion, finely chopped
    1/2 cup mayonnaise
        1 tablespoon Dijon mustard
    1/4 teaspoon salt
Pinch pepper

        1 drop hot pepper sauce
        5 English muffins, split and toasted

In a bowl, combine cheese, ham, green pepper and onion. Stir in mayonnaise, mustard, salt, pepper and hot pepper sauce. Spread 1/4 cup on each muffin half; place on an ungreased baking sheet. Broil 5 in. from the heat for 2 minutes or until lightly browned and bubbly. **Yield:** 5 servings.

Tortilla Roll-Ups

Anna Eiler, El Cajon, California

I came up with this recipe when I was looking for a sandwich that combined foods my young son enjoys. These roll-ups also make a nice appetizer...simply slice before serving.

        8 flour tortillas (7 inches)
        1 carton (8 ounces) soft cream cheese with
          chives and onion
        8 slices (1 ounce *each*) fully cooked ham
    1-1/3 cups shredded cabbage
    2/3 cup shredded carrot
    1/2 cup honey Dijon salad dressing
        1 cup (4 ounces) shredded cheddar cheese

Spread each tortilla with 1 tablespoon cream cheese. Top with a slice of ham. Combine cabbage, carrot and dressing; divide evenly between tortillas. Sprinkle with cheese. Roll tightly; wrap in plastic wrap. Chill at least 1 hour before serving. **Yield:** 8 servings.

Mock Monte Cristos

Diana Brown, Portland, Oregon

Instead of being fried, these sandwiches are baked, so they're a little different than the traditional version. The crunchy coating contrasts nicely with the sweet strawberry sauce.

        3 tablespoons mayonnaise
      12 slices white bread
        6 ounces fully cooked ham, thinly sliced
        6 slices process Swiss cheese
        6 ounces cooked turkey, thinly sliced
        2 tablespoons Dijon mustard
        3 eggs, beaten
    3/4 cup milk
        2 tablespoons confectioners' sugar, optional
    1/4 teaspoon salt, optional
        2 cups crushed crisp rice cereal
    1/2 cup sour cream
    1/4 cup strawberry jam

Spread mayonnaise on six slices of bread; top each with ham, cheese and turkey. Spread mustard on remaining bread; place over turkey. In a shallow dish, combine eggs, milk, and confectioners' sugar and salt if desired. Dip each sandwich into egg mixture, then into crushed cereal. Place on a greased 15-in. x 10-in. x 1-in. baking pan. Bake at 425° for 7 minutes. Turn and bake 5-7 minutes more or until golden brown. Combine sour cream and jam; serve as a dip with hot sandwiches. **Yield:** 6 servings.

Porkettas

Pauline Kauppi, Roswell, New Mexico
(PICTURED AT RIGHT)

For as long as I can remember, these flavorful sandwiches have been part of our Christmas Eve buffet. Now our daughters carry on the tradition with their own families.

    1 boneless pork shoulder roast (5 to 5-1/2
        pounds), trimmed
    2 teaspoons fennel seed
    2 teaspoons *each* dried celery flakes, basil, parsley
        flakes, oregano and rosemary, crushed
    2 teaspoons garlic salt
    1 teaspoon salt
    1 teaspoon pepper
1-3/4 to 2 cups chicken broth
    16 to 20 hard rolls, split
Applesauce, optional

Cut about five deep slits across top of roast. Combine seasonings; stuff some into the slits. Reserve remaining seasoning mixture. Tie meat securely and place in a roasting pan. Pour 1-3/4 cups broth around roast. Bake, uncovered, at 325° for 2-3/4 to 3-1/4 hours or until a meat thermometer reads 170° and meat is very tender. Measure drippings, adding additional broth to make 1-1/4 cups; set aside. Remove tie from meat. Cut meat into bite-size pieces; trim and discard fat. Place meat in a large saucepan. Add reserved drippings and seasoning mixture; mix well. Heat through. Serve on hard rolls. Top meat with applesauce if desired. **Yield:** 16-20 servings (6-2/3 cups meat).

 Quick & Easy

Ham 'n' Cheese Melts

Myra Innes, Auburn, Kansas
(PICTURED AT RIGHT)

These one-of-a-kind sandwiches are a new twist on traditional ham and cheese sandwiches without a lot of extra work. Prepared spaghetti sauce provides a tasty dipping sauce.

    8 slices Italian bread (1/2 inch thick)
    4 slices provolone cheese, halved
    4 slices (1 ounce *each*) fully cooked ham
    2 eggs
    2 tablespoons milk
1/4 cup fine dry bread crumbs
1/4 cup grated Parmesan cheese
1/4 cup butter *or* margarine
    1 cup spaghetti sauce, warmed

On four slices of bread, layer cheese, ham, then cheese. Top with remaining bread. In a shallow dish, beat eggs and milk. In another shallow dish, combine bread crumbs and Parmesan cheese. Dip sandwiches into egg mixture, then into crumb mixture. In a large skillet over low heat, cook sandwiches in butter for 4 minutes per side or until golden brown. Serve with spaghetti sauce for dipping. **Yield:** 4 servings.

South-of-the-Border Submarine

Rhoda Curphy, Grinnell, Iowa
(PICTURED AT RIGHT)

This open-faced sandwich has been a family favorite for years, especially with the grandchildren. It has a zesty Mexican flavor that will really wake up your taste buds.

    2 pounds ground pork
1/2 cup chopped onion
    1 envelope taco seasoning mix
    1 teaspoon salt
    1 can (8 ounces) tomato sauce
1-1/2 cups (6 ounces) shredded sharp cheddar cheese,
        divided
1/2 cup chopped stuffed olives
    1 unsliced loaf (1 pound) French *or* Italian bread

In a large skillet, cook pork and onion until meat is no longer pink; drain. Add taco seasoning and salt. Stir in tomato sauce, 1/2 cup cheese and olives; cook over medium heat for 5-10 minutes, stirring occasionally. Cut bread in half lengthwise. Remove center from each half to form a 1-in. shell. Crumble removed bread to make 1 cup crumbs; stir into meat mixture. Place bread shells on a baking sheet; toast lightly under broiler. Fill with meat mixture and top with remaining cheese. Tent loosely with foil. Bake at 350° for 20 minutes or until cheese is melted and filling is heated through. Cut into slices. **Yield:** 6-8 servings.

Rosemary's Ham Reubens

Rosemary Smith, Fort Bragg, California

I never cared much for pork products when I was young because that's all we ever seemed to eat on our farm. Now I love ham—the leftovers are versatile and make delicious recipes.

    8 ounces fully cooked ham, julienned
    8 ounces Swiss cheese, julienned
3/4 cup mayonnaise
    1 can (8 ounces) sauerkraut, drained
    1 teaspoon caraway seed
    8 slices rye bread
Dijon mustard, optional

Combine ham, cheese, mayonnaise, sauerkraut and caraway. Lightly toast the bread. Spread mustard on toast if desired; top with filling. Place on a baking sheet; broil 6 in. from the heat for 2-3 minutes or until cheese melts. **Yield:** 4-8 servings.

SANDWICH SPREAD. *Pictured at right, top to bottom: Porkettas, Ham 'n' Cheese Melts and South-of-the-Border Submarine (all recipes on this page).*

Stuffed Ham Slices

Beverly Calfee, McDonald, Ohio

Any occasion is perfect to present these tasty slices. The great combination of a seasoned cheese spread, hearty ham and zesty pickle appeals to folks of all ages.

✓ This tasty dish uses less sugar, salt and fat. Recipe includes *Diabetic Exchanges*.

    1 package (8 ounces) cream cheese, softened
  3/4 cup minced celery
  1/2 cup shredded cheddar cheese
  1/3 cup minced fresh parsley
  1/4 cup mayonnaise
    2 tablespoons minced onion
    1 unsliced loaf (1 pound) Italian bread
    8 slices (1 ounce *each*) fully cooked ham
    3 to 4 whole dill pickles, sliced lengthwise

In a bowl, combine the first six ingredients. Cut bread in half lengthwise; spread each half with the cheese mixture. On the bottom half, layer half the ham, pickle slices and remaining ham. Replace top of loaf. Wrap tightly in plastic wrap; chill for at least 2 hours before serving. **Yield:** 8 servings. **Diabetic Exchanges:** One serving (prepared with fat-free cream cheese, cheddar cheese and mayonnaise and low-fat ham) equals 2 starch, 1-1/2 lean meat; also, 233 calories, 1,361 mg sodium, 17 mg cholesterol, 34 gm carbohydrate, 16 gm protein, 3 gm fat.

  Quick & Easy

Ham and Onion Squares

Lauriana Audette, Lac du Bonne, Manitoba

One of my favorite things about this recipe is that it can be assembled the night before. These squares have appeared on many a lunch table, but my family also enjoys them for breakfast.

DOUGH:
    1 package (1/4 ounce) active dry yeast
  1/4 cup warm water (110° to 115°)
    2 cups all-purpose flour
    1 teaspoon sugar
  1/4 teaspoon salt
  1/2 cup shortening
  1/2 cup sour cream
    2 eggs
TOPPING:
    1 cup chopped onion
  1/4 cup butter *or* margarine
    2 cups diced fully cooked ham
    2 eggs, lightly beaten
  1/2 cup sour cream
    2 tablespoons minced chives
  1/2 teaspoon salt
  1/2 teaspoon caraway seed

In a small bowl, dissolve yeast in water; set aside. In a large bowl, combine the flour, sugar and salt; cut in shortening until mixture resembles coarse crumbs. Add yeast mixture. Combine sour cream and eggs; stir into flour mixture until a smooth dough forms (do not knead). Cover and chill over-

night. Roll dough to fit a greased 15-in. x 10-in. x 1-in. baking pan. Form a rim around edges; set aside. In a skillet, saute onion in butter until tender. Remove from the heat; stir in remaining topping ingredients. Spread over dough. Bake at 350° for 25 minutes or until golden brown. **Yield:** 8-10 servings.

  Quick & Easy

Liverwurst Deluxe

Adrienne Bagnall, Chester, Massachusetts

These sandwiches are eye-catching with their colorful layers. Even folks not fond of liverwurst will savor this light meal.

    4 onion rolls, split
    4 teaspoons prepared mustard
 1/3 to 1/2 pound liverwurst, sliced 1/4 inch thick
  1/2 pound cooked turkey breast, sliced
    8 bacon strips, cooked and drained
    2 slices onion, separated into rings
Dill pickle slices
    4 slices cheddar cheese

Spread rolls with mustard. On bottoms of rolls, layer liverwurst, turkey, bacon, onion, pickles and cheese; replace tops. **Yield:** 4 servings.

Meaty Mexican Sandwiches

Teri Spaulding, Durham, California

I like to serve these hearty sandwiches on Super Bowl Sunday along with a green salad, rice and beans. Everyone raves about the great combination of flavors and textures.

  1/2 pound ground pork
  1/2 pound ground beef
    1 small onion, chopped
    1 garlic clove, minced
  3/4 cup ketchup
  1/2 cup raisins
    1 teaspoon red wine vinegar
  1/2 teaspoon ground cinnamon
  1/2 teaspoon chili powder
  1/2 teaspoon salt
  1/4 teaspoon pepper
  1/8 teaspoon ground cumin
Pinch ground cloves
  1/2 cup slivered almonds, toasted
    6 hard rolls, split
1-1/2 cups (6 ounces) shredded cheddar cheese
    2 cups shredded lettuce

In a skillet, cook pork, beef, onion and garlic until meat is no longer pink and vegetables are tender; drain. Stir in the ketchup, raisins, vinegar and seasonings. Cover and simmer for 20-25 minutes, stirring occasionally. Stir in almonds. Hollow out the top and bottom of each roll, leaving a 1/2-in. shell. (Discard removed bread or save for another use.) Fill each roll with about 1/2 cup meat mixture. Top with cheese and lettuce; replace top of roll. **Yield:** 6 servings.

Meat Loaf Sandwiches

Michael Arnestad, Tacoma, Washington

My philosophy is that life's too short to eat bland, boring foods, so I created this recipe. With salsa and cayenne pepper, these sandwiches pack a little punch.

    1/2 cup salsa
      1 tablespoon Worcestershire sauce
    1/8 teaspoon hickory smoke salt
    1/8 teaspoon cayenne pepper
    1/8 teaspoon pepper
    1/2 cup diced sharp cheddar cheese
    1/2 cup diced Swiss cheese
    1/2 cup chopped dill pickle
      1 can (2-1/4 ounces) sliced ripe olives, drained
    1/3 cup chopped red onion
    1/3 cup dry bread crumbs
      1 egg
      3 tablespoons crumbled blue cheese
      2 pounds bulk pork sausage
     14 to 16 hard rolls, split
Dijon mustard

In a large bowl, combine the first five ingredients. Add the next eight ingredients; mix well. Add the sausage; mix well. Press into an ungreased 9-in. x 5-in. x 3-in. loaf pan. Bake at 350° for 1 hour; drain often. Increase temperature to 375° and bake 30 minutes longer or until a meat thermometer reads 160°-170°; drain. Cool in pan for 30 minutes. Remove from pan; cover and chill overnight. Cut into 1/2-in.-thick slices. Spread rolls with mustard and top with meat loaf slices. **Yield:** 14-16 servings.

Humpty-Dumpty Sandwich Loaf

Martha Price, Swartz Creek, Michigan

When they were young, our three boys came to expect this loaf stuffed with egg and ham salad on Sunday evenings. Folks will gobble it up whether you serve it hot or cold.

      1 unsliced loaf (1 pound) Italian bread
    1/3 cup mayonnaise
    1/3 cup sweet pickle relish
      4 teaspoons prepared mustard
      1 garlic clove, minced
Pinch pepper
      4 hard-cooked eggs, chopped
      1 cup diced celery
      1 cup diced fully cooked ham
      3 tablespoons chopped onion
      2 tablespoons butter *or* margarine, melted, optional

Slice off the top third of the loaf; set top aside. Hollow out the bottom of the loaf, leaving a 1-in. shell. Crumble part of the removed bread to measure 3/4 cup; set aside. (Discard remaining bread or save for another use.) In a bowl, com-

bine mayonnaise, relish, mustard, garlic and pepper. Stir in eggs, celery, ham, onion and reserved bread. Stuff loaf; replace top. To serve immediately, cut into 4-in. pieces. To serve hot, brush with butter; wrap in foil. Place on a baking sheet. Bake at 400° for 25 minutes. **Yield:** 4 servings.

Coffee House Sandwiches

Ethel Mott, Sidney, New York

My daughter developed this recipe after trying a similar sandwich at a local restaurant. Apples add a pleasing tartness and crunch to these hearty sandwiches.

      8 submarine rolls, split
Mayonnaise
Spicy brown Dijon mustard
      1 pound fully cooked ham, thinly sliced
      1 pound sliced provolone cheese
     16 slices tomato
      1 package (4 ounces) alfalfa sprouts
     16 slices tart apple (1/4 inch thick)

Place rolls, cut side up, on an ungreased baking sheet. Spread bottom halves with mayonnaise and mustard; top with ham and cheese. Broil 4 in. from the heat for 1-2 minutes or until cheese is melted and roll tops are toasted. Remove from broiler. Layer tomato, alfalfa sprouts and apple over cheese; replace tops. **Yield:** 8 servings.

Sweet 'n' Sour Pockets

Kathy Harris, Old Hickory, Tennessee

This recipe combines two great foods that are fabulous together—ham and pineapple. I first made these for a ladies luncheon and was asked many times for the recipe.

✓ This tasty dish uses less sugar, salt and fat. Recipe includes *Diabetic Exchanges.*

    1/3 cup mayonnaise
    1/3 cup sour cream
    1/2 teaspoon Dijon mustard
      1 can (8 ounces) pineapple tidbits, drained
      5 pita pocket breads (6 inches), halved
     10 lettuce leaves
     10 slices (1 ounce *each*) fully cooked ham
    1/2 cup chopped green pepper
    1/2 cup chopped red onion

In a small bowl, combine mayonnaise, sour cream and mustard. Cover and chill for 1 hour. Just before serving, stir pineapple into mayonnaise mixture. Fill each pita half with lettuce, ham, 2 tablespoons pineapple mixture, green pepper and onion. **Yield:** 5 servings. **Diabetic Exchanges:** One serving of two pita halves (prepared with fat-free mayonnaise and sour cream, unsweetened pineapple and low-fat ham) equals 2-1/2 starch, 1-1/2 very lean meat, 1 vegetable, 1 fruit; also, 291 calories, 1,166 mg sodium, 30 mg cholesterol, 49 gm carbohydrate, 16 gm protein, 3 gm fat.

Pork Pocket Pasties

Dolores Haynie, Banning, California
(PICTURED AT LEFT)

I'm in my 70's and have spent many happy hours in the kitchen. I most often cook from scratch, but I can't resist these delectable pasties that call for frozen hash browns.

        1 pound bulk pork sausage
        2 cups frozen hash browns, thawed
        1 large carrot, finely diced
    1/4 cup chopped onion
    1/2 teaspoon salt
    1/4 teaspoon pepper
1-1/2 cups (6 ounces) shredded Monterey Jack cheese
        4 pita breads (6 inches), halved
        1 tablespoon butter *or* margarine

In a skillet, cook sausage until no longer pink; drain. Add hash browns, carrot, onion, salt and pepper. Cook until vegetables are tender, stirring occasionally. Remove from the heat; stir in cheese. Spoon into pitas. Place on an ungreased baking sheet; brush outside of pitas with butter. Bake at 400° for 4-5 minutes or until heated through. **Yield:** 8 servings.

Ham Wafflewiches

Jnell Willford, Piedmont, Missouri
(PICTURED AT LEFT)

Now that I'm retired, it seems I'm busier than ever. But I always make the time to cook for the family. My kids and grandchildren think these sandwiches are a fun treat.

1-1/2 cups finely chopped fully cooked ham
        1 can (4 ounces) mushroom stems and pieces, drained and finely chopped
    1/3 cup mayonnaise
    1/4 cup chopped celery
        1 tablespoon chopped onion
      16 frozen waffles
        2 tablespoons butter *or* margarine
        2 tablespoons all-purpose flour
    1/4 teaspoon salt
1-1/2 cups milk
        4 teaspoons prepared mustard, optional
    1/2 cup shredded cheddar cheese, optional

In a bowl, combine ham, mushrooms, mayonnaise, celery and onion. Spread on half of the waffles; top with remaining waffles. Place on a greased baking sheet. Bake at 400° for 15-20 minutes or until browned. Meanwhile, melt but-

---

MORNING GLORY. *Pictured at left, top to bottom: Pork Pocket Pasties, Ham Wafflewiches and Bacon Breakfast Sandwiches (all recipes on this page).*

---

ter in a saucepan over medium heat. Stir in flour and salt until smooth. Gradually add milk. Bring to a boil; boil and stir for 2 minutes. Remove from the heat. Add mustard and cheese if desired; stir until smooth. Serve over wafflewiches. **Yield:** 8 servings.

Bacon Breakfast Sandwiches

Rose Carol Brown, Park Forest, Illinois
(PICTURED AT LEFT)

This recipe is a standby when I need to make dinner in a snap. Our five children eat these sandwiches eagerly without complaint and agree they're better than any fast-food variety.

        1 tablespoon butter *or* margarine
        4 eggs
        2 tablespoons snipped chives *or* green onion tops
        1 tablespoon water
    1/4 teaspoon salt
Dash pepper
        2 English muffins, split and toasted
        8 bacon strips, cooked and drained
        4 slices tomato
        4 slices American cheese
Additional chives, optional

Melt butter in a skillet. Beat eggs, chives, water, salt and pepper; pour into skillet. Cook and stir gently until eggs are set. Top each muffin half with eggs, bacon, tomato and cheese. Broil for 1-2 minutes or until cheese melts. Garnish with chives if desired. **Yield:** 2 servings.

Pork Tenderloin Sandwiches

Margarete Muhle, Pewaukee, Wisconsin

Chutney and pears add a distinctive touch to these sandwiches, making them perfect for special luncheons. But they're so simple that you won't mind making them anytime.

        2 pork tenderloins (about 1 pound *each*), trimmed
        1 teaspoon seasoned salt
    1/2 teaspoon pepper
        1 to 2 tablespoons cooking oil
        6 thick slices sourdough *or* white bread
        3 tablespoons mango chutney
        1 can (15 ounces) sliced pears in natural juices, drained
        6 slices process American cheese

Cut pork crosswise into six slices; sprinkle with seasoned salt and pepper. Flatten to 1/4-in. thickness; cook in oil in a large skillet over medium heat for about 4 minutes per side or until no longer pink. Meanwhile, toast bread and spread each slice with about 2 teaspoons chutney. Top with tenderloin, pears and cheese; place on an ungreased baking sheet. Bake at 300° for 2-3 minutes or until cheese is melted. **Yield:** 6 servings.

Brat Hoagies with Coleslaw

Tammara Lindsey-Cain, Green Valley, Arizona

Served with a side of potato salad and pickles, these sandwiches are a standby on our lunch menu. For a little lighter version, you can substitute turkey bratwurst.

        4 uncooked bratwurst
        3 tablespoons water
        4 tablespoons butter *or* margarine, *divided*
        1 tablespoon sugar
1-1/2 teaspoons lemon juice
        3 cups shredded cabbage
    1/4 cup chopped onion
    1/2 teaspoon salt
    1/4 cup sour cream
        4 brat *or* hoagie buns, split
    1/4 teaspoon garlic salt
        4 slices brick cheese, halved

Place bratwurst and water in a skillet; cover and cook over medium heat for 10-12 minutes. Uncover; turn bratwurst and cook 13-17 minutes longer or until browned and centers are no longer pink. Cut bratwurst in half lengthwise; set aside and keep warm. Meanwhile, in another skillet, cook 2 tablespoons butter, sugar and lemon juice over medium heat until sugar is dissolved. Add cabbage, onion and salt. Cook and stir for 3-5 minutes or until cabbage is crisp-tender; drain. Remove from the heat; stir in sour cream. Set aside and keep warm. Spread cut sides of rolls with remaining butter; sprinkle with garlic salt. Broil 5 in. from the heat for 1-2 minutes or until golden brown. Divide cabbage mixture between roll halves. Place one bratwurst half, cut side down, on each half; top with cheese. Broil for 1-2 minutes or until cheese is melted. **Yield:** 4 servings.

Curry Cheddar Grill

Mary Engelmeyer, West Point, Nebraska

As a farm wife with three active teenagers, I need recipes that call for common ingredients and that can be put together quickly. I've come to rely on these snappy sandwiches.

1/2 cup mayonnaise
1/4 cup mango chutney
    1 to 1-1/2 teaspoons curry powder
3/4 teaspoon salt
    2 cups finely shredded cabbage
  12 slices rye bread
  12 slices (1 ounce *each*) fully cooked ham
1/2 pound cheddar cheese, cut into 6 thin slices
1/4 cup butter *or* margarine, softened

In a bowl, combine the mayonnaise, chutney, curry powder and salt; stir in cabbage. On six slices of bread, layer two slices of ham, one slice of cheese and 1/4 cup cabbage mixture; top with remaining bread. Butter outsides of each sandwich. In a large skillet over medium heat, toast

sandwiches on both sides until lightly browned. **Yield:** 6 servings.

Zesty Italian Loaf

Molly Dankowski, San Dimas, California

My husband and I entertain quite a bit, either around our pool at home or at our log cabin. I especially like to serve this zesty sandwich loaf during the cooler months.

        3 tablespoons mayonnaise
        2 tablespoons butter *or* margarine, softened
        1 teaspoon prepared mustard
        1 garlic clove, minced
    1/8 teaspoon crushed red pepper flakes
        1 unsliced loaf (1 pound) Italian bread
        6 slices mozzarella cheese
        6 thin slices tomato
        6 thin slices salami
        6 thin slices red onion
      12 thin slices pepperoni

In a small bowl, combine the first five ingredients; set aside. Make 11 slices in the bread, not cutting all the way through bottom crust. Place loaf on a piece of foil large enough to wrap it completely. Gently separate every other slice and spread 1 tablespoon mayonnaise mixture on cut surfaces. Insert cheese, tomato, salami, onion and pepperoni between every other slice. Wrap the foil tightly around loaf; place on a baking sheet. Bake at 350° for 25 minutes. To serve, cut bread between unstuffed slices; serve warm. **Yield:** 6 servings. **Editor's Note:** This loaf can be made ahead and refrigerated before baking.

Sausage 'n' Spinach Pockets

Denise Stapleton, Fort Collins, Colorado

I've found that these appetizing pockets are the perfect way to sneak some vegetables into my kids' meals. They are a favorite weekend snack around our house.

1/2 pound bulk pork sausage
1/3 cup chopped onion
    1 garlic clove, minced
    1 cup chopped fresh spinach
1/4 cup chopped fresh mushrooms
3/4 cup shredded mozzarella cheese
1/2 teaspoon salt
1/4 teaspoon pepper
    2 tablespoons grated Parmesan cheese, optional
    2 tubes (8 ounces *each*) refrigerated crescent rolls
    1 egg
    1 tablespoon water
    1 tablespoon cornmeal

In a large skillet, brown sausage, onion and garlic; drain. Remove from the heat; stir in spinach and mushrooms. Add mozzarella cheese, salt, pepper and Parmesan cheese if desired; mix well and set aside. Separate crescent dough into eight rectangles; seal perforations and flatten slightly to 5-in. x 4-1/2-in. rectangles. Place about 1/3 cup sausage mixture on half of each rectangle to within 1/2 in. of edges. Beat egg and water; brush on edges of dough. Bring unfilled half of dough over filling; press edges with a fork to seal. Brush tops with egg mixture. Sprinkle the cornmeal on a greased baking sheet; place pockets on baking sheet. Bake at 350° for 15-20 minutes or until golden brown. **Yield:** 8 servings.

Tomato-Bacon Rarebit

Linda May, Mogadore, Ohio

I've had an interest in cooking and baking since I was a young girl and love to experiment with recipes. With bacon and tomatoes, this is a tasty takeoff on a classic Welsh dish.

    1 tablespoon butter *or* margarine
    1 tablespoon all-purpose flour
  2/3 cup milk
    1 teaspoon Worcestershire sauce
  1/4 teaspoon ground mustard
  1/4 teaspoon salt
  1/8 teaspoon pepper
  1/8 teaspoon paprika
    2 cups (8 ounces) shredded sharp cheddar
      cheese
    4 slices white bread, toasted
   12 bacon strips, cooked and drained
    2 medium tomatoes, sliced

In a saucepan, melt butter over medium heat. Stir in the flour to form a smooth paste. Gradually stir in milk. Bring to a boil; cook and stir for 2 minutes. Reduce heat to low; add Worcestershire sauce, mustard, salt, pepper, paprika and cheese. Cook and stir until cheese is melted. Place toast on plates; top each piece with three bacon strips, two slices of tomato and cheese sauce. **Yield:** 4 servings.

Saucy Italian Sausage Sandwiches

Gloria Warczak, Cedarburg, Wisconsin

I created this recipe years ago as a way to satisfy my sons' hearty appetites. I still make them for my husband and me. Any leftovers freeze well for a fast meal in the future.

    8 uncooked Italian sausage links (about 2 pounds)
    2 tablespoons olive *or* vegetable oil, *divided*
  1/2 cup chopped onion
  1/4 cup chopped green pepper
  1/4 cup sliced celery
    2 tablespoons minced fresh celery leaves
    2 tablespoons minced fresh parsley

    1 garlic clove, minced
    1 can (28 ounces) diced tomatoes, undrained
    1 can (12 ounces) tomato paste
    2 cups water
  1/4 cup grated Parmesan cheese
    2 teaspoons sugar
    2 teaspoons browning sauce
    1 teaspoon dried basil
    1 teaspoon beef bouillon granules
    1 teaspoon Worcestershire sauce
  1/2 teaspoon dried oregano
  1/2 teaspoon chili powder
    1 bay leaf
    1 large green pepper, cut into 16 strips
    8 crusty Italian rolls, split
Butter *or* margarine
Additional Parmesan cheese, optional

In a large kettle or Dutch oven, brown sausages in 1 tablespoon oil; remove and set aside. In the same kettle, saute onion, chopped green pepper and celery until tender. Stir in celery leaves, parsley and garlic; saute for 2 minutes. Add the next 12 ingredients. Bring to a boil, stirring frequently. Return sausage to kettle; reduce heat and simmer, uncovered, for 1 hour. Remove bay leaf. In a skillet, saute pepper strips in remaining oil for 5 minutes or until tender. Butter bottom halves of rolls; top with sausage, 1/4 cup sauce and two pepper strips. Replace tops. Sprinkle with Parmesan cheese if desired. Freeze extra sauce for later use. **Yield:** 8 servings.

Pork and Corn Barbecue

Juanita Myres, Lake Charles, Louisiana

Traditional barbecued pork sandwiches are livened up with cumin and corn. Alongside a green salad and chips, this is a hot and hearty meal that's sure to please.

    1 boneless pork shoulder roast (about 4 pounds),
      trimmed
    1 tablespoon cooking oil
    3 medium onions, chopped
    3 garlic cloves, minced
    1 teaspoon salt
    1 teaspoon ground cumin
    1 teaspoon dried oregano
  1/3 cup water
  1/4 cup cider vinegar
    2 cups barbecue sauce
    1 can (15-1/4 ounces) whole kernel corn,
      drained
   16 hard rolls, split

In a Dutch oven, brown roast in oil; remove and set aside. Saute onions and garlic in drippings until onions are tender. Return roast to Dutch oven. Add salt, cumin, oregano, water and vinegar. Cover and bake at 350° for 2-1/2 to 3 hours or until meat falls apart easily. Remove meat and shred; set aside. Skim off excess fat from pan juices. Stir in barbecue sauce, corn and reserved pork; heat through. Serve on rolls. **Yield:** 16 servings.

Country Soups & Stews

Sauerbraten Stew

Joanne Recker, West Point, Nebraska

(PICTURED AT LEFT)

Our kids typically don't care for cabbage, but they can't get enough of this dish. I often put this stew on the stove before doing chores so we can come inside to a hearty meal.

2 pounds boneless pork, trimmed and cut into 1-1/2-inch cubes
2 tablespoons cooking oil
1-1/2 quarts water
2 cups ketchup
1 large onion, chopped
2 medium potatoes, peeled and cubed
3 medium carrots, cut into 1/2-inch slices
1 cup fresh *or* frozen cut green beans (1-inch pieces)
1 cup shredded cabbage
2 celery ribs, cut into 1/2-inch slices
1/4 to 1/2 teaspoon ground allspice
1/4 teaspoon pepper
1 cup crushed gingersnaps (about 16 cookies)

In a Dutch oven or soup kettle, brown pork in oil. Add the next 10 ingredients. Cover and simmer for 1-1/2 hours. Stir in gingersnap crumbs; simmer, uncovered, for 30 minutes or until stew is thickened and pork is tender. **Yield:** 12-14 servings (3-1/2 quarts).

Canadian Cheese Soup

Jolene Roudebush, Troy, Michigan

(PICTURED AT LEFT)

My family loves Canadian bacon, but I don't run across a lot of dishes that call for this pork product. Everyone was thrilled the first time I offered this succulent soup.

✓ **This tasty dish uses less sugar, salt and fat. Recipe includes *Diabetic Exchanges*.**

3 cups chicken broth
4 medium potatoes, peeled and diced
2 celery ribs, diced
1 medium carrot, diced
1 small onion, diced
6 ounces Canadian bacon, trimmed and diced
2 tablespoons butter *or* margarine

> **KETTLE CREATIONS.** *Pictured at left, top to bottom: Sauerbraten Stew, Ham and Vegetable Soup and Canadian Cheese Soup (all recipes on this page).*

2 tablespoons all-purpose flour
1 cup milk
2 cups (8 ounces) shredded cheddar cheese
1/8 teaspoon pepper

In a Dutch oven or soup kettle, combine the first five ingredients; bring to a boil. Reduce heat; cover and simmer for 20 minutes or until vegetables are very tender. With a potato masher, mash vegetables several times. Add bacon; continue to simmer. Meanwhile, melt butter in a small saucepan; stir in the flour and cook, stirring constantly, for 1 minute. Gradually whisk in milk. Bring to a boil; boil and stir for 2 minutes (mixture will be thick). Add to vegetable mixture, stirring constantly. Remove from the heat; add cheese and pepper. Stir just until cheese is melted. **Yield:** 8 servings (2 quarts). **Diabetic Exchanges:** One 1-cup serving (prepared with low-sodium chicken broth, margarine, skim milk and low-fat cheese) equals 2 meat, 1 starch, 1 vegetable; also, 252 calories, 402 mg sodium, 33 mg cholesterol, 22 gm carbohydrate, 19 gm protein, 11 gm fat.

> **ONION ODOR.** To get rid of the smell of onions from your hands, knife or chopping board, rub them with lemon juice or salt.

Ham and Vegetable Soup

Helen Peterson, Rives Junction, Michigan

(PICTURED AT LEFT)

The basis for this soup's broth conveniently comes from canned bean soup. Everyone who tries this comments on how nicely the smoky flavor of ham blends with the vegetables.

2 pounds smoked ham shanks
4 medium carrots, sliced
1 cup thinly sliced celery
1 medium onion, chopped
2 quarts water
2-1/2 cups diced unpeeled red potatoes
1 cup *each* frozen corn, peas and cut green beans
1 can (11-1/2 ounces) condensed bean and bacon soup, undiluted
1/4 teaspoon pepper

Place ham shanks, carrots, celery, onion and water in a Dutch oven or soup kettle; bring to a boil. Reduce heat; cover and simmer for 2-1/2 hours or until meat starts to fall off the bones. Add potatoes and vegetables; bring to a boil. Reduce heat; cover and simmer for 1 hour. Remove shanks; allow to cool. Remove meat from bones and cut into bite-size pieces; discard bones. Return meat to kettle. Stir in bean and bacon soup and pepper; heat through. **Yield:** 14-16 servings (4 quarts).

Smoked Sausage Stew

Ella Jay Tubbs, Fort Worth, Texas

I like to volunteer my time by sharing dishes like this with others. It's a down-home one-pot dinner that appeals to all. Corn bread and a green salad really round out the meal.

> 2 cans (11-1/2 ounces *each*) condensed bean and
>   bacon soup, undiluted
> 1 can (14-1/2 ounces) diced tomatoes, undrained
> 2 cups water
> 2 medium potatoes, diced
> 1 cup sliced carrots
> 1 cup sliced celery
> 1 teaspoon chili powder
> 12 ounces fully cooked smoked sausage, thinly sliced

In a saucepan, combine soup, tomatoes and water. Add potatoes, carrots, celery, and chili powder. Cover and bring to a boil; reduce heat and simmer for 20 minutes. Add sausage; simmer 40 minutes longer. **Yield:** 6-8 servings (2 quarts).

Pork and Pasta Stew

Margaret Bossuot, Carthage, New York

I especially like to make this stew in summer when I can use vegetables from my own garden. Because it doesn't simmer for hours, I often reach for this recipe when I need dinner in a hurry.

✓ **This tasty dish uses less sugar, salt and fat. Recipe includes** *Diabetic Exchanges*.

> 1 pound lean boneless pork, cut into 1-inch strips
> 1/2 teaspoon lemon-pepper seasoning
> 1 tablespoon olive *or* vegetable oil
> 1 medium onion, sliced into thin wedges
> 1 garlic clove, minced
> 1 cup chicken broth
> 3/4 cup salsa
> 1 tablespoon brown sugar
> 3 quarts water
> 1 teaspoon salt, optional
> 1 package (8 ounces) spiral pasta
> 1 cup fresh cut green beans (1-inch pieces)
> 1 cup sliced yellow summer squash
> 1 cup sliced zucchini
> 1 cup sliced fresh mushrooms
> 1 tablespoon cornstarch
> 2 tablespoons cold water

Toss pork and lemon pepper; brown in oil in a skillet over medium heat. Add onion and garlic; saute until tender. Stir in broth, salsa and brown sugar; bring to a boil. Reduce heat; cover and simmer for 15-20 minutes or until pork is tender. Meanwhile, in a large saucepan over medium heat, bring water and salt if desired to a boil. Add pasta and beans; return to a boil. Cook, uncovered, for 7 minutes. Add the squash, zucchini and mushrooms. Cook, uncovered, 6-7 minutes more or until pasta and vegetables are tender. Drain; set aside and keep warm. Combine cornstarch with cold water until smooth; add to the pork mixture and mix

well. Bring to a boil; boil and stir for 2 minutes. To serve, place pasta and vegetables in a serving dish; top with pork mixture. **Yield:** 6 servings. **Diabetic Exchanges:** One 1-1/2-cup serving (prepared with salt-free lemon-pepper seasoning and low-sodium chicken broth and without salt) equals 2 starch, 2 meat, 1 vegetable; also, 309 calories, 371 mg sodium, 46 mg cholesterol, 35 gm carbohydrate, 22 gm protein, 9 gm fat.

Ham and Chicken Gumbo

Jean Leonard, Farmington, New Mexico

I've always enjoyed spending time in the kitchen and worked as a home economist for a utility company in the 1940's. With two kinds of meat, this gumbo makes a hearty supper.

> 6 bacon strips, cut into 1/2-inch pieces
> 3/4 cup chopped onion
> 2 garlic cloves, minced
> 1 cup diced fully cooked ham
> 1/2 cup diced cooked chicken
> 2 cups frozen cut okra
> 1 can (14-1/2 ounces) diced tomatoes, undrained
> 2 cups chicken broth
> 1 teaspoon Worcestershire sauce
> 1/4 teaspoon salt
> 8 drops hot pepper sauce
> Hot cooked rice

In a large skillet, cook bacon just until crisp. Add onion and cook, stirring constantly, until bacon is crisp and onion is soft. Add garlic, ham and chicken; cook for 2 minutes, stirring constantly. Stir in okra, tomatoes and broth; bring to a boil. Reduce heat; cover and simmer for 30 minutes. Add Worcestershire sauce, salt and hot pepper sauce. Serve over rice. **Yield:** 4 servings.

Sweet 'n' Snappy Chili

Joanne Withers, Osakis, Minnesota

I created this dish by combining two different recipes and some of my own ideas. Folks are pleasantly surprised to see this chili brimming with ground pork instead of beef.

> 2 pounds ground pork
> 2 celery ribs, diced
> 1 medium onion, chopped
> 1 small green pepper, chopped
> 2 garlic cloves, minced
> 2 cans (16 ounces *each*) chili beans, undrained
> 1 can (28 ounces) diced tomatoes, undrained
> 1 can (4 ounces) chopped green chilies
> 3 cups water
> 1/4 cup packed brown sugar
> 3 tablespoons chili powder
> 2 teaspoons ground cumin
> 3/4 teaspoon ground ginger

In a Dutch oven or soup kettle, cook pork until no longer pink; drain. Remove and set aside. In the same kettle, saute celery, onion, green pepper and garlic until vegetables are tender; drain. Add pork and remaining ingredients; bring to a boil. Reduce heat; cover and simmer for 45 minutes. **Yield:** 6-8 servings (2-1/4 quarts).

Lima Bean Sunshine Stew

Mrs. Robert Scofield, Van Wert, Ohio

This fresh, flavorful stew features a nice light broth instead of a typical thickened base. My family has been regularly requesting this one-pot meal for as long as I can remember.

✓ **This tasty dish uses less sugar, salt and fat. Recipe includes** *Diabetic Exchanges.*

1-1/2 cups cubed fully cooked ham
    2 medium potatoes, peeled and cut into 3/4-inch cubes
    2 medium onions, cut into eighths
    2 medium tomatoes, cut into 3/4-inch pieces
    1 cup frozen lima beans
    1 cup frozen whole kernel corn
  1/4 cup diced green pepper
    1 teaspoon sugar
  1/2 teaspoon salt, optional
  1/4 teaspoon pepper

Combine all ingredients in an ungreased 2-qt. baking dish. Cover and bake for 50-60 minutes or until potatoes are tender. **Yield:** 6 servings. **Diabetic Exchanges:** One 1-cup serving (prepared with low-fat ham and without salt) equals 1 starch, 1 lean meat, 1 vegetable; also, 139 calories, 522 mg sodium, 16 mg cholesterol, 21 gm carbohydrate, 10 gm protein, 2 gm fat.

Quick Wild Rice Soup

Jane Meyer, Linn, Kansas

While my mother helped out on the family farm, I took over in the kitchen and have been cooking ever since. I often serve this soup with a loaf of warm bread.

 10 bacon strips
   1 medium onion, chopped
   1 box (6-3/4 ounces) quick-cooking long grain and wild rice mix
   2 cans (10-3/4 ounces *each*) condensed cream of potato soup, undiluted
   4 cups milk
   2 cups cubed process American cheese

In a large skillet, cook bacon until crisp; remove to paper towels to drain. Reserve 1 teaspoon drippings; saute onion in drippings. In a large kettle or Dutch oven, cook rice according to package directions; stir in soup, milk, cheese and onion. Crumble eight strips of bacon; add to soup. Cook and stir over low heat until cheese is melted. Crumble remaining bacon and sprinkle over soup. **Yield:** 6-8 servings (2-1/2 quarts).

Corn and Ham Stew

Lili Lanz, Coral Gables, Florida

When I was a little girl, my grandmother would use home-grown vegetables to prepare this old-fashioned stew. I was thrilled when she passed the family recipe on to me.

    1 medium onion, chopped
    1 medium green pepper, chopped
    1 cup cubed fully cooked ham
    3 garlic cloves, minced
    3 tablespoons cooking oil
  1/2 pound bulk pork sausage
2-1/2 cups water
    1 can (8 ounces) tomato sauce
    2 cups fresh, canned *or* frozen corn
    1 cup cubed peeled butternut squash
    1 cup cubed peeled potatoes
    1 bay leaf
  1/8 teaspoon pepper

In a 3-qt. saucepan, saute onion, green pepper, ham and garlic in oil until vegetables are tender. In a skillet, cook sausage until no longer pink; drain and add to ham mixture. Add remaining ingredients; bring to a boil. Reduce heat; cover and simmer for 30 minutes or until potatoes and squash are tender. Remove bay leaf before serving. **Yield:** 4 servings.

Hearty Ham and Cabbage Chowder

Sharyl Mathis, Byron, Michigan

Ketchup and brown sugar add an appealing sweetness to this chowder. I make this frequently throughout the year, but my family especially looks forward to it on winter evenings.

    1 cup thinly sliced celery
  1/2 cup chopped onion
    2 garlic cloves, minced
    2 tablespoons cooking oil
    3 cups shredded cabbage
    2 cups (1 pound) cubed fully cooked ham
    1 can (28 ounces) diced tomatoes, undrained
    1 can (15-1/4 ounces) whole kernel corn, drained
    1 can (15 ounces) whole potatoes, drained and quartered
    1 can (10-1/2 ounces) condensed chicken broth, undiluted
    1 cup water
  1/2 cup ketchup
  1/4 cup packed brown sugar

In a Dutch oven or soup kettle over medium heat, saute celery, onion and garlic in oil for 2 minutes, stirring constantly. Add remaining ingredients; bring to a boil. Reduce heat; cover and simmer for 1-1/2 hours. **Yield:** 8-10 servings (2-3/4 quarts).

Creamy Ham and Asparagus Soup

Maurine Kent, Kilgore, Texas

(PICTURED AT RIGHT)

Like most country cooks, I often bake a large ham so that I can use leftovers in tasty dishes like this. Fresh asparagus is wonderful in this soup's creamy broth.

1-1/2 cups fresh asparagus pieces
   1 medium carrot, julienned
   2 tablespoons butter *or* margarine
   3 small white onions, quartered
   2 tablespoons all-purpose flour
   1 cup milk
   1 cup chicken broth
   1 cup cubed fully cooked ham
   1 jar (2-1/2 ounces) sliced mushrooms, drained
   1 cup half-and-half cream
Salt and pepper to taste
Grated Parmesan cheese, optional
Chopped fresh parsley, optional

Place asparagus in a saucepan with enough water to cover; cook until crisp-tender. Drain and set aside. In a heavy saucepan, saute carrot in butter for 3-5 minutes; add onions and saute 2 minutes longer or until tender. Stir in flour; gradually add milk. Bring to a boil; boil and stir for 2 minutes. Add broth, ham, mushrooms and reserved asparagus. Reduce heat; add cream. Heat through but do not boil. Add salt and pepper. Garnish with Parmesan cheese and parsley if desired. **Yield:** 4 servings.

Wild Rice and Ham Chowder

Elma Friesen, Winnipeg, Manitoba

The rich, comforting taste of this chowder appeals to everyone who tries it. I have my younger sister to thank for sharing this recipe with me years ago.

1/2 cup chopped onion
   2 garlic cloves, minced
1/4 cup butter *or* margarine
   6 tablespoons all-purpose flour
1/2 teaspoon salt
1/4 teaspoon pepper
   4 cups chicken broth
1-1/2 cups cubed peeled potatoes
1/2 cup chopped carrots
   1 bay leaf
1/2 teaspoon dried thyme
1/4 teaspoon ground nutmeg
   3 cups cooked wild rice
2-1/2 cups cubed fully cooked ham
   2 cups half-and-half cream
   1 can (15-1/4 ounces) whole kernel corn, drained
Minced fresh parsley

In a Dutch oven or soup kettle over medium heat, saute onion and garlic in butter until tender. Add flour, salt and pepper; stir to form a smooth paste. Gradually add broth. Bring to a boil; boil and stir for 2 minutes. Add potatoes, carrots, bay leaf, thyme and nutmeg; bring to a boil. Reduce heat; cover and simmer for 30 minutes or until vegetables are tender. Add rice, ham, cream and corn; heat through (do not boil). Remove bay leaf. Sprinkle with parsley just before serving. **Yield:** 8-10 servings (2-3/4 quarts).

Dublin Dumpling Stew

Annette Fisher, Marion, Ohio

I've come a long way with my cooking since getting married some 40 years ago...and the credit goes to my older sister. Through the years, she's passed on many delicious recipes like this.

   1 pound boneless pork, trimmed and cut into
     1-inch cubes
   2 tablespoons butter *or* margarine
1/2 cup chopped onion
1/2 cup chopped celery
   1 garlic clove, minced
   5 medium carrots
   3 cups water
   1 tablespoon beef bouillon granules
   1 teaspoon salt
1/4 cup all-purpose flour
1/2 cup cold water
   1 package (10 ounces) frozen mixed vegetables
DUMPLINGS:
1-1/2 cups all-purpose flour
   1 tablespoon sugar
   2 teaspoons baking powder
   1 teaspoon caraway seed
1/2 teaspoon salt
1/4 teaspoon ground mustard
   1 egg
2/3 cup milk
   2 tablespoons vegetable oil

In a Dutch oven or soup kettle over high heat, brown pork in butter. Add onion, celery and garlic; reduce heat to medium and cook until vegetables are tender. Cut carrots into 2-in. pieces, then quarter lengthwise; add to pork mixture. Add water, bouillon and salt. Reduce heat; cover and simmer for 45 minutes or until the meat and vegetables are tender. Combine flour and cold water until smooth; stir into stew. Bring to a boil; boil and stir for 2 minutes. Add mixed vegetables; reduce heat to low. In a bowl, combine the first six dumpling ingredients. Beat egg, milk and oil; add to dry ingredients all at once. Mix just until moistened. Drop by tablespoonfuls into bubbling stew. Cover tightly and simmer for 25 minutes or until the dumplings are cooked through. **Yield:** 6-8 servings (2-1/2 quarts).

A SOUP FOR SPRING. *Pictured at right: Creamy Ham and Asparagus Soup (recipe on this page).*

Sweet Potato Pork Stew

Susan Klein, Waukesha, Wisconsin

I'm an avid recipe collector and have fun trying new dishes. Fortunately, my family doesn't mind experimenting with new tastes. Everyone loves the blend of flavors in this stew.

```
    2 pounds boneless pork, trimmed and cut into
        1-inch cubes
    3 tablespoons Dijon mustard
  1/2 cup all-purpose flour
    3 tablespoons brown sugar
    2 garlic cloves, minced
    3 tablespoons cooking oil
2-1/3 cups chicken broth
    4 to 5 small onions, quartered
    2 medium sweet potatoes, peeled and cubed
  1/2 teaspoon salt
  1/4 teaspoon pepper
  1/4 cup minced fresh parsley
```

Toss pork and mustard. In a large resealable plastic bag, combine flour and brown sugar; add pork and shake to coat. In a large skillet over medium-high heat, brown pork and garlic in oil. Add broth; bring to a boil. Scrape bottom of skillet to loosen any browned bits. Reduce heat; cover and simmer for 30 minutes. Add onions, sweet potatoes, salt and pepper; cover and simmer 30 minutes more or until the pork and potatoes are tender. Stir in parsley. **Yield:** 6-8 servings (2 quarts).

Navy Bean Soup

Melissa Stuchlik, Lincolnville, Kansas

My kids can't resist their grandmother's bean soup. A touch of nutmeg sets it apart from all other kinds.

```
    1 pound dry navy beans
    2 quarts water
1-1/2 to 2 pounds smoked ham hocks
    1 cup chopped onion
  1/4 cup chopped fresh parsley
1-1/2 teaspoons salt
    1 teaspoon dried basil
  1/2 teaspoon dried oregano
  1/2 teaspoon pepper
  1/4 teaspoon ground nutmeg
    1 bay leaf
    2 cups thinly sliced carrots
    1 cup chopped celery
  3/4 cup mashed potato flakes
```

Place beans and enough water to cover in a Dutch oven or soup kettle. Bring to a boil; boil for 2 minutes. Remove from the heat; let stand for 1 hour. Drain beans and discard liquid. Return beans to kettle; add water, ham hocks, onion, parsley and seasonings. Bring to a boil. Reduce heat; cover and simmer for 1 hour or until beans are tender. Add carrots, celery and potato flakes; mix well. Cover and simmer for

30 minutes or until vegetables are tender. Remove bay leaf. Remove ham hocks; allow to cool. Remove meat from bones and cut into bite-size pieces. Discard bones. Return meat to kettle; heat through. **Yield:** 12-14 servings (3-1/2 quarts).

Company's Coming Soup

Roberta McHam, Hurst, Texas

This soup is great for entertaining because it can be assembled ahead and left to simmer. Plus, with fresh bread and salad, it's a hearty meal that won't leave anyone hungry.

```
    1 pound (about 2 cups) dry 10-bean mix
    2 quarts water
    3 cups diced fully cooked ham
    1 teaspoon salt
  1/2 teaspoon pepper
    1 can (10 ounces) diced tomatoes and green
        chilies, undrained
    1 large onion, chopped
  1/4 cup lemon juice
    1 teaspoon garlic powder
```

Place beans and enough water to cover in a Dutch oven or soup kettle. Bring to a boil; boil for 2 minutes. Remove from the heat; let stand for 1 hour. Drain beans and discard liquid. Return beans to kettle; add water, ham, salt and pepper. Bring to a boil. Reduce heat; cover and simmer for 60-70 minutes or until beans are tender. Add remaining ingredients; cover and simmer for 30 minutes or until onion is tender. **Yield:** 10-12 servings (3 quarts).

Okanagan Pork Stew

Monica Wilcott, Sturgis, Saskatchewan

This stew gets its name from the area where my mom lives in British Columbia. She dries fruit from her orchards and sends it to me for my family to enjoy in this terrific recipe.

```
    2 packages (8 ounces each) dried mixed fruit
    3 cups boiling water
    3 pounds boneless pork, trimmed and cut into
        3/4-inch cubes
    3 tablespoons cooking oil
    3 large onions, chopped
    2 garlic cloves, minced
    2 tablespoons tomato paste
    2 tablespoons honey
    2 tablespoons vinegar
    1 teaspoon ground ginger
  1/2 teaspoon ground coriander
  1/2 teaspoon salt
  1/4 teaspoon pepper
  1/4 cup slivered almonds, toasted
```

Combine fruit and water; cover and let stand 1 hour. Drain, reserving liquid; set aside. In an ovenproof Dutch oven or soup kettle over medium heat, brown pork in oil until no longer pink; drain. Add onions and garlic; cook and stir until onions are tender. Add enough water to reserved fruit liquid to make

3 cups; add to kettle along with fruit, tomato paste, honey, vinegar and spices. Mix well. Cover and bake at 325° for 1-1/2 hours or until pork is tender. Sprinkle with almonds. **Yield:** 8-10 servings (2-1/2 quarts).

Cauliflower Pork Soup

Loretta Wohlenhaus, Cumberland, Iowa

This recipe was given to me by a friend several years ago. Everyone enjoys it, even my husband, who typically doesn't care for cauliflower.

  1 pound ground pork
  1 small head cauliflower, broken into florets
  2 cups water
1/2 cup chopped onion
  2 cups milk, *divided*
1/4 cup all-purpose flour
  2 cups (8 ounces) shredded sharp cheddar cheese
1/2 teaspoon salt
1/8 teaspoon pepper
Chopped chives, optional

In a skillet, cook pork until no longer pink; drain and set aside. In a large kettle or Dutch oven, cook cauliflower in water for 10 minutes or until tender. Do not drain. Add pork, onion and 1-1/4 cups milk to cauliflower. In a small bowl, combine flour and remaining milk until smooth; stir into cauliflower mixture. Bring to a boil; boil and stir for 2 minutes. Remove from the heat; add cheese, salt and pepper, stirring until cheese melts. Garnish with chives if desired. **Yield:** 6-8 servings (2 quarts).

Hearty Ham Borscht

Joanne Kukurudz, River Hills, Manitoba

I like to keep a big pot of this borscht simmering on the stove during busy times on the farm. That way, folks can dip into the kettle when they have a chance to sit down for a quick meal.

  1 meaty ham bone *or* 2 smoked ham hocks
  6 cups water
  2 cups diced fully cooked ham
  3 cups chopped cooked beets
  1 can (14 ounces) pork and beans
  1 can (10-3/4 ounces) condensed tomato soup, undiluted
  1 cup frozen peas
  1 cup chopped carrots
  1 cup frozen cut green beans
  1 medium onion, chopped
  2 to 3 tablespoons snipped fresh dill *or* 1 tablespoon dill weed
Sour cream, optional

Place ham bone and water in a Dutch oven or soup kettle; bring to a boil. Reduce heat; cover and simmer for 1-1/2 hours. Remove ham bone; allow to cool. Remove meat from bone and cut into bite-size pieces; discard bone. Return meat to kettle. Add ham, beets, pork and beans, soup, peas, carrots,

beans, onion and dill. Cover and simmer for 45 minutes or until vegetables are tender. Garnish with sour cream if desired. **Yield:** 12-14 servings (3-1/2 quarts).

Woodcutter's Stew

Patricia Gunning, Highland, Illinois

I originally found this recipe in one of my many cookbooks and modified it to suit my family's tastes. It's the only soup or stew they regularly ask me to prepare.

  1 can (14-1/2 ounces) stewed tomatoes
  2 celery ribs, sliced
1/2 chopped onion
  1 tablespoon butter *or* margarine
  5 cups water
  1 cup dry lentils
  2 medium potatoes, cubed
  2 medium carrots, sliced
  5 teaspoons chicken bouillon granules
1/2 teaspoon dried thyme
1/2 teaspoon pepper
  1 bay leaf
  8 ounces fully cooked Polish sausage

In a blender or food processor, process the tomatoes until smooth; set aside. In a large saucepan, saute celery and onion in butter until tender. Add the next eight ingredients; cover and bring to a boil. Reduce heat and simmer for 35-40 minutes or until lentils are tender. Meanwhile, cut sausage into 1/2-in. slices; cut each slice into quarters. In a skillet over medium heat, brown sausage; drain. Add to lentil mixture with reserved tomatoes; heat through. Remove bay leaf. **Yield:** 6-8 servings (2-1/4 quarts).

Surprise Clam Chowder

Evelyn Whalin, Denver, Colorado

When family and friends first sampled this stew some 40 years ago, they were pleasantly surprised by the combination of ingredients. Now it's a dish they frequently request.

✓ This tasty dish uses less sugar, salt and fat. Recipe includes *Diabetic Exchanges*.

  1 can (14-1/2 ounces) diced tomatoes, undrained
  1 cup water
1/2 cup diced peeled potato
1/4 cup diced green pepper
1/4 cup diced onion
1/4 teaspoon garlic salt
1/4 teaspoon chili powder
  1 cup diced fully cooked ham
  1 can (7-1/2 ounces) minced clams, undrained

In a saucepan, combine the first seven ingredients. Cover and simmer for 25-30 minutes or until vegetables are tender. Add ham and clams; heat through. **Yield:** 4 servings. **Diabetic Exchanges:** One 1-cup serving (prepared with no-salt-added tomatoes and low-fat ham) equals 2 vegetable, 1 lean meat, 1/2 starch; also, 135 calories, 694 mg sodium, 35 mg cholesterol, 13 gm carbohydrate, 16 gm protein, 3 gm fat.

Potato Bacon Chowder

Jacque Manning, Burbank, South Dakota

(PICTURED AT LEFT)

This chowder is like a bacon-topped baked potato in a bowl. On cold winter days, my family is thrilled to see this meal on the table.

    2 cups cubed peeled potatoes
    1 cup water
    8 bacon strips
    1 cup chopped onion
  1/2 cup chopped celery
    1 can (10-3/4 ounces) condensed cream of
      chicken soup, undiluted
1-3/4 cups milk
    1 cup (8 ounces) sour cream
  1/2 teaspoon salt
Dash pepper
    1 tablespoon minced fresh parsley

In a covered 3-qt. saucepan, cook potatoes and water until tender. Meanwhile, cook bacon in a skillet until crisp; remove to paper towel to drain. In the same skillet, saute onion and celery in drippings until tender; drain. Add to undrained potatoes. Stir in soup, milk, sour cream, salt and pepper. Cook over low heat for 10 minutes or until heated through (do not boil). Crumble bacon; set aside 1/4 cup. Add remaining bacon to soup along with parsley. Sprinkle with remaining bacon. **Yield:** 6 servings.

Lumberjack Stew

Bonnie Tetzlaff, Scandinavia, Wisconsin

(PICTURED AT LEFT)

I found this recipe many years ago in a brochure put out by the state of Wisconsin. This stew makes appearances on our table throughout the year, especially during hunting season.

    2 pounds boneless pork, trimmed and cut into
      1-inch cubes
    1 teaspoon salt
    1 teaspoon sugar
  1/2 teaspoon pepper
  1/2 teaspoon paprika
    2 tablespoons cooking oil
    1 cup sliced onion
    1 garlic clove, minced
    3 cups water
    1 tablespoon lemon juice
    1 teaspoon Worcestershire sauce
    2 chicken bouillon cubes
    2 bay leaves
    6 medium carrots, cut into 1-inch pieces
    1 package (10 ounces) pearl onions, peeled
    3 cups frozen cut green beans

COOL-WEATHER CUISINE. *Pictured at left, clockwise from top: Potato Bacon Chowder, Lumberjack Stew and Zucchini Soup (all recipes on this page).*

---

    3 tablespoons cornstarch
  1/2 cup cold water

Toss pork with salt, sugar, pepper and paprika; brown in oil in a Dutch oven or soup kettle over medium-high heat. Add sliced onion and garlic; cook over medium heat for 5 minutes. Add water, lemon juice, Worcestershire sauce, bouillon and bay leaves; cover and simmer for 1 hour. Add the carrots and pearl onions; cover and simmer for 40 minutes. Add beans; cover and simmer for 10 minutes. Combine cornstarch and cold water until smooth; stir into stew. Bring to a boil; boil and stir for 2 minutes. Remove bay leaves. **Yield:** 6 servings.

Zucchini Soup

Lindsay Gibson, New Springfield, Ohio

(PICTURED AT LEFT)

I've received numerous 4-H cooking awards over the past few years and often cook for the family...much to my mom's delight!

   12 ounces pork breakfast sausage links
    1 cup chopped celery
  1/2 cup chopped onion
    1 pound zucchini, sliced
    3 cans (14-1/2 ounces *each*) stewed tomatoes
    1 can (14-1/2 ounces) chicken broth
    2 teaspoons garlic powder
    1 teaspoon salt
  1/2 teaspoon dried oregano
  1/2 teaspoon Italian seasoning
  1/2 teaspoon sugar
  1/4 teaspoon dried basil
    1 medium green pepper, chopped

Cut sausage into 1/4-in. slices; brown in a Dutch oven or soup kettle. Add celery and onion; saute until tender. Drain. Stir in the next nine ingredients. Bring to a boil; reduce heat and simmer for 35 minutes. Add green pepper and simmer for 10 minutes. **Yield:** 6-8 servings (2 quarts).

Bologna and Sauerkraut Stew

Gladie Delaney, West Allis, Wisconsin

This old-fashioned stew conveniently bakes in the oven, so I can put it together and forget about it.

    1 large onion, chopped
    1 garlic clove, minced
    1 tablespoon cooking oil
    1 can (14-1/2 ounces) diced tomatoes, undrained
    1 can (14 ounces) sauerkraut, undrained
    6 small potatoes, peeled and halved
    1 teaspoon caraway seed
    1 teaspoon sugar, optional
    1 pound fully cooked ring bologna

In a skillet, saute onion and garlic in oil until tender. Transfer to a 2-1/2-qt. baking dish. Add tomatoes, sauerkraut, potatoes, caraway and sugar if desired; mix gently. Cover and bake at 350° for 30 minutes. Cut bologna into 1-in. chunks; arrange over vegetables. Cover and bake 20 minutes longer or until potatoes are tender. **Yield:** 6-8 servings (2 quarts).

Split Pea and Ham Soup

Lucille Schreiber, Gleason, Wisconsin

Not a winter goes by that I don't fix at least one batch of this traditional pea soup. It's a hot and hearty meal that really warms up my family.

✓ **This tasty dish uses less sugar, salt and fat. Recipe includes** *Diabetic Exchanges.*

1 pound (about 2 cups) dry green split peas
7 cups water
1 teaspoon vegetable oil
1 teaspoon salt, optional
2 cups diced fully cooked ham
2 cups chopped carrots
1 cup chopped celery
1 cup chopped onion
1 cup diced peeled potato
1/2 teaspoon garlic powder
1/2 teaspoon pepper
1/4 cup chopped fresh parsley

In a Dutch oven or soup kettle, bring peas, water, oil and salt if desired to a boil. Reduce heat; cover and simmer for 2 hours, stirring occasionally. Add the next seven ingredients; cover and simmer for 30 minutes or until vegetables are tender. Stir in parsley. **Yield:** 8-10 servings (2-3/4 quarts). **Diabetic Exchanges:** One 1-cup serving (prepared with low-fat ham and without salt) equals 1-1/2 starch, 1 lean meat, 1 vegetable; also, 205 calories, 389 mg sodium, 12 mg cholesterol, 32 gm carbohydrate, 16 gm protein, 2 gm fat.

Pork Stew with Corn-Bread Dumplings

Shelly Gresham, Dawson, Illinois

Corn-bread dumplings add a delectable down-home flavor to this truly country meal. I frequently make a double batch of this stew on Sunday so that we can have leftovers all week long.

2 pounds boneless pork, trimmed and cut into 3/4-inch cubes
2 tablespoons cooking oil
1 can (28 ounces) stewed tomatoes
1-1/4 cups chicken broth, *divided*
1 medium onion, quartered
2 bay leaves
1 teaspoon Worcestershire sauce
1 teaspoon dried thyme
3/4 teaspoon sugar
3/4 teaspoon salt
1/4 teaspoon pepper
1/4 teaspoon garlic powder
1/8 teaspoon ground nutmeg
2 tablespoons all-purpose flour
DUMPLINGS:
1/2 cup all-purpose flour
1/3 cup yellow cornmeal
1-1/2 teaspoons baking powder

1/4 teaspoon salt
Dash pepper
1 egg
3 tablespoons milk
2 tablespoons vegetable oil
1 can (8-3/4 ounces) whole kernel corn, drained

In a large skillet over medium heat, brown pork in oil; drain. Stir in tomatoes, 1 cup broth, onion and seasonings; bring to a boil. Reduce heat; cover and simmer for 60-70 minutes or until pork is tender. Combine flour and remaining broth until smooth; gradually add to stew, stirring constantly. Bring to a boil; boil and stir for 2 minutes. Remove bay leaves. For dumplings, in a bowl, combine flour, cornmeal, baking powder, salt and pepper. Beat egg, milk and oil; add to flour mixture and mix until just moistened. Stir in corn. Drop by rounded tablespoonfuls into simmering stew. Cover and cook for 10-12 minutes or until dumplings are tender. **Yield:** 6 servings.

Country Ham Stew

Paula Pelis, Rocky Point, New York

I've come to discover that everyone enjoys this chunky stew, especially during the winter months. Whenever I offer it to family and friends, I'm asked to share the recipe as well.

1 jar (12 ounces) chicken gravy
1 cup water
1-1/2 pounds fully cooked ham, cut into 1/2-inch cubes
6 small red potatoes, quartered
1 cup fresh sugar snap peas
1 cup frozen lima beans
1 cup fresh baby carrots *or* frozen tiny whole carrots
1 cup frozen small whole onions

In a large saucepan over medium heat, stir gravy and water until smooth. Add remaining ingredients; mix well. Bring to a boil. Reduce heat; cover and simmer for 20-30 minutes or until vegetables are tender. **Yield:** 6 servings.

Maltese Stew

Jannet Sanden, Tempe, Arizona

While growing up on the island of Malta, my mother ate this slightly spicy stew often. The recipe has been in the family for generations. Now I'm passing it on to my children...and you!

1 pork shoulder roast (1-1/2 to 2 pounds), trimmed and cut into 1-inch cubes
2 medium onions, quartered
2 tablespoons cooking oil
2 cups chicken broth, *divided*
3 tablespoons tomato paste
1 tablespoon red wine vinegar
1 teaspoon browning sauce
1/2 to 3/4 teaspoon curry powder

1/2 teaspoon salt
1/4 teaspoon pepper
1/4 to 1/2 teaspoon ground allspice
1/4 to 1/2 teaspoon ground nutmeg
Pinch ground cloves
3 medium potatoes, peeled and cut into 1-inch cubes
1 cup frozen peas

In a Dutch oven or soup kettle over medium heat, cook pork and onions in oil for 10-12 minutes or until pork is browned and onions are soft. In a bowl, combine 1 cup broth and tomato paste until smooth; add to pork mixture. Cook, uncovered, for 10 minutes. Stir in vinegar, browning sauce and seasonings; cook, uncovered, for 15 minutes. Add potatoes, peas and remaining broth; bring to a boil. Reduce heat; cover and simmer for 50-60 minutes or until pork and potatoes are tender. **Yield:** 6-8 servings (2 quarts).

Confetti Chowder

Donna Valen, Stonewall, Manitoba

My mom always had flavorful soups simmering on the stove during a long workday on our cattle ranch. She inspired me to create my own rib-sticking recipes like this.

4 cups water
1-1/2 cups diced fully cooked ham
1-1/2 cups frozen *or* canned whole kernel corn
1/2 cup diced celery
1/2 cup shredded carrot
1/4 cup diced cabbage
1/4 cup diced onion
2 tablespoons chicken bouillon granules
1/4 cup cornstarch
2 cups milk, *divided*

In a 3-qt. saucepan, combine the first eight ingredients; bring to a boil over medium heat. Reduce heat; cover and simmer for 10-12 minutes or until vegetables are tender. Combine cornstarch with 1/2 cup milk until smooth; gradually add to soup, stirring constantly. Bring to a boil; boil and stir for 2 minutes. Add remaining milk; heat through, stirring frequently. **Yield:** 6-8 servings (2 quarts).

Hot Pot Stew

Sandra Allen, Leadville, Colorado

This full-bodied stew is ideal for chilly rainy days. So I often try— unsuccessfully—to sneak some into the freezer before my family can eat it all! I hope you enjoy it, too.

✓ This tasty dish uses less sugar, salt and fat. Recipe includes *Diabetic Exchanges.*

1 cup cubed lean boneless pork (1/2-inch pieces)
1 cup cubed fully cooked ham
1 cup coarsely chopped green pepper
1/2 cup chopped onion
1/2 cup chopped celery

1 garlic clove, minced
3 cups cubed red potatoes
3 cups water
1 can (16 ounces) pinto beans, rinsed and drained
1 can (15.8 ounces) great northern beans, rinsed and drained
1-1/4 teaspoons sugar
1 teaspoon chicken bouillon granules
1 teaspoon beef bouillon granules
1/4 teaspoon ground nutmeg
1/4 teaspoon coarsely ground pepper
1 package (10 ounces) frozen chopped spinach *or* turnip greens *or* 1 can (14-1/2 ounces) spinach *or* turnip greens, drained

In a Dutch oven or soup kettle coated with nonstick cooking spray, brown pork over medium-high heat. Add ham, green pepper, onion, celery and garlic. Reduce heat to medium; cook for 8-10 minutes or until vegetables are just tender, stirring occasionally. Add the next nine ingredients. Reduce heat; cover and simmer for 20 minutes or until potatoes are tender. Add spinach and cook until heated through. **Yield:** 8-10 servings (2-1/2 quarts). **Diabetic Exchanges:** One 1-cup serving (prepared with low-fat ham, low-sodium bouillon and frozen spinach) equals 1-1/2 starch, 1 lean meat; also, 165 calories, 528 mg sodium, 15 mg cholesterol, 25 gm carbohydrate, 12 gm protein, 2 gm fat.

Southwestern Pork Stew

Pam Gordon, Neptune Beach, Florida

I grew tired of preparing the same old beef stew, so this pork variety was a welcome change. It has a fun combination of colors and flavors along with the right amount of zip.

1 pound boneless pork, trimmed and cut into 3/4-inch cubes
1-1/2 teaspoons ground cumin
1/4 teaspoon salt
1/8 teaspoon cayenne pepper
2 teaspoons cooking oil
2 medium green peppers, cut into 3/4-inch pieces
2 small onions, quartered
2 garlic cloves, minced
2 medium potatoes, peeled and cubed
1 can (14-1/2 ounces) Mexican-style stewed tomatoes
1-1/2 cups V-8 juice
1/2 cup water
1 package (10 ounces) frozen whole kernel corn
Minced fresh cilantro *or* parsley, optional

In a large resealable plastic bag, combine pork, cumin, salt and cayenne; shake to coat evenly. In a Dutch oven or soup kettle over medium heat, brown pork in oil; drain. Add green peppers, onions and garlic; saute for 3 minutes. Add potatoes, tomatoes, V-8 and water; mix well. Bring to a boil. Reduce heat; cover and simmer for 45 minutes. Add corn; cover and simmer for 10-15 minutes or until vegetables and pork are tender. Garnish with cilantro or parsley if desired. **Yield:** 6-8 servings (2 quarts).

Skillet Main Dishes

Ham and Broccoli Divan

Mrs. L.M. Renfrow, Shawnee Mission, Kansas

(PICTURED AT LEFT)

I worked for years in a school cafeteria and exchanged many recipes with co-workers. I'm happy to pass on this tasty, simple-to-prepare dish.

- 1 can (10-3/4 ounces) condensed cream of mushroom soup, undiluted
- 1/4 cup milk
- 1 teaspoon prepared mustard
- 1/2 teaspoon Worcestershire sauce
- Pinch pepper
- 2 packages (10 ounces *each*) frozen broccoli pieces, cooked and drained
- 2 cups cubed fully cooked ham
- 1 can (6 ounces) french-fried onions, *divided*
- 1 cup (4 ounces) shredded cheddar cheese

Combine soup, milk, mustard, Worcestershire sauce and pepper; spoon half into a skillet. Top with the broccoli, ham, half of the onions and cheese. Spoon remaining soup mixture over cheese and top with remaining onions. Cover and cook over low heat for 20-25 minutes or until heated through. Do not stir. **Yield:** 4-6 servings.

Pork Chops Deluxe

Sandy Krin, Watertown, Connecticut

(PICTURED AT LEFT)

With its one-pan convenience, I enjoy preparing this recipe often for hearty weekday meals.

✓ This tasty dish uses less sugar, salt and fat. Recipe includes *Diabetic Exchanges*.

- 6 boneless pork chops (4 ounces *each*), trimmed
- 2 tablespoons water
- 1 can (14-1/2 ounces) diced tomatoes, undrained
- 1 can (10-3/4 ounces) condensed golden mushroom soup, undiluted
- 1/3 cup chopped onion
- 2 teaspoons Dijon mustard
- 1 pound fresh mushrooms, sliced
- 1/4 teaspoon salt, optional
- 3 cups hot cooked rice
- 2 tablespoons minced fresh parsley

Coat a skillet with nonstick cooking spray; brown pork chops on both sides. Remove and set aside. Add water, scraping

---

bottom of the skillet to loosen any browned bits. Drain tomatoes, reserving juice; set tomatoes aside. Add juice, soup, onion, mustard, mushrooms and salt if desired to skillet; mix well. Return chops to skillet. Cover and simmer for 30 minutes or until pork is tender. Stir in tomatoes; heat through. Combine rice and parsley. Serve the pork chops and sauce over rice. **Yield:** 6 servings. **Diabetic Exchanges:** One serving (prepared with no-salt-added tomatoes and without salt) equals 2-1/2 meat, 2 starch, 2 vegetable; also, 331 calories, 475 mg sodium, 54 mg cholesterol, 42 gm carbohydrate, 24 gm protein, 7 gm fat.

Cheesy Bratwurst

Kim Miers, Rock Island, Illinois

(PICTURED AT LEFT)

I'll admit that the combination of ingredients in this recipe is unusual, but I guarantee the flavor is fabulous!

- 4 medium potatoes, peeled and cut into 1/2-inch cubes
- 2 cups water, *divided*
- 6 fully cooked bratwurst links (1 pound), cut into 1/2-inch slices
- 1 can (10-3/4 ounces) condensed cream of mushroom soup, undiluted
- 2 cups frozen cut green beans
- 1 small onion, chopped
- 1 cup (4 ounces) shredded cheddar cheese

Place potatoes and 1 cup water in a deep skillet or large saucepan; cook for 15 minutes or until almost tender. Drain and set aside. In the same pan, brown bratwurst; add soup, beans, onion, potatoes and remaining water. Cover and simmer for 15 minutes or until the vegetables are tender. Stir in cheese; heat until melted. **Yield:** 6 servings.

Sausage Gravy

Marcia Zeiger, Kalamazoo, Michigan

My parents love ordering biscuits and sausage gravy at restaurants. One day when they visited us, I offered them my version. They said mine couldn't be beat!

- 1/2 pound bulk pork sausage
- 1/2 pound bulk hot pork sausage
- 1/2 pound bulk sage sausage
- 3/4 to 1 cup all-purpose flour
- 1 tablespoon chicken bouillon granules
- 5 cups milk
- Warm baking powder biscuits

In a large skillet over medium heat, cook all of the sausage until no longer pink; drain. Stir in flour and bouillon. Gradually add milk, stirring constantly. Bring to a boil; boil and stir for 2 minutes. Serve over biscuits. **Yield:** 8-10 servings (6 cups).

DOWN-HOME DINNERS. *Pictured at left, top to bottom: Ham and Broccoli Divan, Pork Chops Deluxe and Cheesy Bratwurst (all recipes on this page).*

Mom's Chinese Dish

Patricia Harroun, Las Vegas, Nevada

Recently when I was looking for a different pork dish, I remembered this family favorite that was accidentally filed away. Now it's back on our menus...much to my family's delight.

- 4 bacon strips, diced
- 2 pork tenderloins (3/4 pound *each*)
- 1 garlic clove, minced
- 3/4 cup water, *divided*
- 3 tablespoons soy sauce
- 1/4 teaspoon ground ginger
- 1/4 teaspoon pepper
- 1 large green *or* sweet red pepper, julienned
- 1 medium onion, julienned
- 3 celery ribs, cut into thin diagonal slices
- 2 tablespoons cornstarch
- 1 can (8 ounces) sliced water chestnuts, drained
- 1 can (8 ounces) sliced bamboo shoots, drained

Hot rice *or* chow mein noodles

In a large skillet, cook bacon until crisp; remove to paper towel to drain. Cut pork into 3-in. x 1/2-in. strips. In the bacon drippings, stir-fry pork and garlic over medium-high heat for 2-3 minutes. Stir in 1/2 cup water, soy sauce, ginger and pepper. Reduce heat; cover and simmer for 3 minutes. Add green pepper, onion and celery; stir-fry over medium-high heat for 3 minutes or until vegetables are crisp-tender. Combine cornstarch and remaining water until smooth; add to skillet. Bring to a boil; boil and stir for 2 minutes. Add water chestnuts, bamboo shoots and bacon; heat through. Serve over rice or chow mein noodles. **Yield:** 6 servings.

Pork 'n' Potato Skillet

Fern Leinweber, Longmont, Colorado

This was one of the specials I offered in my small cafe years ago. Diners were always surprised to hear that boxed potatoes were the basis for this down-home dish.

1-1/2 to 2 pounds boneless pork, cut into 3/4-inch cubes
- 1 tablespoon cooking oil
- 1 cup chopped celery
- 1/2 cup milk
- 1/2 cup mayonnaise
- 1 package (5 ounces) scalloped potato mix with sauce packet
- 2 cups hot water
- 1 medium green pepper, cut into rings
- 1 medium tomato, cut into wedges

In a skillet over medium heat, brown pork in oil; add celery. Cook until celery is tender; drain. Combine milk and mayonnaise until smooth; add to the skillet. Stir in potatoes, contents of sauce packet and water; mix well. Bring to a boil. Reduce heat; cover and simmer for 15-20 minutes or

until potatoes are tender, stirring occasionally. Arrange green pepper and tomato on top. Cover and simmer for 10-15 minutes or until peppers are tender. **Yield:** 4-6 servings.

Sausage Stroganoff

Barbara Berkow, Northbrook, Illinois

This recipe calls for sausage instead of beef, making it an enticing economical meal. My family loves this dish served with salad and oven-fresh rolls.

- 1 pound bulk pork sausage
- 1 medium onion, chopped
- 1/2 pound fresh mushrooms, sliced
- 1-1/4 cups chicken broth, *divided*
- 1 tablespoon Worcestershire sauce
- 1/4 teaspoon pepper
- 1/4 cup all-purpose flour
- 1 cup (8 ounces) sour cream
- 2 tablespoons minced fresh parsley, optional

Hot cooked noodles

In a large skillet, cook sausage and onion until meat is no longer pink and onion is tender; drain. Add mushrooms; cook for 1 minute. Add 1 cup broth, Worcestershire sauce and pepper; cover and simmer for 5 minutes. Gradually stir remaining broth into flour; mix until smooth. Stir into skillet. Bring to a boil; boil and stir for 2 minutes. Reduce heat; add sour cream. Stir until heated through (do not boil). Add parsley if desired. Serve over noodles. **Yield:** 4 servings.

Apple-Topped Ham Steak

Eleanor Chore, Athena, Oregon

(PICTURED ON THE FRONT COVER)

Sweet apples combine nicely with tangy mustard in this dish to create a luscious topping for skillet-fried ham steak. I especially like to serve this to guests in fall.

✓ **This tasty dish uses less sugar, salt and fat. Recipe includes** *Diabetic Exchanges.*

- 1 fully cooked ham steak (2 pounds)
- 1 cup chopped onion
- 3 cups apple juice
- 2 teaspoons Dijon mustard
- 2 medium green apples, cored and thinly sliced
- 2 medium red apples, cored and thinly sliced
- 2 tablespoons cornstarch
- 1/4 cup cold water
- 1 tablespoon minced fresh sage *or* 1 teaspoon rubbed sage
- 1/4 teaspoon pepper

In a large skillet coated with nonstick cooking spray, brown ham steak on both sides over medium heat; set aside and keep warm. In the same skillet, saute onion until tender. Stir in apple juice and mustard; bring to a boil. Add apples. Reduce heat; cover and simmer for 4 minutes or until apples are tender. Combine cornstarch and water until smooth;

stir into apple juice mixture. Bring to a boil; boil and stir for 2 minutes. Stir in sage and pepper. Return ham steak to the skillet; heat through. **Yield:** 8 servings. **Diabetic Exchanges:** One serving (prepared with extra-lean ham steak and rubbed sage) equals 3-1/2 very lean meat, 1-1/2 fruit; also, 240 calories, 1,474 mg sodium, 51 mg cholesterol, 25 gm carbohydrate, 23 gm protein, 5 gm fat.

Ham Balls with Mustard Dill Sauce

Doris Kitzman, Marion, Wisconsin

My husband and I both come from large families, so I'm always cooking up something in the kitchen. These hearty ham balls with a tangy sauce are a hit served over noodles.

- 1 pound ground fully cooked ham
- 1 pound ground pork
- 2 eggs
- 1/2 cup crushed cornflakes
- 2-1/3 cups milk, *divided*
- 1/4 cup chopped onion
- 6 teaspoons prepared mustard, *divided*
- Dash pepper
- 2 tablespoons cooking oil
- 3 tablespoons butter *or* margarine
- 3 tablespoons all-purpose flour
- 1 cup (8 ounces) sour cream
- 1 teaspoon salt
- 1/2 teaspoon dill weed

In a bowl, combine ham, pork, eggs, cornflake crumbs, 1/3 cup milk, onion, 2 teaspoons mustard and pepper; shape into 1-in. balls. In a large skillet over medium heat, brown ham balls in oil. Cook for 15-20 minutes or until juices run clear. Meanwhile, in a saucepan, melt butter; stir in flour. Add remaining milk, stirring constantly. Bring to a boil; boil and stir for 2 minutes. Stir in sour cream, salt, dill and remaining mustard; heat through but do not boil. Place ham balls on a serving patter and top with sauce. **Yield:** 8-10 servings.

Pork Fajitas

Dianne Esposite, New Middletown, Ohio

My family likes to take a break from traditional beef dishes by substituting pork. Since we are big fans of Mexican food, these fajitas are a much-requested menu item.

- 1 pound boneless pork
- 2 tablespoons orange juice
- 2 tablespoons vinegar
- 2 garlic cloves, minced
- 1 teaspoon dried oregano
- 1 teaspoon ground cumin
- 1/2 teaspoon seasoned salt
- 1/2 teaspoon hot pepper sauce
- 1 medium onion, cut into thin wedges
- 1 medium green pepper, julienned
- 1 tablespoon cooking oil
- 6 flour tortillas (7 inches), warmed
- Shredded lettuce, diced tomatoes, salsa *and/or* sour cream, optional

Cut pork into 4-in. x 1/2-in. x 1/4-in. strips; set aside. In a bowl or resealable plastic bag, combine orange juice, vinegar, garlic, oregano, cumin, seasoned salt and hot pepper sauce; mix well. Add pork; cover or close bag and chill for 1-2 hours. In a skillet over medium heat, cook pork with marinade, onion and green pepper in oil until pork is no longer pink and vegetables are tender; drain. Place about 3/4 cup filling down the center of each tortilla; top with lettuce, tomatoes, salsa and sour cream if desired. Fold in sides of tortilla and serve immediately. **Yield:** 6 servings.

Ginger Pork Chops with Caramelized Onions

Amelia Meaux, Crowley, Louisiana

(PICTURED ON THE FRONT COVER)

I created this recipe in my kitchen as a way to add a little Oriental flavor to my pork chops. The caramelized onions were an afterthought, but I think they add a nice touch.

- 1/3 cup water
- 1/3 cup soy sauce
- 4 teaspoons brown sugar
- 1/2 teaspoon ground ginger
- 1 garlic clove, minced
- Dash cayenne pepper
- 4 pork chops (1 inch thick)
- 2 tablespoons cooking oil
- 1 tablespoon cornstarch
- 1/4 cup cold water
- CARAMELIZED ONIONS:
- 2 large sweet onions, sliced and separated into rings
- 2 tablespoons cooking oil
- 1/4 cup ginger ale *or* chicken broth
- 1/4 teaspoon salt
- Dash cayenne pepper

In a large resealable plastic bag or shallow glass container, combine the first six ingredients. Add pork chops; seal bag or cover container and chill for 2 hours, turning once. Remove pork chops from marinade; set marinade aside. In a large skillet over medium heat, cook pork chops in oil for 3 minutes per side or until golden brown. Add reserved marinade; bring to a boil. Reduce heat; cover and simmer for 30 minutes. Remove chops from skillet; set aside and keep warm. Combine cornstarch and cold water until smooth; add to skillet. Bring to a boil; boil and stir for 2 minutes or until sauce is thickened and clear. Meanwhile, toss onions in oil in a large skillet. Cover and cook over medium heat for 10 minutes, stirring occasionally. Uncover; cook and stir for 15 minutes or until golden brown. Add ginger ale, salt and cayenne; cook 5 minutes longer. Top each chop with caramelized onions and serve with sauce. **Yield:** 4 servings.

STOVETOP SPECIALTIES. *Clockwise from lower left: Cajun Chops, Mom's Paella, Creamy Ham Fettucini, Pork Schnitzel and Sweet-and-Sour Pork (all recipes on pages 50 and 51).*

Cajun Chops

Cindy Schaefer, Carey, North Carolina
(PICTURED ON PAGE 48)

If you like spicy foods, you'll surely want to try these chops. I've never served them to friends without being asked for the recipe before the meal ended!

    4 teaspoons paprika
    2 teaspoons salt
    2 teaspoons rubbed sage
    3/4 teaspoon cayenne pepper
    3/4 teaspoon pepper
    3/4 teaspoon garlic powder
    4 boneless pork chops (1-1/2 inches thick)
    2 tablespoons butter *or* margarine

In a shallow dish, combine the first six ingredients. Make a horizontal cut through each pork chop from one side to within 1/4 in. of the opposite side. Open chops and flatten to form "butterfly" chops. Dip each chop into the seasoning mixture and press into both sides. In a heavy skillet, heat butter on high until browned. Reduce heat to medium; cook the chops for 2-3 minutes per side or until browned and juices run clear. **Yield:** 4 servings.

Mom's Paella

Ena Quiggle, Goodhue, Minnesota
(PICTURED ON PAGE 48)

I enjoy cooking ethnic foods, especially those that call for lots of rice. Like my mom, I often prepare this dish for special Sunday get-togethers.

1-1/2 cups cubed cooked chicken
    1 cup cubed fully cooked smoked ham
    1/2 cup sliced fully cooked smoked sausage (1/4-inch slices)
    1 medium onion, chopped
    1 small green pepper, chopped
    4 tablespoons olive *or* vegetable oil, *divided*
    1/4 cup stuffed olives, halved
    1/2 cup raisins, optional
    1 cup uncooked converted rice
    2 garlic cloves, minced
    1 tablespoon ground turmeric
1-1/2 teaspoons curry powder
2-1/4 cups chicken broth
1-1/2 cups frozen mixed vegetables

In a large skillet, saute chicken, ham, sausage, onion and green pepper in 2 tablespoons oil for 3-5 minutes or until onion is tender. Add olives and raisins if desired. Cook 2-3 minutes longer or until heated through, stirring occasionally; remove meat and vegetable mixture from pan and keep warm. In the same skillet, saute rice in remaining oil for 2-3 minutes or until lightly browned. Add garlic, turmeric and curry; mix well. Return meat and vegetables to pan; toss lightly. Add broth and mixed vegetables; bring to a boil.

Reduce heat; cover and simmer for 25-30 minutes or until rice is tender. **Yield:** 6-8 servings.

Creamy Ham Fettucini

Anna Walker, Ashley, North Dakota
(PICTURED ON PAGE 48)

I often prepare this dish as a fast and flavorful way to bring a "taste of Italy" to the dinner table. The creamy sauce dresses up ordinary ham and asparagus.

    1/2 cup sliced green onions
    1 can (4 ounces) sliced mushrooms, drained
    1/4 cup butter *or* margarine
    1 package (8 ounces) cream cheese, softened
1-3/4 cups milk
    1 pound fully cooked ham, julienned
    1 cup cut fresh asparagus (3/4-inch pieces), cooked, optional
    12 ounces fettucini, cooked and drained
    1/2 cup grated Parmesan cheese
Additional green onions, optional

In a large skillet over medium heat, cook onions and mushrooms in butter until onions are tender. Reduce heat to low; stir in cream cheese and milk. Cook and stir until cheese is melted. Add ham, asparagus if desired and fettucini; heat through. Sprinkle with Parmesan cheese. Garnish with additional onions if desired. **Yield:** 4-6 servings.

Pork Schnitzel

Joyce Folker, Parowan, Utah
(PICTURED ON PAGE 49)

My husband is of German descent, and this is one of his favorite meals. I like to serve it with mashed potatoes and cinnamon applesauce. This is an attractive dish to serve to company.

    1/2 cup all-purpose flour
    2 teaspoons seasoned salt
    1/2 teaspoon pepper
    2 eggs
    1/4 cup milk
1-1/2 cups dry bread crumbs
    2 teaspoons paprika
    6 boneless pork cutlets (1/2 inch thick)
    6 tablespoons cooking oil
DILL SAUCE:
1-1/2 cups chicken broth, *divided*
    2 tablespoons all-purpose flour
    1/2 teaspoon dill weed
    1 cup (8 ounces) sour cream

In a shallow bowl, combine flour, seasoned salt and pepper; set aside. In another bowl, beat eggs and milk; set aside. In another bowl, combine bread crumbs and paprika; set aside. Flatten pork cutlets to 1/4-in. thickness. Dip cutlets into flour mixture, then into egg mixture, then into crumb mixture. In a large skillet, cook pork in oil, a few pieces at a time, for 3-4 minutes per side or until meat is no longer pink. Remove to a serving platter; keep warm. For sauce, pour 1 cup broth into skillet, scraping bottom of pan to loosen browned bits. Combine flour and remaining broth until smooth; add to skillet. Bring to a boil; boil and stir for 2 minutes. Stir in dill and sour cream; heat through (do not boil). Pour over pork. **Yield:** 6 servings.

Sweet-and-Sour Pork

Faye Johnson, Alexander City, Alabama

(PICTURED ON PAGE 49)

From start to finish, this dish can be prepared in less than 30 minutes using ingredients I typically have on hand. I've been making this for 15 years or so and have yet to tire of it!

    1 medium onion, sliced into thin wedges
    1 small green pepper, thinly sliced
    1 small sweet red pepper, thinly sliced
    1 garlic clove, minced
    2 tablespoons cooking oil, *divided*
    1 pound pork loin
    2 cans (8 ounces *each*) unsweetened pineapple
      chunks, undrained
    3 tablespoons cornstarch
  1/2 cup corn syrup
  1/4 cup vinegar
    3 tablespoons soy sauce
    2 tablespoons ketchup
Hot cooked rice

In a large skillet or wok over medium-high heat, stir-fry onion, peppers and garlic in 1 tablespoon oil for 3-4 minutes or until crisp-tender. Remove vegetables; set aside and keep warm. Cut pork into 3-in. x 1/2-in. x 1/8-in. strips; stir-fry over medium-high heat in remaining oil for 5-7 minutes or until no longer pink. Drain pineapple, reserving juice; set pineapple aside. Combine juice and cornstarch; add corn syrup, vinegar, soy sauce and ketchup. Add to skillet with vegetables and pineapple. Bring to a boil; boil and stir for 2 minutes. Serve over rice. **Yield:** 4 servings.

Braised Pork Chops

Helen Mason, Victor, West Virginia

Simple seasonings in this recipe let the wonderful natural flavor of pork chops really shine through. With homemade bread and a salad, this makes a delightful meal.

  1/4 cup all-purpose flour
  1/4 teaspoon salt
  1/4 teaspoon pepper
    4 pork chops (3/4 inch thick)
    2 tablespoons cooking oil
    1 medium onion, sliced
  3/4 cup sliced celery

    1 garlic clove, minced
    1 can (13-3/4 ounces) beef broth
    1 teaspoon dried thyme
    1 bay leaf

In a large resealable plastic bag, combine flour, salt and pepper. Add chops; seal bag and shake to coat. In a skillet over medium-high heat, cook chops in oil for about 3 minutes per side or until well browned. Remove chops and set aside. Cook onion, celery and garlic in drippings until tender. Return chops to the skillet; add broth, thyme and bay leaf. Simmer, uncovered, for 30 minutes or until pork juices run clear. Remove bay leaf. Transfer chops to a serving plate. With a slotted spoon, remove celery and onion; spoon over chops. Thicken juices for gravy if desired. **Yield:** 4 servings.

Paprika Pork with Dumplings

Kathryn Schubert, Sun City, Arizona

The first time I made this dish, my family gave it two thumbs up. I knew I had a hit on my hands when it passed that test! Through the years, I've used this recipe often when entertaining.

    3 tablespoons all-purpose flour
  1/2 teaspoon salt
    4 pork steaks (1/2 inch thick)
    3 tablespoons cooking oil
    2 medium onions, thinly sliced
    1 cup water
    2 teaspoons chicken bouillon granules
1-1/2 teaspoons paprika
DUMPLINGS:
    4 quarts water
    1 package (12 ounces) frozen shredded hash
      browns, thawed
    2 eggs
    2 tablespoons chopped fresh parsley *or* 2
      teaspoons dried parsley flakes
2-1/4 teaspoons salt
1-1/2 cups all-purpose flour
  1/4 teaspoon baking powder
  1/2 cup sour cream

Combine flour and salt; coat pork. Set remaining flour mixture aside. In a large skillet over medium heat, brown pork in oil for 8 minutes per side. Remove pork and set aside. Saute onions in pan drippings for 2 minutes. Stir in reserved flour mixture. Gradually stir in water, bouillon and paprika; bring to a boil. Return pork to skillet. Reduce heat; cover and simmer for 45 minutes or until pork is tender. Meanwhile, for dumplings, bring water to a boil in a large kettle. In a large bowl, combine hash browns, eggs, parsley and salt. Stir in flour and baking powder until mixture forms a soft dough. Turn dough onto a floured surface. With floured hands, shape dough into 1-3/4-in. balls; gently drop into boiling water. Reduce heat; cover and simmer for 15-18 minutes or until dumplings are tender but firm. Remove with a slotted spoon to a serving platter. Remove pork to the platter; cover and keep warm. Stir sour cream into pan juices; heat through but do not boil. Pour over dumplings and pork. **Yield:** 4 servings.

Garden Pork Skillet

Kathryn Bockus, Tuscumbia, Alabama

This is deliciously different than any other sweet-and-sour recipes because it's packed with produce. It makes a pretty presentation on the table, so it's great for special dinners.

✓ This tasty dish uses less sugar, salt and fat. Recipe includes *Diabetic Exchanges*.

    1 pound lean boneless pork
    1 can (8 ounces) unsweetened pineapple chunks, undrained
    2 tablespoons soy sauce
1-1/2 teaspoons ground ginger
    1 garlic clove, minced
    3 drops hot pepper sauce
    1 cup julienned celery
    1 cup julienned carrots
    1 cup julienned green pepper
    1 cup thinly sliced red onion
  1/2 pound fresh mushrooms, sliced
    1 cup julienned yellow squash
    1 cup julienned zucchini
    1 package (6 ounces) frozen snow peas
Hot cooked rice, optional

Cut pork into 1/8-in. x 1/2-in. x 2-in. strips; set aside. Drain juice from pineapple into a medium bowl; set pineapple aside. Add soy sauce, ginger, garlic and hot pepper sauce to juice; mix well. Add pork; cover and chill at least 1 hour. With a slotted spoon, transfer pork to a large skillet that has been sprayed with nonstick cooking spray. Brown pork over medium-high heat, stirring constantly; add marinade. Bring to a boil. Reduce heat; cover and simmer for 20-25 minutes or until pork is tender. Add celery, carrots, green pepper and onion. Cook, uncovered, over medium heat until vegetables are crisp-tender. Add mushrooms, squash, zucchini, peas and pineapple; cook for 1-2 minutes or until vegetables are crisp-tender. Serve over rice if desired. **Yield:** 6 servings. **Diabetic Exchanges:** One 1-1/3-cup serving (prepared with light soy sauce and without rice) equals 2 lean meat, 2 vegetable, 1/2 fruit; also, 201 calories, 227 mg sodium, 45 mg cholesterol, 18 gm carbohydrate, 20 gm protein, 6 gm fat.

Scalloped Potatoes 'n' Ham

Marie Schuh, Festus, Missouri

Because this potato dish comes out perfect every time, I often rely on it for casual entertaining. My guests are thrilled to sit down to a country-style supper.

    1 small onion, chopped
    1 small green pepper, thinly sliced
    1 tablespoon butter *or* margarine
    2 tablespoons all-purpose flour
  1/2 teaspoon salt
  1/8 teaspoon pepper
    1 cup milk

1-1/2 cups (6 ounces) shredded cheddar cheese, *divided*
    4 medium potatoes, peeled, cooked and sliced
1-1/2 cups diced fully cooked ham

In a skillet, saute onion and green pepper in butter until tender. Stir in flour, salt and pepper. Gradually add milk, stirring constantly. Bring to a boil; boil and stir for 2 minutes. Remove from the heat; stir in half of the cheese until melted. Gently stir in potatoes and ham. Cover and cook over low heat for 10 minutes or until heated through, stirring occasionally. Sprinkle with remaining cheese; cover and let stand until cheese melts. **Microwave Directions:** In a covered microwave-safe bowl, cook onion, green pepper and butter on high for 4 minutes. Stir in flour, salt and pepper; gradually stir in milk. Cook on medium for 4-5 minutes or until thickened, stirring occasionally. Stir in half of the cheese; set aside. In a 1-1/2-qt. microwave-safe baking dish, layer half the potatoes, ham and cheese sauce. Repeat layers. Cover and cook on high for 3-4 minutes or until heated through, stirring occasionally. Sprinkle with remaining cheese. Cover and let stand until cheese melts. This recipe was tested in a 700-watt microwave. **Yield:** 4 servings.

One-Pan Pork a la Orange

Shirley Smith, Orange, California

When I want to serve family and friends something special without a lot of fuss, this is the recipe I reach for.

    2 cups dry instant chicken stuffing mix
1-1/2 cups orange juice, *divided*
    4 pork cutlets
  1/4 cup all-purpose flour
    2 tablespoons cooking oil
    2 cups frozen tiny whole carrots
    2 cups frozen broccoli cuts
  1/8 teaspoon salt
  1/8 teaspoon pepper

Combine stuffing mix and 3/4 cup orange juice; let stand for 3-4 minutes or until liquid is absorbed, stirring occasionally. Flatten cutlets to 1/4-in. thickness; top each with about 1/3 cup stuffing. Roll up jelly-roll style and secure with toothpicks; coat with flour. In a large skillet, brown roll-ups in oil; drain. Add remaining orange juice; bring to a boil. Reduce heat; cover and simmer for 7 minutes. Add remaining ingredients; cover and simmer 7-10 minutes more or until vegetables are tender. Remove toothpicks. **Yield:** 4 servings.

Southwestern Stir-Fry

Marion Delp, Sidney, Nebraska

Our family likes pork in a variety of recipes, but this is probably at the top of the list. It's a quick and easy way to bring a little Mexican flair to your table.

    1 pork tenderloin (1 pound)
    2 tablespoons chicken broth *or* water

    2 teaspoons cornstarch
    3 garlic cloves, minced
    1 teaspoon ground cumin
1/2 teaspoon seasoned salt
    1 tablespoon cooking oil
   15 cherry tomatoes, halved
    1 medium onion, cut into thin wedges
    1 medium green pepper, cut into thin strips
Hot cooked rice or flour tortillas, warmed, optional
Shredded cheddar cheese and salsa, optional

Slice tenderloin into 3-in. x 1/2-in. x 1/8-in. strips; set aside. In a bowl, combine broth, cornstarch, garlic, cumin and seasoned salt. Add pork; toss to coat. In a large skillet, stir-fry pork in oil over medium-high heat for 5-7 minutes or until no longer pink. Add tomatoes, onion and green pepper; cover and cook for 3-4 minutes or until onion is tender. Serve over rice, or spoon into tortillas and top with cheese and salsa if desired. **Yield:** 6 servings.

Mexican Pork and Pasta

Phyllis Brooks, Auburn, Illinois

On a cold Midwestern evening, this hot and spicy dish really warms us up. It's a fun, festive change from spaghetti. Plus, everyone loves the leftovers—if there are any!

    1 pound bulk hot pork sausage
    1 medium onion, chopped
1/2 cup chopped green pepper
    1 can (14-1/2 ounces) stewed tomatoes
    1 can (8 ounces) tomato sauce
    1 cup uncooked spiral pasta
    2 tablespoons brown sugar
    1 to 2 teaspoons chili powder
    1 teaspoon salt
Parmesan cheese, optional

In a large skillet, cook sausage until no longer pink; drain. Add onion and green pepper; cook until tender. Add tomatoes, tomato sauce, pasta, brown sugar, chili powder and salt; cover and simmer for 20 minutes or until pasta is tender. Sprinkle with Parmesan cheese if desired. **Yield:** 4 servings.

Pork Chops Parmesan

Virginia Clark, Pembroke, Kentucky

My family loves Chicken Parmesan, so I was thrilled to find this recipe using pork chops. It's so good and quite different from any other pork recipe I've ever tried.

    1 cup crushed potato chips
1/4 cup grated Parmesan cheese
1/4 cup minced fresh parsley
    2 tablespoons all-purpose flour
1/4 teaspoon pepper
    4 pork chops (1/2 to 3/4 inch thick)
    2 tablespoons butter or margarine

In a shallow bowl, combine potato chips, cheese, parsley, flour and pepper. Dip pork chops into mixture, pressing firmly. In a large skillet over medium-high heat, cook pork chops in butter for about 7 minutes per side or until juices run clear. **Yield:** 4 servings.

Sausage and Zucchini

Fran Sprain, Westfield, Wisconsin

This fast, flavorful dish appears on our table many times in summer when zucchini is abundant. The combination of zucchini, sausage and cheese is a real taste treat.

    1 pound fully cooked smoked sausage
    4 cups cubed zucchini
    2 cups chopped fresh tomatoes
1/2 cup chopped onion
    1 teaspoon lemon juice
1/4 teaspoon dried oregano
1/4 teaspoon salt
1/4 teaspoon hot pepper sauce, optional
    1 teaspoon all-purpose flour
1/2 cup shredded cheddar cheese

Cut sausage in half lengthwise, then into 1/2-in. slices; brown in a large skillet over medium heat. Drain. Add the zucchini, tomatoes, onion, lemon juice, oregano, salt and hot pepper sauce if desired. Cook for 15 minutes or until zucchini is just crisp-tender. Sprinkle with flour; toss to coat. Bring to a boil; boil and stir for 2 minutes. Sprinkle with cheese. Remove from the heat; cover and let stand until cheese is melted. **Yield:** 6 servings.

Fruited Pork Picante

Anita Schebler, Phoenix, Arizona

I received this recipe from my mother-in-law, who's a great cook. Colorful peaches, salsa, sweet red pepper and peas make this dish attractive as well as great tasting.

✓ This tasty dish uses less sugar, salt and fat. Recipe includes *Diabetic Exchanges*.

    1 pound boneless pork loin, trimmed and cut into
        1/2-inch cubes
    1 tablespoon taco seasoning mix
    1 cup julienned sweet red pepper
1-1/2 cups chunky salsa
1/3 cup peach preserves or spreadable peach fruit
    1 package (6 ounces) frozen snow peas
Hot cooked rice, optional

Toss pork with taco seasoning mix. In a skillet sprayed with nonstick cooking spray, brown pork over medium heat. Add red pepper; cook for 1 minute. Add salsa and preserves; mix well. Bring to a boil. Reduce heat; cover and simmer for 15-20 minutes or until pork is tender. Add peas; cook and stir over medium heat until tender. Serve over rice if desired. **Yield:** 4 servings. **Diabetic Exchanges:** One 1-cup serving (prepared with sodium-reduced taco seasoning mix and spreadable peach fruit and without rice) equals 3 lean meat, 1 vegetable, 1 fruit; also, 271 calories, 505 mg sodium, 68 mg cholesterol, 21 gm carbohydrate, 26 gm protein, 8 gm fat.

Peasant Skillet

Lisbeth Whitehead, Watertown, South Dakota
(PICTURED AT RIGHT)

I prepare this supper frequently throughout the year, substituting whatever vegetables are in season. No matter how often I make it, I'm always asked for the recipe.

       6 bacon strips
       4 medium potatoes, thinly sliced
       3 cups broccoli florets
       3 medium carrots, thinly sliced
   1/2 cup thinly sliced celery
       1 medium onion, chopped
   1/4 teaspoon salt
   1/8 teaspoon pepper
       1 pound fully cooked Polish sausage

In a large skillet, cook bacon until crisp. Remove bacon to paper towel to drain. Reserve 2 tablespoons drippings in skillet. Add potatoes, broccoli, carrots, celery and onion to drippings; cover and cook over medium heat for 30 minutes or until vegetables are crisp-tender. Sprinkle with salt and pepper. Cut sausage diagonally into 1/2-in. slices; place on top of vegetables. Cover and simmer for 10 minutes. Crumble bacon; sprinkle on top. **Yield:** 8 servings.

Stovetop Pork Dinner

Connie Moore, Medway, Ohio
(PICTURED AT RIGHT)

Sometimes it's nice to combine a recipe's ingredients into one pan and simmer it on the stove, instead of turning on the oven. That's why I appreciate this recipe.

       4 pork steaks (1/2 inch thick)
       8 small new potatoes, optional
       1 small onion, chopped
       1 can (10-3/4 ounces) condensed cream of chicken soup, undiluted
       1 can (4 ounces) sliced mushrooms, drained
   1/4 cup water
   1/2 teaspoon garlic salt
   1/2 teaspoon Worcestershire sauce
   1/4 teaspoon dried thyme
       1 package (10 ounces) frozen peas and carrots

In a large skillet, brown steaks; drain. Add potatoes if desired and onion. Combine soup, mushrooms, water, garlic salt, Worcestershire sauce and thyme; pour into skillet. Bring to a boil. Reduce heat; cover and simmer for 1 hour. Stir in peas and carrots; cover and simmer for 10 minutes or until heated through. **Yield:** 4 servings.

Pork Patties Oriental

Shirley Nordblum, Youngsville, Pennsylvania

While on the road, my husband can't find a lot of good Chinese restaurants. So when he's home, I offer him a variety of Oriental dishes, including this one.

       1 pound ground pork
       1 egg
   1/2 cup bread crumbs
       2 tablespoons soy sauce
   3/4 teaspoon ground ginger
   3/4 teaspoon ground mustard
       1 can (20 ounces) unsweetened pineapple chunks, undrained
       1 medium green pepper, cut into chunks
       3 green onions, sliced
       3 tablespoons vinegar
       3 tablespoons water
       3 tablespoons brown sugar
       2 tablespoons cornstarch
Hot cooked rice

In a bowl, combine the first six ingredients; mix well. Shape into four patties. In a large greased skillet over medium heat, brown patties on both sides; drain. Add pineapple and juice, green pepper and onions; bring to a boil. Reduce heat; cover and simmer for 10 minutes. In a small bowl, combine vinegar, water, brown sugar and cornstarch; mix well. Add to pineapple mixture. Bring to a boil; boil and stir for 2 minutes. Serve over rice. **Yield:** 4 servings.

Ham Steak with Potatoes and Onions

Mrs. Maynard Robinson, Cleveland, Minnesota
(PICTURED AT RIGHT)

The browned potato and onion mixture is a nice complement to ham in this country-style dinner. This recipe has made the rounds in my family for a number of years.

       1 large baking potato
       1 medium red onion
       2 tablespoons cooking oil
       1 tablespoon red wine vinegar
   1/2 teaspoon salt
   1/8 to 1/4 teaspoon pepper
   1/8 teaspoon dried thyme
       1 ham steak (about 1/2 pound)

Peel potato; slice lengthwise into quarters, then crosswise into 1/4-in. slices. Repeat with onion. In a skillet over medium heat, saute potato and onion in oil for 2 minutes. Reduce heat; cover and cook for 10 minutes or until potato is crisp-tender. Uncover; increase heat to high. Cook and stir for 6-8 minutes or until potato is browned. Sprinkle with vinegar, salt, pepper and thyme. Meanwhile, in another skillet, saute ham steak over medium heat until browned and heated through. To serve, place ham on a platter and spoon potato and onion over the top. **Yield:** 2 servings.

GRANDMA'S KITCHEN. *Pictured at right, top to bottom: Peasant Skillet, Stovetop Pork Dinner and Ham Steak with Potatoes and Onions (all recipes on this page).*

Citrus Pork Skillet

Shirley Nordblum, Youngsville, Pennsylvania

Our grandchildren often ask me to prepare this stir-fry when they come to visit, so I keep the recipe close at hand. I'm happy to serve them this healthy meal.

✓ This tasty dish uses less sugar, salt and fat. Recipe includes *Diabetic Exchanges*.

    1/2 pound pork tenderloin, trimmed
    1/2 to 3/4 teaspoon ground cumin
    1/4 teaspoon pepper
    1/4 teaspoon salt, optional
      2 garlic cloves, minced
      1 cup chicken broth
    2/3 cup orange juice
      2 tablespoons cider vinegar
  1-1/2 teaspoons brown sugar
      1 cup julienned carrots
      2 tablespoons cornstarch
    1/2 cup thinly sliced green onions
Hot cooked noodles, optional

Cut pork into 1/2-in. x 1/2-in. x 2-in. strips. In a large resealable plastic bag, combine cumin, pepper and salt if desired. Add pork; seal bag and shake to coat. In a large skillet coated with nonstick cooking spray, stir-fry pork and garlic over medium heat until pork is browned. In a bowl, combine broth, orange juice, vinegar and brown sugar; mix well. Add carrots and 1-1/2 cups of the broth mixture to skillet; bring to a boil. Reduce heat; cover and simmer for 5 minutes or until carrots are tender. Combine cornstarch and remaining broth mixture until smooth; add to skillet, stirring constantly. Bring to a boil; boil and stir for 2 minutes. Add green onions; cook for 1 minute. Serve over noodles if desired. **Yield:** 4 servings. **Diabetic Exchanges:** One serving (prepared with low-sodium chicken broth and without salt and noodles) equals 2 lean meat, 1 vegetable, 1/2 fruit; also, 152 calories, 63 mg sodium, 35 mg cholesterol, 14 gm carbohydrate, 14 gm protein, 5 gm fat.

Pork Chop Suey

Garnett Johnson, Williamsburg, Kentucky

I make this fast recipe often for weekday dinners. There are never any leftovers when this is the featured fare.

  1-1/2 pounds pork chop suey meat
      2 tablespoons cooking oil
      1 cup sliced onion
  2-1/2 cups water
  1-1/2 cups sliced celery
      1 can (4 ounces) mushroom stems and pieces, drained
      2 chicken bouillon cubes
      1 teaspoon ground ginger
    1/4 cup cornstarch
    1/4 cup soy sauce
Hot cooked rice *or* mashed potatoes

In a skillet over medium heat, brown pork in oil. Add onion and saute for 10 minutes. Add water, celery, mushrooms, bouillon and ginger; cover and cook for 30-40 minutes or until pork is tender. Combine cornstarch and soy sauce until smooth; stir into skillet and simmer for 10 minutes. Serve over rice or mashed potatoes. **Yield:** 6 servings.

Curried Pork Chops

Ordell Erdaw, Gresham, Oregon

My mother was a very traditional cook, except when it came to this recipe! My sisters and I enjoyed it when we were growing up. Now it's a favorite of our own kids'.

      4 pork chops (1/2 inch thick)
      2 tablespoons butter *or* margarine, *divided*
    1/2 cup chopped onion
      1 cup water
  1-1/2 cups diced unpeeled cooking apples
    1/2 cup raisins, optional
      3 tablespoons orange marmalade
      2 tablespoons lemon juice
      1 to 2 tablespoons curry powder
      4 teaspoons sugar
    1/2 teaspoon pepper
      2 tablespoons all-purpose flour
    1/4 cup cold water
Hot cooked rice *or* macaroni

In a large skillet over medium heat, brown pork chops in 1 tablespoon of butter; drain and aside. In the same skillet, saute onion in remaining butter until tender. Add water, apples, raisins if desired, marmalade, lemon juice, curry, sugar and pepper; mix well. Bring to a boil. Return pork chops to skillet. Reduce heat; cover and simmer for 10-15 minutes or until pork juices run clear and apples are crisp-tender. Remove pork chops; keep warm. Combine flour and cold water until smooth; add to skillet, stirring constantly. Bring to a boil; boil and stir for 2 minutes. Serve over rice or macaroni. **Yield:** 4 servings.

Pork with Peanuts

Carol Gaus, Itasca, Illinois

Restaurant eating is a treat for us. So when we enjoy a meal out, I try to re-create it at home. My family enjoys my version of this Chinese dish even more than the original.

      1 pound pork cutlets (1/4 inch thick)
      4 green onions, cut into 1-inch pieces
      1 garlic clove, minced
      1 tablespoon cooking oil
      1 can (14 ounces) bean sprouts, drained
    1/2 cup thinly sliced celery
    1/2 cup thinly sliced carrots
    1/2 cup thinly sliced green *or* sweet red pepper
      1 tablespoon cornstarch
      1 cup chicken broth
      2 tablespoons soy sauce
    1/4 to 1/2 teaspoon crushed red pepper flakes
    1/2 cup dry roasted peanuts
Hot cooked rice *or* thin spaghetti

Cut pork into 1/2-in. strips. In a skillet over medium-high heat, stir-fry pork, onions and garlic in oil for 2-3 minutes or until pork is no longer pink. Add bean sprouts, celery, carrots and green pepper; stir-fry for 2-3 minutes. Combine cornstarch, broth and soy sauce until smooth; add to skillet. Stir in red pepper flakes. Bring to a boil; boil and stir for 2 minutes. Stir in peanuts. Serve over rice or spaghetti. **Yield:** 4-6 servings.

Jambalaya

Gloria Kirchman, Eden Prairie, Minnesota

This Southern dish is my family's favorite. They love the hearty combination of sausage, shrimp and rice. I appreciate the fact that it cooks in one pot for a marvelous meal.

    3/4 pound bulk hot *or* mild Italian sausage
    1/2 cup chopped onion
    1/2 cup chopped green pepper
      1 garlic clove, minced
      1 can (14-1/2 ounces) diced tomatoes, undrained
      1 can (14-1/2 ounces) chicken broth
      2 cups diced fully cooked ham
    3/4 cup uncooked long grain rice
      1 bay leaf
    1/4 teaspoon dried thyme
      1 pound fresh medium shrimp, peeled and deveined

In a large skillet, cook sausage until browned; drain. Stir in onion, green pepper and garlic; cook until vegetables are tender. Add tomatoes, broth, ham, rice, bay leaf and thyme; cover and simmer for 20-25 minutes or until tender. Stir in shrimp; cover and cook for 3-4 minutes or until shrimp turns pink. Remove bay leaf. **Microwave Directions:** In a 3-qt. microwave-safe baking dish, combine sausage, onion, green pepper and garlic; cover and cook on high for 5-6 minutes or until vegetables are tender. Stir in tomatoes, broth, ham, rice, bay leaf and thyme; cover and cook on high for 14-15 minutes or until rice is tender, stirring occasionally. Stir in shrimp; cover and cook on high for 3 minutes. Cover and let stand for 10 minutes. Remove bay leaf. This recipe was tested in a 700-watt microwave oven. **Yield:** 6-8 servings.

Pork Chops with Sauteed Plums

Tammi Lewis, Bellevue, Ohio

I frequently rely on fast, flavorful recipes like this that look like I fussed in the kitchen all day. What an easy way to please my family…and to impress dinner guests!

      4 pork chops (1 inch thick)
      1 teaspoon salt, *divided*
    1/4 teaspoon pepper
      1 tablespoon cooking oil
      1 pound fresh plums, pitted and sliced
    1/2 cup chopped onion
      2 tablespoons water
    1/2 teaspoon dried thyme

Sprinkle pork chops with 1/2 teaspoon salt and pepper. In a skillet over medium heat, brown pork chops in oil; set chops

aside. Reserve 1 tablespoon drippings; saute plums and onion for 4-6 minutes or until plums begin to brown. Stir in water, thyme and remaining salt. Return pork chops to pan. Reduce heat; cover and simmer for 13-16 minutes or until pork is tender. **Yield:** 4 servings.

Old-Fashioned Kraut Dinner

Bridget Coles, Roanoke, Virginia

Although I've collected countless cookbooks, I enjoy creating my own recipes even more. I came up with this recipe as an easy way to put dinner on the table after a long day's work.

      1 pound fully cooked smoked Polish sausage, cut into 1-inch pieces
      6 pork chops (3/4 inch thick)
      1 tablespoon cooking oil
    1/2 cup chopped onion
    1/4 cup chopped green pepper
    1/2 teaspoon garlic powder
    1/2 teaspoon pepper
    1/2 teaspoon curry powder
      1 can (15 ounces) tomato sauce
    1/4 cup water
      2 cans (14 ounces *each*) sauerkraut, rinsed and drained
      1 teaspoon sugar

In a large skillet, brown sausage and pork chops in oil; drain. Add the next five ingredients; cook until vegetables are tender. Stir in tomato sauce and water; cover and simmer for 40 minutes. Remove pork chops to a serving platter; keep warm. Add sauerkraut and sugar to skillet; mix well. Heat through. Serve with pork chops. **Yield:** 6 servings.

Saucy Ham and Rice

Janice Christofferson, Milwaukee, Wisconsin

This recipe is a tasty takeoff on beef Stroganoff. It is my husband's favorite way to eat leftover ham, so I prepare it for him at least once a month.

    1-1/2 pounds fully cooked ham, julienned
        1 tablespoon butter *or* margarine
        1 cup chopped celery
        1 cup julienned green pepper
        1 small onion, cut into thin wedges
        1 can (10-3/4 ounces) condensed cream of mushroom soup, undiluted
        2 tablespoons prepared mustard
      3/4 teaspoon dill weed
      1/8 teaspoon celery salt
        1 cup (8 ounces) sour cream
Hot cooked rice

In a skillet over medium heat, saute ham in butter for 2 minutes. Add celery, green pepper and onion; saute until tender. Add the soup, mustard, dill and celery salt; stir until smooth and heated through. Stir in sour cream; heat through (do not boil). Serve over rice. **Yield:** 4-6 servings.

Homemade Pork Sausage

Bertha Bench, Mineral Wells, Texas
(PICTURED AT LEFT)

These country-style patties are so simple to prepare. You'll never again settle for store-bought versions that are loaded with preservatives and not nearly as good.

- 2 pounds ground pork
- 2 teaspoons ground sage
- 1-1/2 teaspoons salt
- 1-1/2 teaspoons pepper
- 1/2 teaspoon cayenne pepper
- 1/2 teaspoon brown sugar

In a bowl, combine all ingredients; mix well. Shape into eight 4-in. patties. In a skillet over medium heat, fry patties for 3-4 minutes per side until browned or until no longer pink in the center. **Yield:** 8 servings.

Creamed Ham 'n' Cornmeal Cakes

Louise Bodziony, Gladstone, Missouri
(PICTURED AT LEFT)

This recipe really captures the terrific taste of the country. Whether served for breakfast, lunch or dinner, the cakes are a nice change from traditional sweet-topped pancakes.

CREAMED HAM:
- 1/2 cup chopped carrot
- 1/2 cup chopped celery
- 1/2 cup chopped onion
- 1/4 cup butter *or* margarine
- 1/4 cup all-purpose flour
- 1/4 teaspoon salt
- 1/4 teaspoon white pepper
- 2 cups milk
- 2 cups diced fully cooked ham
- 1/2 cup frozen peas
- 1 tablespoon minced fresh parsley
- 1/2 teaspoon Worcestershire sauce

CORNMEAL CAKES:
- 1-3/4 cups self-rising white cornmeal
- 1-1/2 cups buttermilk
- 1 egg
- 2 tablespoons butter *or* margarine, melted

In a skillet over medium heat, saute carrot, celery and onion in butter until tender. Add flour, salt and pepper; mix well. Gradually add milk, stirring constantly. Bring to a boil; boil and stir for 2 minutes. Stir in ham, peas, parsley and Worcestershire sauce; heat through and keep warm over low heat. Meanwhile, in a bowl, combine cornmeal, buttermilk, egg and

> **SUNNY-SIDE SKILLETS.** *Pictured at left, Homemade Pork Sausage, Zesty Breakfast Burritos and Creamed Ham 'n' Cornmeal Cakes (all recipes on this page).*

butter; mix until moistened. Pour batter by 1/4 cupfuls onto a lightly greased hot griddle; turn when bubbles form on top of pancakes. Cook until second side is golden brown. Place on plates and top with creamed ham. **Yield:** 4-6 servings.

Zesty Breakfast Burritos

Angie Ibarra, Stillwater, Minnesota
(PICTURED AT LEFT)

My husband grew up in Mexico and prefers his food extra spicy. Special seasonings added to ordinary ground pork give a little life to standard sausage and eggs.

- 1 pound ground pork
- 2 tablespoons vinegar
- 1 tablespoon chili powder
- 1 teaspoon dried oregano
- 1 teaspoon salt
- 1 garlic clove, minced
- 6 eggs
- 1/4 cup milk
- 1 tablespoon cooking oil
- 6 flour tortillas (7 inches), warmed

Taco sauce

Combine pork, vinegar, chili powder, oregano, salt and garlic; mix well. Cover and chill overnight. In a skillet over medium heat, cook pork mixture until no longer pink. Drain; keep warm. Beat eggs and milk. In another skillet, heat oil. Cook eggs over low heat until set, stirring occasionally. Spoon about 1/4 cup pork mixture and 1/4 cup eggs down the center of each tortilla. Top with taco sauce and roll up. **Yield:** 6 servings.

Pork Tenderloin with Raspberry Sauce

Norma Pimental, Acushnet, Massachusetts

Here's an easy, elegant dinner that's perfect for special occasions. The colorful fruit sauce adds just the right amount of sweetness to moist and tender pork.

- 1 pork tenderloin (1 pound)
- 1/8 teaspoon cayenne pepper, optional
- 2 teaspoons butter *or* margarine
- 1/4 cup raspberry preserves
- 2 teaspoons red wine vinegar
- 1 tablespoon ketchup
- 1/2 teaspoon soy sauce
- 1/8 to 1/4 teaspoon prepared horseradish
- 1 garlic clove, minced

Fresh raspberries, optional

Cut tenderloin into eight pieces; flatten each piece to 1-in. thickness. Sprinkle cayenne on both sides if desired. Melt butter in a skillet over medium heat; add pork and cook for 3-4 minutes per side or until juices run clear. Meanwhile, in a saucepan, combine preserves, vinegar, ketchup, soy sauce, horseradish and garlic. Simmer for 3 minutes, stirring occasionally. Serve over tenderloin; garnish with raspberries if desired. **Yield:** 4 servings.

Green Chili Burritos

Joy Margaret Gilbert, Corpus Christi, Texas

My husband introduced me to this recipe when we were engaged. It's become our family's favorite dish for birthday meals, informal get-togethers and everyday dinners.

- 1 pound boneless pork, cut into 3/4-inch cubes
- 1 tablespoon olive *or* vegetable oil
- 1 can (10 ounces) diced tomatoes and green chilies, undrained
- 2 garlic cloves, minced
- 1 cup water
- 1 cup diced fresh tomato
- 1/2 cup chopped onion
- 1/4 cup chopped green pepper
- 1/2 teaspoon dried oregano
- 1/2 teaspoon salt
- 1/4 teaspoon pepper
- 1/4 teaspoon ground cumin
- 5 teaspoons cornstarch
- 2 tablespoons cold water
- 1 can (16 ounces) refried beans
- 10 flour tortillas (7 inches), warmed

In a skillet over medium heat, brown pork in oil; drain. Add the next 10 ingredients; bring to a boil. Reduce heat; cover and simmer for 1 hour or until pork is tender. Combine cornstarch and cold water until smooth; add to pork mixture, stirring constantly. Bring to a boil; boil and stir for 2 minutes. Meanwhile, heat refried beans; spread evenly on tortillas. Spoon pork mixture down the center of tortillas; fold in sides. **Yield:** 4-6 servings.

Italian Cabbage and Rice

Betty Masarone, West Valley City, Utah

The whole family enjoys pitching in to assemble this delicious dish. They especially like the fact that they can sit back and taste the fruits of their labor in no time!

- 1-1/2 pounds ground pork
- 1 cup chopped onion
- 2 garlic cloves, minced
- 4 cups shredded cabbage
- 1 can (8 ounces) tomato sauce
- 1 cup chicken broth
- 2 tablespoons red wine vinegar
- 1/2 teaspoon dried oregano
- 1/2 teaspoon dried basil
- 1/2 teaspoon fennel seed
- 1/4 teaspoon pepper
- 1/4 teaspoon sugar
- 3 cups cooked long grain rice
- 6 bacon strips, cooked and crumbled
- 1/4 teaspoon crushed red pepper flakes, optional

Grated Parmesan cheese, optional

In a large skillet, cook pork, onion and garlic until pork is browned; drain. Add the next nine ingredients; cover and simmer for 5 minutes. Stir in rice, bacon and red pepper flakes if desired; cover and simmer 5 minutes more or until cabbage is tender. Sprinkle with Parmesan cheese if desired. **Yield:** 6 servings.

Pork Lo Mein

Billie Bethel, Waynesville, North Carolina

My husband teases me about using him as the guinea pig in the kitchen. But he's always an eager participant whenever I present attractive, tasty meals like this at dinnertime.

- 1 pound ground pork
- 1 cup thinly sliced carrots
- 1 cup chopped onion
- 1 garlic clove, minced
- 2 packages (3 ounces *each*) Oriental *or* chicken-flavored Ramen noodles
- 1-1/2 cups water
- 1 cup frozen peas
- 6 cups shredded romaine

In a large skillet coated with nonstick cooking spray, cook pork, carrots, onion and garlic over medium heat until pork is no longer pink; drain. Break noodles into skillet; stir in seasoning packets. Add water and peas; mix well. Bring to a boil; reduce heat and simmer for about 6-8 minutes or until noodles and vegetables are tender, stirring several times. Add romaine; heat and stir until wilted. **Yield:** 4 servings.

Apple Scrapple

Marion Lowery, Medford, Oregon

Just the aroma of this cooking at breakfast takes me back to my days growing up in Pennsylvania. This recipe was a favorite at home and at church breakfasts.

- 3/4 pound bulk pork sausage
- 1/2 cup finely chopped onion
- 2 tablespoons butter *or* margarine
- 1/2 cup diced unpeeled red apple
- 3/4 teaspoon dried thyme
- 1/2 teaspoon ground sage
- 1/4 teaspoon pepper
- 3 cups water, *divided*
- 3/4 cup cornmeal
- 1 teaspoon salt
- 2 tablespoons all-purpose flour

Additional butter for frying
Maple syrup

In a skillet, cook the sausage and onion until sausage is no longer pink and onion is tender. Remove from skillet with a slotted spoon; set aside. Reserve 2 tablespoons drippings in skillet. Add butter, apple, thyme, sage and pepper to drippings; cook over low heat for 5 minutes or until apple is tender. Remove from the heat; stir in sausage and onion mixture. Set aside. In a heavy saucepan, bring 2 cups water to a boil. Combine cornmeal, salt and remaining water; stir into boiling water. Return to a boil, stirring constantly. Reduce heat; cover and simmer for 1 hour, stirring occasionally. Stir in the sausage mixture. Pour into a greased 8-in. x 4-in. x 2-in. loaf pan. Cover and chill 8 hours or overnight. Slice 1/2 in. thick. Sprinkle both sides of slices with flour. Fry in a buttered skillet until browned on each side. Serve with syrup. **Yield:** 6-8 servings.

Curried Pork and Green Tomatoes

Colleen Frederick, Redwater, Alberta

When the tomatoes are green in the garden, my husband and sons are thrilled to know this dish will appear on several weekly menus. I've passed the recipe on more times than I can count.

>   1 large onion, minced
>   2 tablespoons butter *or* margarine
>   4 large fresh green tomatoes, cubed
> 1/4 cup all-purpose flour
>   1 to 2 teaspoons curry powder
> 1/2 teaspoon salt
> 1/4 teaspoon pepper
> 1/4 teaspoon sugar
> Pinch ground cardamom, optional
>   2 cups chicken broth
>   2 cups cubed cooked pork
> Hot cooked rice

In a medium skillet, saute onion in butter. Add tomatoes; cover and simmer for 10-12 minutes or until tender. Combine flour, curry, salt, pepper, sugar and cardamom if desired; slowly stir into tomatoes. Add broth and pork; simmer, uncovered, for 3-5 minutes or until sauce thickens. Serve over rice. **Yield:** 3-4 servings.

Bacon and Macaroni

Stephanie Savage, Rushville, Missouri

I've prepared this dish on the stovetop and in the microwave ...either way, it's a down-home dinner that my husband can't resist. The blend of bacon and cheese is unbeatable.

>   14 bacon strips, diced
>   1 can (15 ounces) tomato sauce
>   1 can (6 ounces) tomato paste
>   3 tablespoons minced fresh parsley, *divided*
> 1/2 teaspoon sugar
> 1/4 teaspoon garlic powder
> 1/8 teaspoon pepper
>   2 cups elbow macaroni, cooked and drained
> 1/4 cup grated Parmesan cheese

In a skillet, cook bacon; drain. Reserve 1 tablespoon drippings in skillet. Add tomato sauce, tomato paste, 2 tablespoons parsley, sugar, garlic powder and pepper to drippings; cover and simmer for 8-10 minutes. Stir in macaroni; heat through, stirring occasionally. Combine cheese and remaining parsley; sprinkle on top. **Microwave Directions:** In a 2-qt. microwave-safe baking dish, heat bacon on high for 4 minutes; discard fat. Microwave on high 4-5

minutes more or until bacon is crisp. Reserve 1 tablespoon drippings; stir in tomato sauce, tomato paste, 2 tablespoons parsley, sugar, garlic powder and pepper. Mix well. Cover and cook on high for 4-5 minutes, stirring occasionally. Stir in macaroni; cover and cook on high for 2-3 minutes or until heated through. Combine cheese and remaining parsley; sprinkle on top. This recipe was tested in a 700-watt microwave. **Yield:** 8 servings.

Ham Fried Rice

Grace Clark, Geneseo, Illinois

My husband and I lived in Japan for a few years and came to love that country's ethnic dishes. This dish captures the Oriental flavor better than any other recipes I've tried.

>   3 tablespoons olive *or* vegetable oil, *divided*
>   4 eggs, lightly beaten
> 1/2 cup chopped onion
>   1 cup chopped celery
>   4 cups cooked long grain rice
>   3 cups cubed fully cooked ham (3/4-inch cubes)
>   1 package (10 ounces) frozen peas
>   1 package (10 ounces) frozen corn
>   2 tablespoons soy sauce

In a large skillet over medium-high heat, heat 1 tablespoon of oil. Pour eggs into skillet. As eggs set, lift edges, letting uncooked portion flow underneath. Remove eggs to a plate; set aside. In the same skillet, saute onion and celery in remaining oil until crisp-tender. Reduce heat. Add rice and ham; heat through. Stir in peas and corn; heat through. Meanwhile, chop egg into small pieces; gently fold into rice mixture. Sprinkle with soy sauce. **Yield:** 4-6 servings.

Inside-Out Pork Chops

Jill Cooper, Riverdale, Georgia

This recipe gets its name because the corn bread serves as a coating instead of a stuffing. You can easily vary the amount of chili powder, so these slightly spicy chops appeal to all.

>   4 pork chops (1 inch thick)
>   1 tablespoon butter *or* margarine
> 1/4 cup water
>   1 package (8-1/2 ounces) corn bread/muffin mix
>   1 egg
> 1/2 cup milk
>   1 to 2 teaspoons chili powder
>   2 to 3 tablespoons cooking oil

In a skillet over medium heat, brown pork chops in butter. Add water; bring to a boil. Reduce heat; cover and simmer for 20 minutes or until juices run clear and pork is tender. Drain pork chops on paper towels. Drain all drippings from pan. In a bowl, combine muffin mix, egg, milk and chili powder; mix until blended. Immediately coat chops with batter. In the same skillet over medium heat, fry chops in oil until batter is golden brown and cooked through. **Yield:** 4 servings.

Slow-Cooked Specialties

Sunday Pot Roast

Brandy Schaefer, Glen Carbon, Illinois
(PICTURED AT LEFT)

This recipe proves you don't have to slave over a hot stove to prepare a delicious down-home dinner like Grandma used to make. The roast turns out tender and savory every time.

      1 teaspoon dried oregano
  1/2 teaspoon onion salt
  1/2 teaspoon pepper
  1/2 teaspoon caraway seed
  1/4 teaspoon garlic salt
      1 boneless pork loin roast (3-1/2 to 4 pounds), trimmed
      6 medium carrots, peeled and cut into 1-1/2-inch pieces
      3 large potatoes, peeled and quartered
      3 small onions, quartered
1-1/2 cups beef broth
  1/3 cup all-purpose flour
  1/3 cup cold water
  1/4 teaspoon browning sauce, optional

Combine the seasonings; rub over roast. Wrap in plastic wrap and refrigerate overnight. Place carrots, potatoes and onions in a slow cooker; add broth. Unwrap roast and place in the slow cooker. Cover and cook on high for 2 hours. Reduce heat to low and cook 6 hours longer. Transfer roast and vegetables to a serving platter; keep warm. Pour broth into a saucepan. Combine flour and water until smooth; stir into broth. Bring to a boil; boil and whisk for 2 minutes. Add browning sauce if desired. Serve with roast. **Yield:** 12-14 servings.

Chalupa

Ginny Becker, Torrington, Wyoming
(PICTURED AT LEFT)

This is such a refreshing change of pace from traditional chili. It's also fun to serve to guests. Nearly everyone who's sampled it has requested the recipe.

      1 cup dry pinto beans
3-1/2 cups water
  1/4 cup chopped onion
      1 can (4 ounces) chopped green chilies

---

      1 garlic clove, minced
      1 tablespoon chili powder
1-1/2 teaspoons salt
1-1/2 teaspoons ground cumin
  1/2 teaspoon dried oregano
      1 boneless pork shoulder roast (1-1/2 pounds), trimmed
      1 bag (10-1/2 ounces) corn chips
  1/4 cup sliced green onions
Shredded lettuce
Shredded cheddar cheese
Chopped fresh tomatoes
Salsa

Place beans and enough water to cover in a 3-qt. saucepan. Bring to a boil; boil for 2 minutes. Remove from the heat; let stand for 1 hour. Drain beans and discard liquid. In a slow cooker, combine water, onion, chilies, garlic, chili powder, salt, cumin and oregano. Add roast and beans. Cover and cook on high for 2 hours. Reduce heat to low and cook 6 hours longer or until pork is very tender. Remove roast and shred with a fork. Drain beans, reserving cooking liquid in a saucepan. Combine beans and meat; set aside. Skim and discard fat from cooking liquid; bring to a boil. Boil, uncovered, for 20 minutes or until reduced to 1-1/2 cups. Add meat and bean mixture; heat through. To serve, spoon meat mixture over corn chips; top with green onions, lettuce, cheese, tomatoes and salsa. **Yield:** 6-8 servings.

Pork Chili

Linda Temple, St. Joseph, Missouri
(PICTURED AT LEFT)

My husband usually tries to avoid spending time in the kitchen, but he'll frequently offer to prepare this easy chili. Of course, he always eagerly serves as taste-tester!

2-1/2 pounds boneless pork, cut into 1-inch cubes
      2 tablespoons cooking oil
      1 can (28 ounces) diced tomatoes, undrained
      1 can (15-1/2 ounces) chili beans, undrained
      1 can (8 ounces) tomato sauce
  1/4 cup salsa
  1/4 cup chopped onion
  1/4 cup chopped green pepper
      1 tablespoon chili powder
      1 teaspoon minced jalapeno pepper
  1/4 teaspoon garlic powder
  1/4 teaspoon cayenne powder
  1/4 teaspoon pepper
  1/4 teaspoon salt

In a large skillet over medium-high heat, brown pork in oil; drain. Place in a slow cooker; add remaining ingredients. Cover and cook on high for 2 hours. Reduce heat to low and cook 4 hours longer. **Yield:** 10-12 servings.

ONE-POT WONDERS. *Pictured at left, clockwise from top right: Sunday Pot Roast, Chalupa and Pork Chili (all recipes on this page).*

Pork and Sauerkraut With Potatoes

Valerie Hay, Longmont, Colorado

This is a wintertime favorite in our home. The down-home flavors of pork and sauerkraut are complemented by potatoes and apples. The aroma is irresistible as it cooks.

    2 cans (16 ounces *each*) sauerkraut, undrained
    1 cup thinly sliced onion
    2 medium baking apples, peeled and sliced
  1/2 cup dark corn syrup
    2 bay leaves
    1 teaspoon caraway seed
  1/2 teaspoon pepper
    3 large potatoes, peeled and cut into 2-inch
       chunks
    6 pork chops (3/4 inch thick)

In a bowl, combine sauerkraut, onion, apples, corn syrup, bay leaves, caraway and pepper. Spoon half into a slow cooker; top with potatoes. Broil pork chops 6 in. from the heat for 3-4 minutes per side or until browned; place over potatoes. Spoon remaining sauerkraut mixture over pork. Cover and cook on high for 1 hour. Reduce heat to low; cook 4-5 hours longer or until vegetables and meat are tender. Remove bay leaves. **Yield:** 6 servings.

Country Cassoulet

Suzanne McKinley, Lyons, Georgia

This bean stew goes great with fresh dinner rolls and your favorite green salad. It's a hearty meal that's perfect after a long day in the garden.

    1 pound (2 cups) dry great northern beans
    2 fresh garlic sausage links
    3 bacon strips, diced
1-1/2 pounds boneless pork, cut into 1-inch cubes
    1 pound boneless lamb, cut into 1-inch cubes
1-1/2 cups chopped onion
    3 garlic cloves, minced
    2 teaspoons salt
    1 teaspoon dried thyme
    4 whole cloves
    2 bay leaves
2-1/2 cups chicken broth
    1 can (8 ounces) tomato sauce

Place beans and enough water to cover in a Dutch oven or soup kettle. Bring to a boil; boil for 2 minutes. Remove from the heat and let stand for 1 hour. Drain beans and discard liquid. In a large skillet over medium-high heat, brown sausage; remove with a slotted spoon to a slow cooker. Add bacon to skillet; cook until crisp. Remove with a slotted spoon to slow cooker. In bacon drippings, cook pork and lamb until browned on all sides. Remove pork and lamb with a slotted spoon to slow cooker. Stir in beans and

remaining ingredients. Cover and cook on high for 2 hours. Reduce heat to low and cook 3-4 hours longer. Remove cloves and bay leaves. Remove sausage and slice into 1/4-in. pieces; return to slow cooker and stir gently. **Yield:** 8-10 servings.

Southwestern Stew

Virginia Price, Cheyenne, Wyoming

Slow cooking allows the flavors in this recipe to blend beautifully. Over the past few years, it's become our traditional Super Bowl Sunday meal.

1-1/2 pounds boneless pork, trimmed and cut into
       1/2-inch cubes
    2 tablespoons cooking oil
    1 medium onion, chopped
    1 can (15-1/2 ounces) yellow hominy, drained
    1 can (14-1/2 ounces) diced tomatoes,
       undrained
    1 can (4 ounces) chopped green chilies
  1/2 cup water
  1/2 teaspoon chili powder
  1/4 teaspoon garlic powder
  1/4 teaspoon ground cumin
  1/4 teaspoon salt
  1/4 teaspoon pepper

In a large skillet over medium-high heat, brown pork in oil. Add onion and cook for 2 minutes or until tender. Transfer to a slow cooker; add remaining ingredients. Cover and cook on high for 2 hours. Reduce heat to low and cook 4 hours longer. **Yield:** 4-6 servings.

Pork Carnitas

Tracy Byers, Corvallis, Oregon

I use this recipe often when entertaining. I set out all the toppings, and folks have fun assembling their own carnitas. Because I can prepare everything in advance, I get to spend more time with my guests.

    1 boneless pork shoulder *or* loin roast (2 to 3
       pounds), trimmed and cut into 3-inch cubes
  1/2 cup lime juice
    1 teaspoon salt
  1/2 teaspoon pepper
  1/2 teaspoon crushed red pepper flakes
   12 flour tortillas (7 inches), warmed
    2 cups (8 ounces) shredded cheddar *or*
       Monterey Jack cheese
    2 medium avocados, peeled and diced
    2 medium tomatoes, diced
    1 medium onion, diced
Shredded lettuce
Minced fresh cilantro, optional
Salsa

In a slow cooker, combine pork, lime juice, salt, pepper and pepper flakes. Cover and cook on high for 1 hour; stir. Reduce heat to low and cook 8-10 hours longer or until meat is very tender. Shred pork with a fork (it may look somewhat pink). Spoon about 1/3 cup of filling down the center of each tortilla; top with cheese, avocados, tomatoes, onion, lettuce and cilantro if desired. Fold in bottom and sides of tortilla. Serve with salsa. **Yield:** 12 servings.

Barbecued Beans

Diane Hixon, Niceville, Florida

Most members of my family would agree that no picnic is complete until these delicious beans have made their appearance. Preparing them in a slow cooker makes them easy to transport to any gathering.

- 1 pound dry navy beans
- 1 pound sliced bacon, cooked and crumbled
- 1 bottle (32 ounces) tomato juice
- 1 can (8 ounces) tomato sauce
- 2 cups chopped onion
- 2/3 cup packed brown sugar
- 1 tablespoon soy sauce
- 2 teaspoons garlic salt
- 1 teaspoon Worcestershire sauce
- 1 teaspoon ground mustard

Place beans in a 3-qt. saucepan; cover with water. Bring to a boil; boil for 2 minutes. Remove from the heat; let stand for 1 hour. Drain beans and discard liquid. In a 5-qt. slow cooker, combine remaining ingredients; mix well. Add the beans. Cover and cook on high for 2 hours. Reduce heat to low and cook 8-10 hours longer or until beans are tender. **Yield:** 12-15 servings.

Orange Pork Roast

Nancy Medeiros, Sparks, Nevada

Overcooking can cause pork roasts to be dry and tough. But this recipe's succulent orange sauce guarantees that the meat turns out moist and tender.

- 1 pork shoulder roast (3 to 4 pounds), trimmed
- 1/2 teaspoon salt
- 1/8 teaspoon pepper
- 1 can (6 ounces) frozen orange juice concentrate, thawed
- 1/4 cup honey
- 1/8 teaspoon ground cloves
- 1/8 teaspoon ground nutmeg
- 3 tablespoons all-purpose flour
- 1/4 cup cold water

Sprinkle roast with salt and pepper; place in a slow cooker. Combine orange juice concentrate, honey, cloves and nutmeg; pour over pork. Cover and cook on high for 2 hours. Reduce heat to low and cook 6 hours longer. Remove meat to a serving platter; cover and keep warm. Skim and discard fat from cooking liquid; pour into a saucepan. Combine flour and cold water until smooth; stir into cooking liquid. Bring to a boil; boil and stir for 2 minutes. Serve with roast. **Yield:** 8 servings.

Slow-Cooked Spaghetti Sauce

Margaret Shauers, Great Bend, Kansas

This sauce gets a convenient head start from prepared spaghetti sauce. I simply add a few everyday ingredients of my own. Most folks think it's homemade.

- 1 pound bulk Italian sausage
- 1/4 teaspoon cayenne pepper
- 1 small onion, sliced
- 1 medium green pepper, cut into strips
- 1 jar (28 ounces) spaghetti sauce

Hot cooked spaghetti

In a skillet over medium heat, brown sausage and cayenne for about 5 minutes. Add enough water to cover; bring to a boil. Reduce heat; cover and simmer for 10 minutes. Drain; transfer to a slow cooker. Add onion and green pepper. Pour spaghetti sauce on top. Cover and cook on high for 1 hour. Reduce heat to low and cook 2-3 hours longer. Serve over spaghetti. **Yield:** 4-6 servings.

Peachy Pork Steaks

Sandra McKenzie, Braham, Minnesota

My mom has been preparing this pork dish for years. She always found it a surefire way to get picky children to eat meat. No one can refuse these succulent steaks!

- 4 pork steaks (1/2 inch thick), trimmed
- 2 tablespoons cooking oil
- 3/4 teaspoon dried basil
- 1/4 teaspoon salt

Dash pepper

- 1 can (15-1/4 ounces) peach slices in heavy syrup, undrained
- 2 tablespoons vinegar
- 1 tablespoon beef bouillon granules
- 2 tablespoons cornstarch
- 1/4 cup cold water

Hot cooked rice

In a skillet, brown steaks in oil; sprinkle with basil, salt and pepper. Drain peaches, reserving juice. Place peaches in a slow cooker; top with steaks. Combine juice, vinegar and bouillon; pour over steaks. Cover and cook on high for 1 hour. Reduce heat to low and cook 4 hours longer or until meat is tender. Remove steaks and peaches to a serving platter; keep warm. Skim and discard fat from cooking liquid; pour into a saucepan. Combine cornstarch and cold water until smooth; stir into cooking liquid. Bring to a boil; boil and stir for 2 minutes. Serve steaks, peaches and sauce over rice. **Yield:** 4 servings.

Meaty Oven Meals

Pork Chop Potato Bake

Ardis Henning, Montello, Wisconsin
(PICTURED AT LEFT)

Folks who sample my cooking tease me and say I should open a restaurant. But I'm more than happy just cooking comforting meals like this for family and friends.

✓ This tasty dish uses less sugar, salt and fat. Recipe includes *Diabetic Exchanges*.

- 6 pork chops (5 ounces *each*), trimmed
- 1 can (10-3/4 ounces) condensed cream of mushroom soup, undiluted
- 1 can (4 ounces) sliced mushrooms, drained
- 1/4 cup chicken broth
- 1/2 teaspoon garlic salt
- 1/2 teaspoon Worcestershire sauce
- 1/4 teaspoon dried thyme
- 1 can (16 ounces) whole potatoes, drained
- 1 package (10 ounces) frozen peas, thawed
- 1 tablespoon diced pimientos

In a large skillet coated with nonstick cooking spray, brown chops on each side. Place chops in an ungreased 13-in. x 9-in. x 2-in. baking pan. Combine the next six ingredients; mix well. Pour over pork. Cover and bake at 350° for 1 hour. Add potatoes, peas and pimientos. Cover and bake 15 minutes longer or until pork is tender and vegetables are heated through. **Yield:** 6 servings. **Diabetic Exchanges:** One serving (prepared with low-fat soup and low-sodium broth) equals 2-1/2 lean meat, 1 starch, 1 vegetable; also, 232 calories, 787 mg sodium, 63 mg cholesterol, 18 gm carbohydrate, 25 gm protein, 6 gm fat.

Pork Roast with Apple-Mushroom Sauce

Karen Paumen, Buffalo, Minnesota
(PICTURED AT LEFT)

The smooth sauce combines two old recipes from my extensive collection and pairs perfectly with tender pork slices. This is a terrific entree for special dinner parties.

- 1 teaspoon dried thyme
- 1/4 teaspoon pepper
- 1 boneless pork loin roast (3 pounds)

SUMMERTIME ASSORTMENT. *Pictured at left, clockwise from top: Pork Chop Potato Bake, Pork Roast with Apple-Mushroom Sauce and Ham 'n' Swiss Ring (all recipes on this page).*

- 3 small baking apples, cored and cut into eighths
- 3 tablespoons butter *or* margarine
- 12 ounces fresh mushrooms, sliced
- 1/4 teaspoon salt, *divided*
- 1/2 cup apple cider
- 1 cup chicken broth
- 1 cup whipping cream
- 1 teaspoon brown sugar
- 2 tablespoons cornstarch
- 1/4 cup cold water

Fresh thyme sprigs, optional

Sprinkle thyme and pepper over roast and press into the meat. Place in a greased 13-in. x 9-in. x 2-in. baking pan. Bake, uncovered, at 450° for 20 minutes. Reduce heat to 325°; bake 1-1/4 hours longer or until a meat thermometer reads 160°-170°. Fifteen minutes before roast is done, saute apples in butter in a skillet until tender. Remove with a slotted spoon; cover and keep warm. Saute mushrooms in the same skillet until tender; set aside. Remove roast from oven; sprinkle with 1/8 teaspoon salt. Transfer to a serving platter; cover and keep warm. Pour cider into baking pan; stir to loosen browned bits. Transfer to a saucepan; add broth, cream, brown sugar and remaining salt. Combine cornstarch and water until smooth; stir into broth mixture. Bring to a boil; boil gently for 2 minutes or until thickened, stirring frequently. Add mushrooms and heat through. To serve, garnish roast with apples and thyme sprigs if desired. Serve with mushroom sauce. **Yield:** 8-10 servings.

Ham 'n' Swiss Ring

Bobbie Lopez, Bucyrus, Ohio
(PICTURED AT LEFT)

My family loves ham and cheese together, so I came up with this recipe. I like to serve this rich creamy dish with rice and steamed broccoli.

- 1 tube (8 ounces) refrigerated crescent rolls
- 1 cup sliced fresh mushrooms
- 2 tablespoons chopped onion
- 1 tablespoon butter *or* margarine
- 1 cup chopped fully cooked ham
- 3/4 cup shredded Swiss cheese
- 1/4 cup chopped fresh parsley
- 1 tablespoon Dijon mustard
- 1/2 teaspoon lemon juice

Arrange crescent rolls on a 13-in. round pizza pan, forming a ring with wide ends overlapping and pointed ends facing the outer edge of pan. In a skillet, saute mushrooms and onion in butter for 8 minutes or until juices are absorbed. Add remaining ingredients; mix well. Spoon over wide ends of rolls. Fold points of rolls over filling and tuck under wide ends at center (filling will be visible). Bake at 350° for 20-25 minutes or until golden brown. **Yield:** 4 servings.

Rosemary Pork Roast With Vegetables

Suzanne Strocsher, Bothell, Washington

(PICTURED ON THE FRONT COVER)

I found this recipe in a friend's recipe book years ago. Since then, my family has requested it too many times to count! Sometimes I add frozen green beans for additional color.

✓ This tasty dish uses less sugar, salt and fat. Recipe includes *Diabetic Exchanges*.

> 2 garlic cloves, minced
> 5 teaspoons dried rosemary, crushed
> 4 teaspoons dried marjoram
> 1/2 teaspoon pepper
> 1 boneless pork loin roast (2-1/2 pounds), trimmed
> 8 small red new potatoes, quartered
> 1 pound fresh baby carrots
> 1 tablespoon vegetable oil

In a small bowl, combine garlic, rosemary, marjoram and pepper; set aside 1 tablespoon. Rub remaining mixture over roast; place in a shallow roasting pan. Combine potatoes, carrots and oil in a large resealable plastic bag; add reserved spice mixture and toss to coat. Arrange vegetables around roast. Cover and bake at 325° for 1 hour. Uncover and bake 1 hour longer or until a meat thermometer reads 160°-170°. Let stand for 10 minutes before slicing. **Yield:** 8 servings. **Diabetic Exchanges:** One serving equals 4 lean meat, 1 vegetable, 1/2 starch; also, 283 calories, 92 mg sodium, 84 mg cholesterol, 12 gm carbohydrate, 31 gm protein, 12 gm fat.

Hawaiian Pizza

Gena Kuntz, West Springfield, Pennsylvania

When a friend ordered this pizza in a restaurant, I was skeptical. But after trying a slice, I was hooked! My family is thrilled that I serve this at least twice a month.

✓ This tasty dish uses less sugar, salt and fat. Recipe includes *Diabetic Exchanges*.

> 1 package (1/4 ounce) active dry yeast
> 1-1/4 cups warm water (110° to 115°)
> 3 to 3-1/4 cups all-purpose flour
> 1 tablespoon sugar
> 1 teaspoon salt
> 1 can (15 ounces) pizza sauce
> 3 cups (12 ounces) shredded mozzarella cheese
> 1 cup diced fully cooked ham
> 1 can (8 ounces) pineapple tidbits, drained

In a large mixing bowl, dissolve yeast in water. Add 1-1/2 cups flour, sugar and salt; beat until smooth. Add enough remaining flour to form a soft dough. Turn onto a floured surface; knead until smooth and elastic, about 6-8 minutes. Place in a greased bowl, turning once to grease top. Cover and let rise in a warm place until doubled, about 1 hour. Punch dough down; press onto the bottom and up the sides of a greased 15-in. x 10-in. x 1-in. baking pan. Spread with pizza sauce; sprinkle with cheese, ham and pineapple. Bake

at 400° for 20-25 minutes or until the crust is browned and cheese is melted. **Yield:** 12 servings. **Diabetic Exchanges:** One serving (prepared with low-fat cheese and ham and unsweetened pineapple) equals 2 starch, 1 meat; also, 241 calories, 675 mg sodium, 21 mg cholesterol, 31 gm carbohydrate, 14 gm protein, 6 gm fat.

Spanish Pork Steaks

Ramona Stude, Mineral Point, Wisconsin

When I lived on a farm where we prepared our own meat, this recipe was used quite often. Now my own family expects to see this dish on the menu regularly.

> 6 pork shoulder *or* sirloin steaks (1/2 inch thick)
> 3/4 teaspoon salt, *divided*
> 1/8 teaspoon pepper
> 1/2 cup sliced fresh mushrooms
> 1/2 cup sliced stuffed olives
> 1/4 cup chopped green pepper
> 1/4 cup finely chopped onion
> 1 garlic clove, minced
> 1 tablespoon all-purpose flour
> 1 tablespoon sugar
> 2 cups tomato juice

In a skillet over medium-high heat, brown steaks. Place in an ungreased 13-in. x 9-in. x 2-in. baking dish. Sprinkle with 1/4 teaspoon salt and pepper. Top with mushrooms, olives, green pepper, onion and garlic. Combine the flour, sugar and remaining salt; gradually stir in tomato juice until smooth. Pour over vegetables. Bake, uncovered, at 350° for 1 hour or until meat is tender. **Yield:** 6 servings.

Herbed Pork Roast

Margaret Paterson, Marion, Iowa

My nephew from Toronto shared this recipe with me a while back. It is very flavorful, and the accompanying roasted potatoes make it a complete meal.

> 6 garlic cloves, minced
> 1-1/2 teaspoons salt
> 3 tablespoons minced fresh parsley
> 1 tablespoon paprika
> 1/2 teaspoon dried oregano
> 1/4 cup olive *or* vegetable oil
> 1 boneless pork loin roast (3 pounds)
> 14 to 16 unpeeled small red potatoes (about 2 pounds), halved

Combine garlic and salt in a small bowl until a paste forms. Add parsley, paprika and oregano; mix well. Whisk in oil. Rub over roast. Cover and chill overnight. Place roast and any extra oil mixture in a roasting pan. Bake, uncovered, at 450° for 15 minutes. Add potatoes to pan. Reduce heat to 350°; bake for 1 to 1-1/4 hours or until a meat thermometer reads 160°-170°. Spoon drippings over potatoes. Let roast stand for 10 minutes before slicing. **Yield:** 10 servings.

Stuffed Crown Roast of Pork

Pat Panopoulos, Spring Hill, Florida

Tart cranberries and a sweet orange glaze blend beautifully in this timeless recipe. This elegant yet easy roast has made many appearances at special dinners in our home.

- 1 pork crown rib roast (about 7 pounds)
- 1 cup chopped onion
- 1 cup chopped celery
- 6 tablespoons butter *or* margarine
- 1 can (6 ounces) frozen orange juice concentrate, thawed, undiluted, *divided*
- 4 cups soft bread cubes
- 1 teaspoon salt
- 1/4 teaspoon fennel seed, crushed
- 1/8 teaspoon pepper
- 1 cup fresh *or* frozen cranberries, thawed
- 1/2 cup honey

Place the roast with rib ends up in a shallow roasting pan. Bake, uncovered, at 325° for 2 to 2-1/2 hours or until a meat thermometer inserted into meat between ribs reads 150°. Meanwhile, saute onion and celery in butter in a skillet until tender. Stir in 1/4 cup orange juice concentrate; bring to a boil. Remove from the heat. Add bread cubes, salt, fennel and pepper; toss lightly. Stir in cranberries; spoon into the center of roast. Bake 30 minutes longer. Meanwhile, combine honey and remaining orange juice concentrate in a saucepan. Bring to a boil; reduce heat and simmer for 2 minutes. Brush over roast and dressing; bake 30 minutes longer or until meat thermometer reads 160°-170°. Let stand for 15 minutes before slicing. **Yield:** 14 servings.

Pork Chops with Pear Stuffing

Mrs. Michael Dryden, Pollock, Louisiana

My husband loves pork and stuffing, so this recipe combines the best of both worlds for him. With a vegetable and salad, this dish really perks up our dinner table during the week.

- 8 pork chops (1/2 inch thick)
- 2 tablespoons cooking oil
- 2 tablespoons butter *or* margarine
- 1/4 cup chopped celery
- 1/4 cup chopped onion
- 1-3/4 cups corn-bread stuffing mix
- 1 fresh pear, diced
- 2 tablespoons chopped pecans
- 2 tablespoons chopped fresh parsley
- 1/8 teaspoon dried thyme
- 1/8 teaspoon salt
- Dash pepper
- 1/2 cup water

In a skillet over medium heat, brown pork chops in oil; drain and set aside. Add butter to skillet; saute celery and onion until tender. Remove from the heat. Add stuffing mix, pear, pecans, parsley, thyme, salt and pepper; mix well. Add water; toss gently to moisten. Spoon a fourth of the stuffing on one pork chop; top with another chop and secure with string. Repeat with remaining chops and stuffing. Stand chops vertically, but not touching, in a deep roasting pan. Add water to a depth of 1/4 in. Cover and bake at 350° for 30-35 minutes or until juices run clear and a meat thermometer reads 160°-170°. Uncover and bake 5 minutes longer to brown. Remove string. **Yield:** 4 servings.

Walnut Pork Chops

Sandra Louth, Burlingame, California

Since my mother worked while I was growing up, I did the lion's share of cooking. I still enjoy spending time in the kitchen preparing foods for my friends and family.

- 4 pork chops (1 inch thick)
- 1/8 teaspoon salt
- 1/8 teaspoon pepper
- 4 teaspoons Dijon mustard
- 3/4 cup ground walnuts *or* pecans

Sprinkle chops with salt and pepper. Spread mustard over chops; coat with nuts, pressing to adhere. Place on an ungreased baking sheet. Bake, uncovered, at 350° for 1 hour or until chops are golden brown and juices run clear. **Yield:** 4 servings.

Holiday Ham Ring

Virginia Alverson, Milroy, Indiana

I always seem to have one of these ham rings in the freezer to share with neighbors during difficult times. Its country-style taste reminds folks of Grandma's kitchen.

- 1-1/2 pounds fully cooked ham, ground
- 1/2 pound ground pork
- 3/4 cup graham cracker crumbs
- 3/4 cup milk
- 1 egg
- 1/4 teaspoon ground allspice
- 1/4 teaspoon pepper
- 1/2 cup condensed cream of tomato soup, undiluted
- 1/4 cup vinegar
- 1/4 cup packed brown sugar
- 1/2 teaspoon prepared mustard

Combine the first seven ingredients; mix well. On a 15-in. x 10-in. x 1-in. baking pan, shape meat mixture into a 9-1/2-in.-diameter ring. Combine soup, vinegar, brown sugar and mustard; pour half over ham ring. Bake, uncovered, at 350° for 30 minutes. Pour remaining soup mixture over the top; bake 30 minutes longer or until a meat thermometer reads 160°-170°. **Yield:** 8 servings.

Pork Roast Provencale

Helen Maddox, Fairfield, Pennsylvania
(PICTURED AT RIGHT)

This is my daughter's favorite meal and she always requests it for her birthday dinner. I give credit to my mother for teaching me to become skilled in the kitchen.

    1 boneless pork loin roast (2-1/2 to 3 pounds)
    3 garlic cloves, sliced
1-1/3 cups chicken broth, *divided*
  2/3 cup lemon juice
  1/4 cup olive *or* vegetable oil
    3 medium onions, chopped
    2 bay leaves
    1 tablespoon dried thyme
    1 teaspoon salt
  1/2 teaspoon pepper
    2 tablespoons cornstarch
  1/4 cup cold water

Cut tiny slits in the roast and insert garlic slices. Place roast in a large resealable plastic bag or shallow glass bowl. Combine 2/3 cup of broth, lemon juice, oil, onions, bay leaves, thyme, salt and pepper; pour over roast. Seal bag or cover; refrigerate overnight, turning occasionally. Place roast, fat side up, in a shallow roasting pan; pour marinade over. Bake, uncovered, at 350° for 2 to 2-1/2 hours or until a meat thermometer reads 160°-170°. Remove roast to a serving platter; keep warm. Skim and discard fat from juices in roasting pan. Remove bay leaves. Combine cornstarch and water until smooth; stir into pan juices. Add remaining broth. Bring to a boil over medium heat; boil for 2 minutes, stirring constantly. Serve with roast. **Yield:** 8-10 servings.

Pork Wellington

Patricia Ferreira, Holyoke, Massachusetts

This meal is a simple and nutritious way for kids to eat their vegetables. With the tender crust and tasty cheese, it's a real hit with everyone who samples it.

    1 boneless pork loin roast (2 to 3 pounds)
  1/4 teaspoon salt
  1/4 teaspoon pepper
    4 garlic cloves, minced, *divided*
    5 tablespoons olive *or* vegetable oil, *divided*
    2 cups torn fresh spinach
1-1/2 cups sliced fresh mushrooms
  1/2 cup shredded mozzarella cheese
    1 tube (11 ounces) refrigerated breadsticks

Slice roast in half horizontally; sprinkle with salt and pepper. In a skillet over low heat, cook roast and two garlic cloves in 3 tablespoons oil for 40 minutes, turning to brown all sides. Meanwhile, in another skillet, cook spinach, mushrooms and remaining garlic in remaining oil for 3-4 minutes or until soft; drain well. Remove from the heat; stir in cheese. Place breadsticks 1/2 in. apart in a greased 15-in. x 10-in. x 1-in. baking pan, stretching dough slightly so each

breadstick is about 13 in. long. Lay one roast half in the center of the dough. Spread spinach filling evenly over roast. Top with other half of roast. Bring ends of a breadstick to the top of the roast, twisting and pinching to seal. Repeat with each breadstick. Bake at 350° for 35-45 minutes or until a meat thermometer reads 160°-170°. Let stand for 10 minutes before slicing. **Yield:** 8-10 servings.

Barbecued Meatballs

Gwen Goss, Garden City, Kansas

The sweet, thick barbecue sauce clings to large tasty meatballs. This recipe is one of my favorites to take to potlucks or to serve as a meal after harvest.

1-1/2 pounds ground pork
    1 cup quick-cooking oats
    1 egg
  1/3 cup evaporated milk
  3/4 teaspoon chili powder
  3/4 teaspoon salt
  1/4 teaspoon pepper
  1/8 teaspoon garlic powder
    1 cup ketchup
  3/4 cup packed brown sugar
2-1/2 teaspoons liquid smoke, optional
  1/2 teaspoon lemon juice

Combine the first eight ingredients; shape into 2-in. balls. Place in an ungreased 13-in. x 9-in. x 2-in. baking pan. Combine the ketchup, brown sugar, liquid smoke if desired and lemon juice; stir until brown sugar is dissolved. Pour over meatballs. Bake, uncovered, at 350° for 50-60 minutes or until a meat thermometer reads 160°-170° and meatballs are no longer pink in the center. **Yield:** 6 servings.

Hungarian Pork Loaf

Sandy Harper, Kalamazoo, Michigan

I found this treasured recipe in my great-aunt's handwritten cookbook. She was a wonderful cook, and the entire family always looked forward to hearty meals at her home.

    2 cups crushed herb-seasoned stuffing mix
    1 cup buttermilk
    2 pounds ground pork
    1 egg
    1 tablespoon minced fresh parsley
    1 teaspoon garlic salt
    1 teaspoon paprika, *divided*

In a bowl, combine stuffing mix and buttermilk; let stand for 15 minutes. Add pork, egg, parsley, garlic salt and 1/2 teaspoon paprika; mix well. Press into a greased 9-in. x 5-in. x 3-in. loaf pan. Bake at 350° for 1-1/2 to 1-3/4 hours or until a meat thermometer reads 160°-170°; drain. Sprinkle with remaining paprika. **Yield:** 8-10 servings.

SPECIAL SUNDAY SUPPER. *Pictured at right: Pork Roast Provencale (recipe on this page).*

Pork and Cabbage Rolls

Barbara Whitehouse, Huntley, Illinois

I received this recipe from my mother-in-law and made some adjustments. Because I'm allergic to tomatoes, I cover the rolls with chicken broth. Either way, they're fabulous!

- 1 medium head cabbage (3 pounds)
- 1 pound ground pork
- 1/2 pound sage-flavored pork sausage
- 1 cup chopped onion
- 2 cups cooked brown rice
- 1/4 teaspoon pepper
- 2 cups chicken broth *or* 2 cans (15 ounces *each*) seasoned tomato sauce

Remove core from the cabbage. Place cabbage in a large saucepan and cover with water. Bring to a boil; boil until outer leaves loosen from head. Remove cabbage; set softened leaves aside. Return cabbage to boiling water to soften more leaves. Repeat until all leaves are softened. Remove tough center stalk from each leaf. Set aside 12 large leaves for rolls. Coarsely chop enough of the remaining leaves to measure 8 cups. Place chopped cabbage in an ungreased 13-in. x 9-in. x 2-in. baking dish. In a skillet over medium heat, cook pork, sausage and onion until meat is no longer pink and onion is tender; drain. Stir in rice. Place 1/2 cup meat mixture on each cabbage leaf. Fold in sides; starting at an unfolded edge, roll up leaf completely to enclose meat. Repeat with remaining meat and leaves. Place rolls, seam side down, in the baking dish. Sprinkle with pepper. Pour broth or tomato sauce over rolls. Cover and bake at 325° for 1 to 1-1/4 hours. **Yield:** 6 servings.

Marinated Pork Loin Roast

Susan Stull, Wanatah, Indiana

Being a hog farmer's wife, I'm always trying recipes that promote the product. I recently ran across this recipe in a church cookbook. My family was delighted with the outstanding flavor.

- 3/4 cup ketchup
- 1/4 cup seedless raspberry jam
- 1/4 cup white wine vinegar
- 1/4 cup packed brown sugar
- 1/4 cup maple-flavored syrup
- 2 tablespoons Worcestershire sauce
- 2 tablespoons lemon juice
- 1 teaspoon *each* dried thyme, oregano and marjoram
- 1 teaspoon salt
- 1 teaspoon pepper
- 1 teaspoon Dijon mustard
- 1 bay leaf
- 1/4 teaspoon ground ginger
- 1 boneless pork loin roast (3 pounds)

In a saucepan, combine all ingredients except pork. Bring to a boil over medium heat. Place roast in an 11-in. x 7-in.

x 2-in. baking dish. Prick surface of roast with a fork; pour sauce over roast. Cover and refrigerate overnight. Bake, uncovered, at 325° for 1-1/2 to 2 hours or until a meat thermometer reads 160°-170°. Let stand 10 minutes before slicing. Remove bay leaf. **Yield:** 10 servings.

Basil Baked Chops for Two

Dominique Petersen, Eden, Ontario

In this recipe, basil enhances the naturally delicious flavors of pork and vegetables. I like to make this dish during the summer months when fresh zucchini is abundant.

✓ This tasty dish uses less sugar, salt and fat. Recipe includes *Diabetic Exchanges*.

- 2 pork chops (7 ounces *each*), trimmed
- 2 sheets heavy-duty aluminum foil (18 inches x 12 inches)
- 1/4 teaspoon garlic powder
- 1/4 teaspoon pepper
- 2 cups sliced zucchini
- 1 cup thinly sliced carrots
- 2 tablespoons chopped onion
- 1 teaspoon dried basil

Place each pork chop in the center of a piece of foil. Sprinkle with garlic powder and pepper. Top with zucchini, carrots and onion. Sprinkle with basil. Bring opposite long edges of foil together over the top of vegetables and fold down several times. Fold the short ends toward the food and crimp tightly to prevent leaks. Place foil pouches on a baking sheet. Bake at 350° for 45-55 minutes or until pork juices run clear and vegetables are tender. **Yield:** 2 servings. **Diabetic Exchanges:** One serving equals 4 very lean meat, 2 vegetable; also, 230 calories, 109 mg sodium, 81 mg cholesterol, 11 gm carbohydrate, 31 gm protein, 7 gm fat.

Stuffed Ham Slices

Elizabeth Bjork, Billings, Montana

Whenever I have leftover ham, my family knows I'll be preparing these ham slices. They love the corn in the moist stuffing.

- 1/4 cup minced onion
- 3 tablespoons butter *or* margarine
- 2 cups soft bread crumbs
- 1/4 cup whole kernel corn
- 3 tablespoons minced celery
- 1 tablespoon minced green pepper
- 1/8 teaspoon poultry seasoning
- 2 pounds fully cooked ham, cut into 1/2-inch slices*
- 1 teaspoon honey

Saute onion in butter until tender; remove from the heat. Stir in bread crumbs, corn, celery, green pepper and poultry seasoning. Place half the ham slices in a greased 13-in. x 9-in. x 2-in. baking dish; spread stuffing over ham. Top with remaining ham. Bake, uncovered, at 350° for 20 minutes. Brush top slices with honey; return to the oven for 5-10 minutes or until heated through. **Yield:** 6-8 servings. ***Editor's Note:** Ask the butcher or deli to slice the ham for you.

Pork-Stuffed Eggplant

Ruth Herrmann, Kenosha, Wisconsin

My father loved to grow eggplant in his wonderful garden. Through the years, Mother learned to use it often in her cooking. We take pride in keeping this traditional fare in the family.

    1 large eggplant (1-1/2 pounds)
    1 pound ground pork
    1 egg
    1/2 cup dry bread crumbs
    1/2 cup grated Parmesan *or* Romano cheese
    1/4 cup chopped fresh parsley
    1-1/2 teaspoons dried oregano
    1/2 teaspoon salt
    1/2 teaspoon pepper
    1 can (15 ounces) tomato sauce

Cut off stem of eggplant; cut eggplant in half lengthwise. Scoop out and reserve center, leaving a 1/2-in. shell. Steam shells for 3-5 minutes or just until tender; drain. Cube reserved eggplant. In a saucepan, cook eggplant cubes in boiling water for 6-8 minutes or just until tender; drain and set aside. In a skillet over medium heat, cook pork until no longer pink; drain. Add eggplant cubes, egg, bread crumbs, cheese, parsley, oregano, salt and pepper; mix well. Fill shells; place in a greased 9-in. square baking dish. Pour tomato sauce over eggplant. Cover and bake at 350° for 25-30 minutes or until heated through. **Yield:** 4 servings.

Pork Chops and Sweet Potatoes

Virginia Bryon, Bellevue, Washington

I grew up on a farm in Ohio where good food like this was a way of life. I've had this recipe for as long as I can remember and consider it a great meal to serve when entertaining.

    4 cups cooked sliced sweet potatoes
    2 tablespoons all-purpose flour
    1/2 teaspoon salt
    1/4 teaspoon pepper
    4 pork chops (1/2 inch thick)
    2 tablespoons butter *or* margarine
    1/2 cup orange juice
    1/2 cup currant jelly
    1 tablespoon lemon juice
    1 teaspoon grated lemon peel
    1 teaspoon ground mustard
    1 teaspoon paprika
    1/2 teaspoon ground ginger

Place potatoes in a greased 13-in. x 9-in. x 2-in. baking pan. In a shallow bowl, combine the flour, salt and pepper; coat pork chops. In a skillet over medium heat, brown chops in butter for 4-5 minutes on each side or until browned; remove chops and place over sweet potatoes. Drain drippings from skillet. Add remaining ingredients; cook and stir until smooth and bubbly. Pour 3/4 cup sauce over pork chops.

Bake, uncovered, at 350° for 30-40 minutes or until pork is tender. Brush chops with remaining sauce. **Yield:** 4 servings.

Ham Loaf Pie

Mary Cook, Parsons, Kansas

We've lived on our farm for nearly 50 years, so I've had lots of experience cooking for my family and hired hands. Everyone looks forward to this meal after working out in the field.

    1-1/2 cups finely crushed cheese crackers
    1/4 cup butter *or* margarine, melted
    2 eggs
    1 can (5 ounces) evaporated milk
    1/2 cup finely chopped onion
    1/4 cup chopped green pepper
    1 tablespoon prepared mustard
    1 tablespoon prepared horseradish
    1 pound fully cooked ham, ground

Combine cracker crumbs and butter; mix well. Reserve 2 tablespoons for topping. Press remaining crumbs into the bottom and up the sides of a 9-in. pie pan. Bake at 350° for 8-10 minutes or until lightly browned. Meanwhile, in a medium bowl, beat eggs. Blend in milk, onion, green pepper, mustard and horseradish; stir in ham. Carefully spoon and spread into crust. Sprinkle with reserved crumbs. Bake at 350° for 45-50 minutes or until set. (A knife inserted halfway between the center and edge will be wet.) Let stand 5 minutes before serving. **Yield:** 6 servings.

Stuffed Banana Peppers

Louise Menzies, Rossville, Georgia

This is a delightful change from traditional stuffed green peppers. Banana peppers and chili powder give a little kick. As a bonus, any leftovers reheat nicely in the microwave.

    6 to 8 banana peppers
    1 pound bulk pork sausage
    1/2 cup cooked rice
    1/3 cup thinly sliced green onions
    3 garlic cloves, minced
    1 teaspoon salt
    1/2 teaspoon pepper
    1 can (8 ounces) tomato sauce
    1 tablespoon water
    1 teaspoon chili powder, optional
    1/2 cup shredded mozzarella cheese, optional

Remove stems of peppers; cut peppers in half lengthwise. Carefully remove seeds and membrane; set aside. Combine sausage, rice, onions, garlic, salt and pepper; mix well. Fill pepper halves. Place in a greased 13-in. x 9-in. x 2-in. baking dish. Combine tomato sauce, water and chili powder if desired; pour over peppers. Cover and bake at 350° for 30 minutes or until filling is cooked and set. Sprinkle with cheese if desired; return to the oven for 5-10 minutes or until cheese is melted. **Yield:** 6-8 servings.

OLD-FASHIONED FAMILY FAVORITES. *Clockwise from lower left: Apricot Pork Loin, Mushroom-Broccoli Stuffed Crown Roast, Vegetable Pork Chop Dinner, Tangy Glazed Ham and Stuffed Pork Chops (recipes on pages 76 and 77).*

Apricot Pork Loin

Jacquelyn Smith, Soperton, Georgia
(PICTURED ON PAGE 74)

This pork dish is pretty to look at and yummy to taste! The stuffing has a great balance of flavors that folks rave about. It's my family's top pick of pork recipes.

  1/2 pound bulk Italian sausage
1-1/3 cups chopped onion
    1 cup dried apricots, finely chopped
  1/3 cup chopped walnuts
    2 garlic cloves, minced
    2 teaspoons grated orange peel
    2 teaspoons dried thyme, *divided*
  1/2 teaspoon salt
    1 boneless pork loin roast (2-1/2 pounds)
    1 cup orange marmalade
  1/3 cup chicken broth
  1/4 cup lemon juice
    2 tablespoons grape juice
    1 teaspoon pepper

In a skillet over medium heat, cook sausage and onion until sausage is no longer pink and onion is tender; drain. Remove from the heat; stir in apricots, walnuts, garlic, orange peel, 1 teaspoon thyme and salt. Cut a pocket along one long side of the roast; stuff with sausage mixture. Place in a shallow roasting pan. Combine marmalade, broth and lemon and grape juices; pour half over roast. Sprinkle with pepper and remaining thyme. Bake, uncovered, at 350° for 45 minutes. Baste with remaining marmalade mixture. Bake 45-60 minutes longer or until a meat thermometer reads 160°-170°. Let stand 10 minutes before slicing. **Yield:** 8-10 servings.

Mushroom-Broccoli Stuffed Crown Roast

Linda Kirby, Burlington, Wisconsin
(PICTURED ON PAGE 74)

A few years ago, I was looking for a unique main dish for Christmas dinner when I stumbled across this recipe. I decided to give it try. It was a big hit with everyone.

    1 pork crown rib roast (about 6 pounds)
    1 teaspoon salt
    3 tablespoons all-purpose flour
    1 teaspoon dried thyme
    1 teaspoon dried parsley flakes
  1/4 teaspoon pepper
STUFFING:
    1 large onion, chopped
    3 tablespoons cooking oil
    4 cups coarsely chopped fresh mushrooms
    4 cups chopped fresh broccoli
  3/4 teaspoon salt
  1/2 teaspoon chicken bouillon granules
  1/4 teaspoon dried thyme

  1/4 teaspoon pepper
    6 cups onion and sage stuffing mix
  1/2 cup water
GRAVY:
    3 tablespoons all-purpose flour
  1/2 teaspoon salt
  1/8 to 1/4 teaspoon pepper

Rub the inside and outside of roast with salt. Combine flour, thyme, parsley and pepper; rub over outside of roast. Place roast with rib ends down in a large roasting pan. Bake at 325° for 2 hours. Meanwhile, in a skillet, saute onion in oil until tender. Add mushrooms, broccoli, salt, bouillon, thyme and pepper; cook for 8 minutes or until broccoli is crisp-tender. Stir in stuffing mix and water. Turn roast over with rib ends up; fill center of roast with about 3 cups stuffing. Bake 1 hour longer or until meat thermometer inserted into meat between ribs reads 160°-170°. Bake remaining stuffing in a greased covered baking dish during the last 40 minutes of baking time. Transfer roast to serving platter; let stand 15 minutes before slicing. For gravy, drain drippings into a measuring cup; skim and discard fat. Add enough water to drippings to measure 3 cups; stir in flour. Pour into skillet, stirring to loosen browned bits. Add salt and pepper. Bring to a boil over medium heat; boil for 2 minutes, stirring constantly. Serve with roast and stuffing. **Yield:** 12 servings.

Vegetable Pork Chop Dinner

MaryAnn Stoppini, Elmhurst, Pennsylvania
(PICTURED ON PAGE 75)

My family loves these savory chops served with mashed potatoes and salad. This meal is perfect for cold winter evenings.

    1 pound carrots, julienned
    1 medium onion, sliced
  1/2 cup raisins
    3 tablespoons olive *or* vegetable oil
    8 pork chops (3/4 inch thick)
  1/4 teaspoon salt
  1/4 teaspoon pepper
  1/8 teaspoon paprika

Layer carrots, onion and raisins in a 13-in. x 9-in. x 2-in. baking dish; drizzle with oil. Cover and bake at 325° for 15 minutes. Sprinkle pork chops with salt, pepper and paprika; place over vegetables. Cover and bake for 30 minutes. Uncover and bake 20 minutes longer or until pork juices run clear. **Yield:** 8 servings.

Tangy Glazed Ham

Florence McCray, Johnson City, Tennessee
(PICTURED ON PAGE 75)

After unsuccessfully looking for a satisfying glaze recipe in a number of cookbooks, my daughter and I came up with this version. It's a simple way to dress up any ham you prepare.

    1 boneless fully cooked ham (3 pounds)
  1/2 cup sweet-and-sour sauce

1/4 cup light corn syrup
3 tablespoons zesty Italian salad dressing

Place ham in an 11-in. x 7-in. x 2-in. baking pan. Pour remaining ingredients over ham in the order listed. Bake, uncovered, at 325°, basting occasionally, for 1-1/4 to 1-1/2 hours or until a meat thermometer reads 140°. **Yield:** 12 servings.

Stuffed Pork Chops

Sheri Smith, Bethlehem, Pennsylvania
(PICTURED ON PAGE 75)

A while ago, my boyfriend requested stuffed chops with a different kind of filling. I came up with this version, which stems from a recipe for stuffed mushrooms. He raved about them for days.

1-1/2 cups chopped fresh mushrooms
4 green onions, finely chopped
1/3 cup finely chopped celery
1 tablespoon butter *or* margarine
1 small tomato, chopped
1/4 to 1/2 teaspoon dried marjoram
1/8 to 1/4 teaspoon garlic salt
1/8 teaspoon pepper
2 slices day-old white bread, cut into 1/4-inch cubes
4 pork chops (1 to 1-1/2 inches thick)

In a skillet over medium heat, saute mushrooms, onions and celery in butter until tender. Add the tomato, marjoram, garlic salt and pepper; cook and stir for 5 minutes. Remove from the heat and stir in bread cubes. Cut a large pocket in the side of each chop. Stuff mushroom mixture into pockets. Place chops in an ungreased shallow baking pan. Bake, uncovered, at 350° for 1 hour or until juices run clear. **Yield:** 4 servings.

Roast Pork with Onion Stuffing

Catherine Lee, San Jose, California

I had the luck of finding this recipe neatly written and tucked inside a cookbook I bought at a garage sale. My family especially likes this in fall when the air takes on a chill.

1 boneless pork loin roast (3 pounds)
1 tablespoon olive *or* vegetable oil
2 teaspoons salt
1 teaspoon dried thyme
1/2 teaspoon pepper
STUFFING:
4 large onions, chopped
1/4 cup butter *or* margarine
1/4 cup all-purpose flour
1 tablespoon lemon juice
1 teaspoon chicken bouillon granules
1 teaspoon salt
1/4 teaspoon ground nutmeg
1/4 teaspoon pepper
1 cup water

Rub roast with oil. Combine salt, thyme and pepper; sprinkle over roast. Place roast in a shallow baking pan. Bake, uncovered, at 325° for 2 to 2-1/2 hours or until a meat thermometer reads 160°-170°. Meanwhile, in a skillet, saute onions in butter for 8-10 minutes or until tender. Stir in flour, lemon juice, bouillon, salt, nutmeg and pepper; add water. Cook over medium heat for 2 minutes, stirring constantly. Cut roast almost all the way through into 3/8-in. slices. Spoon 1 tablespoon of stuffing between each slice. Spoon remaining stuffing over roast. Bake, uncovered, at 325° for 30 minutes. If desired, thicken pan juices to make gravy. **Yield:** 10 servings.

Old-Fashioned Pork Roast

Hazel Fritchie, Palestine, Illinois

A lightly sweet coating keeps the pork roast tender and moist. With just four ingredients, this roast is great for everyday dinners but looks impressive enough to serve guests.

1 boneless pork loin roast (2 to 3 pounds)
1 cup unsweetened applesauce
1 teaspoon salt
1 teaspoon rubbed sage

Place roast, fat side up, on a greased rack in a roasting pan. Combine applesauce, salt and sage; spread over roast. Cover and bake at 350° for 1 hour. Uncover and bake 15 to 30 minutes longer or until a meat thermometer reads 160°-170°. Let stand 10 minutes before slicing. **Yield:** 8-10 servings.

Ham and Spinach Rolls

Betty Dunham, Indianapolis, Indiana

I often prepare these roll-ups for my daughters to take to office brunches—along with many copies of the recipe, of course! Everyone finds the rich cheese sauce irresistible.

1 package (10 ounces) frozen chopped spinach, thawed and well drained
1 cup (8 ounces) sour cream
1 cup corn-bread stuffing mix
1/4 teaspoon garlic powder, *divided*
1/4 teaspoon white pepper, *divided*
12 thin slices fully cooked ham (1 ounce *each*)
1/4 cup butter *or* margarine
1/4 cup all-purpose flour
1/8 teaspoon salt
2 cups milk
1/2 cup shredded sharp cheddar cheese
1/4 cup grated Parmesan cheese
1/4 teaspoon paprika

Combine spinach, sour cream, stuffing mix, 1/8 teaspoon garlic powder and 1/8 teaspoon pepper; mix well. Spread 2 tablespoons on the bottom inch of each ham slice; roll up jelly-roll style. Place, seam side down, in an ungreased 11-in. x 7-in. x 2-in. baking pan. In a small saucepan, melt butter; stir in flour, salt and remaining garlic powder and pepper until smooth. Add milk. Bring to a boil over medium heat; boil and stir for 2 minutes. Remove from the heat; stir in cheddar cheese until melted. Pour over ham rolls. Cover and bake at 350° for 15 minutes. Sprinkle with Parmesan cheese and paprika. Bake, uncovered, 10-15 minutes longer or until bubbly. **Yield:** 6 servings.

Baked Pork Chops and Apples

Naomi Giddis, Longmont, Colorado

I like to make this fruity main dish for company because it can be assembled ahead of time and popped in the oven when guests arrive. Apples and raisins give it a homey flavor.

- 6 pork chops (3/4 inch thick)
- 1/2 teaspoon salt
- 1 tablespoon cooking oil
- 2 medium baking apples, peeled and sliced
- 1/4 cup raisins
- 4 tablespoons brown sugar, *divided*
- 1/4 to 1/2 teaspoon ground cinnamon
- 1/8 teaspoon ground cloves
- 1 tablespoon lemon juice
- 1/4 cup apple juice
- 1/4 cup orange juice

Sprinkle pork chops with salt. In a skillet, brown chops in oil; set aside. Place apples and raisins in a greased 13-in. x 9-in. x 2-in. baking dish. Combine 2 tablespoons brown sugar, cinnamon and cloves; sprinkle over apples. Drizzle with lemon juice. Arrange pork chops on top. Bake, uncovered, at 325° for 40-45 minutes or until chops are tender and juices run clear. In a saucepan, combine apple juice, orange juice and remaining brown sugar; bring to a boil. Reduce heat and simmer for 10 minutes. Pour over pork chops just before serving. **Yield:** 6 servings.

Stuffed Easter Ham

Katherine Featherstone, Spirit Lake, Idaho

I traditionally serve this special ham on Easter. But it's so delicious that my family often requests it for a number of holidays throughout the year. I think you'll enjoy it, too.

- 1/2 cup chopped onion
- 3 tablespoons chopped celery
- 3 tablespoons butter *or* margarine
- 2-3/4 cups cubed French bread (1/4-inch cubes)
- 1 cup chopped baking apple
- 3/4 cup chicken broth
- 3 tablespoons raisins
- 1 tablespoon chopped fresh parsley
- 1/8 teaspoon ground cinnamon
- 1 fully cooked ham (3 pounds), cut into 3/8-inch slices*
- 1/2 cup pineapple preserves, melted

In a skillet, saute onion and celery in butter until tender; add the next six ingredients and mix well. Line an 11-in. x 7-in. x 2-in. baking pan with foil; place string for tying on foil. Place one ham slice on top of string; spread with 1 cup of stuffing. Top with another ham slice. Repeat the process, using two ham slices between stuffing layers. Tie securely with string. Cover loosely with foil. Bake at 350° for 1-1/4 hours. Baste ham with preserves; bake, uncovered, basting several times, for 45 minutes or until a meat thermometer in-

serted into the stuffing in the center of ham reads 140°. Let stand 10 minutes. Remove the string and separate the double ham slices; cut into desired portions. **Yield:** 8-10 servings. ***Editor's Note:** Ask the butcher or deli to slice the ham for you.

Italian Sausage And Sauerkraut

Evalyn Fitton, Santa Monica, California

This is my aunt's recipe. I've made it for many potlucks, and I'm always asked to bring it for church dinners. Even people who normally don't eat sauerkraut enjoy this dish.

- 1-1/2 pounds bulk Italian sausage
- 1 small onion, chopped
- 2 cans (one 16 ounces, one 8 ounces) sauerkraut, undrained
- 1-1/2 teaspoons brown sugar
- 3/4 teaspoon poultry seasoning
- 7 to 8 medium potatoes
- 1/3 cup milk
- Pinch pepper
- 1/2 teaspoon salt, optional
- 2 tablespoons butter *or* margarine
- Paprika and chopped fresh parsley, optional

In a large skillet, cook sausage and onion until sausage is no longer pink; drain. Add sauerkraut, brown sugar and poultry seasoning; cover and simmer for 1 hour. Transfer to an ungreased 13-in. x 9-in. x 2-in. baking dish. Meanwhile, cook potatoes until tender; drain and mash slightly. Add milk, pepper and salt if desired; mash until smooth. Spread evenly over sausage mixture; dot with butter. Bake at 350° for 20-25 minutes or until potatoes are lightly browned. Garnish with paprika and parsley if desired. **Yield:** 8 servings.

Creole-Style Pork Roast

Helen Carpenter, Marble Falls, Texas

We're quite active in our church and find ourselves inviting friends and neighbors over to share supper with us. This slightly spicy pork roast appeals to all palates.

- 1 teaspoon cayenne pepper
- 1/2 teaspoon salt
- 1/4 teaspoon *each* chili powder, paprika, pepper and ground coriander
- Pinch *each* ground cloves and garlic powder
- 1/4 cup finely chopped green pepper
- 1/4 cup finely chopped onion
- 1 tablespoon butter *or* margarine
- 1 can (4 ounces) mushroom stems and pieces, drained
- 1 can (6 ounces) tomato paste, *divided*
- 1 boneless pork shoulder roast (2 to 3 pounds)
- 2 tablespoons all-purpose flour

Combine all of the seasonings; set aside 1/2 teaspoon. In a saucepan over low heat, saute green pepper, onion and remaining seasoning mixture in butter until vegetables are tender. Stir in mushrooms and half the tomato paste. Spread mixture over the roast; place in a shallow baking pan. Bake, uncovered, at 325° for 2-1/2 to 3 hours or until a meat thermometer reads 160°-170°. Place roast on a serving platter; keep warm. Transfer all but 2 tablespoon drippings to a measuring cup. Add enough water to measure 1-1/2 cups; set aside. Stir flour into drippings in pan. Gradually blend the 1-1/2 cups of liquid into flour mixture, stirring until smooth. Add reserved seasoning mixture and remaining tomato paste. Bring to a boil over medium heat; boil for 2 minutes, stirring constantly. Serve with the roast. **Yield:** 8-10 servings.

Creamy Pork Tenderloin

Cathy Meizel, Flanders, New York

My husband learned this recipe while at cooking school. This tenderloin is a great dish for company because it's so elegant, yet folks don't realize how easy it is to prepare.

1/2 pound sliced bacon, cut into 1-inch pieces
1 pork tenderloin (1 pound)
1/2 teaspoon paprika
Dash pepper
1/4 teaspoon salt, optional
1 cup whipping cream

In a medium skillet, cook bacon until it just begins to brown; drain and set aside. Cut pork into 1-1/2-in. slices; flatten slightly. Sprinkle with paprika, pepper and salt if desired. Place pork in an ungreased 8-in. square baking dish. Sprinkle with bacon. Bake, uncovered, at 350° for 25-30 minutes or until pork juices run clear. Pour cream over the top; bake, uncovered, 5-10 minutes longer or until the cream is slightly thickened. **Yield:** 4 servings.

Pork Chop and Rice Dinner

Regina Albright, Southaven, Mississippi

This recipe combines two family favorites—pork and rice. It's a traditional type of meal I've come to rely on for my hurried, hectic weekdays and for casual entertaining.

6 boneless pork chops (3/4 inch thick)
1 tablespoon butter *or* margarine
Salt and pepper to taste, optional
1 cup uncooked long grain rice
1 small onion, chopped
1 garlic clove, minced
1 can (10-3/4 ounces) cream of broccoli soup, undiluted
1-1/2 cups water
1 cup (4 ounces) shredded sharp cheddar cheese
1/2 teaspoon pepper
1/4 teaspoon salt

In a skillet, brown pork chops in butter; season with salt and pepper if desired. Remove from the skillet and set aside. Reserve 2 tablespoons drippings; add rice, onion and garlic. Mix well. Stir in soup, water, cheese, pepper and salt. Transfer to a greased 13-in. x 9-in. x 2-in. baking dish; arrange chops over rice mixture. Cover and bake at 350° for 1 hour; uncover and bake 15 minutes longer or until rice is tender and pork juices run clear. **Yield:** 6 servings.

Ham 'n' Onion Frittata

Debbi Baker, Tiffin, Ohio

Hearty and filling, this dish is one I usually take to potluck brunches. My family asks me to fix this often in the colder months, and I'm always happy to oblige.

1 cup diced peeled potatoes
5 eggs
1 jar (8 ounces) process cheese spread
1/4 cup milk
1 cup diced fully cooked ham
1 can (2.8 ounces) french-fried onions, *divided*
2 tablespoons butter *or* margarine

Cook potatoes in water until almost tender; drain. In a mixing bowl, beat eggs; gradually add cheese spread and milk (mixture will appear lumpy). Stir in potatoes, ham and half the onions. In a 10-in. ovenproof skillet, melt butter over low heat; remove from the heat. Pour egg mixture into skillet. Bake, uncovered, at 350° for 20 minutes. Sprinkle with remaining onions; bake 5-10 minutes longer or until a knife inserted near the center comes out clean. Let stand for 5 minutes before cutting. **Yield:** 6 servings.

Orange Dijon Pork

Wanda Billington, Crossville, Tennessee

My family loves saucy dishes and I love simple recipes—this one combines those two criteria! Sweet orange marmalade blends nicely with tangy mustard.

4 boneless pork chops (1/2 inch thick)
1/4 teaspoon salt
1/4 teaspoon pepper
2 tablespoons butter *or* margarine
1/4 cup Dijon-mayonnaise blend
1/4 cup orange marmalade

Sprinkle chops with salt and pepper. In a skillet over medium heat, brown chops in butter for 3-5 minutes on each side. Remove from the heat; place chops in an 8-in. square baking dish. Add Dijon-mayonnaise blend and marmalade to drippings in the skillet; stir until smooth. Cook over low heat for 2 minutes or until heated through. Pour over chops. Cover and bake at 350° for 20-25 minutes; uncover and bake 5-10 minutes longer or until chops are tender and sauce is thickened. **Yield:** 4 servings.

Citrus Pork Roast

Irene Shiels, Wallingford, Connecticut
(PICTURED AT RIGHT)

Wonderful herb and citrus flavors are light and delicious additions to a traditional pork roast. Guests often comment that this roast looks almost too good to eat.

✓ This tasty dish uses less sugar, salt and fat. Recipe includes *Diabetic Exchanges*.

   1 medium grapefruit
   1 medium orange
   1 medium lemon
   2 tablespoons olive *or* vegetable oil
1-1/2 teaspoons dried rosemary, crushed
  1/2 teaspoon salt, optional
   1 garlic clove, minced
   1 boneless pork loin roast (5 pounds), trimmed

Cut fruit in half; squeeze to remove juice, reserving rinds. In a large resealable plastic bag, combine fruit juices, oil, rosemary, salt if desired and garlic. Make shallow cuts in top of roast. Place roast in bag; seal and turn to coat. Refrigerate overnight. Place roast and marinade in a shallow baking pan. Bake, uncovered, at 325° for 1-1/2 hours, basting with juices every 30 minutes. Meanwhile, slice fruit rinds into 1/4-in. strips; arrange around roast. Bake 30 minutes longer or until a meat thermometer reads 160°-170°. Let stand for 15 minutes before slicing. Arrange pork slices on a platter; drizzle with 1/4 cup of pan juices. **Yield:** 18 servings. **Diabetic Exchanges:** One serving (prepared without salt) equals 3 lean meat; also, 209 calories, 63 mg sodium, 75 mg cholesterol, 2 gm carbohydrate, 26 gm protein, 10 gm fat.

Spicy Pork Tenderloin

Sheryl Hurd-House, Fenton, Michigan
(PICTURED AT RIGHT)

A zesty rub seasons pork tenderloin overnight for exceptional flavor. The next day, it bakes in no time. So it's easy to put a fast yet fancy meal on the table.

✓ This tasty dish uses less sugar, salt and fat. Recipe includes *Diabetic Exchanges*.

   2 pork tenderloins (1 pound *each*), trimmed
  1/3 cup olive *or* vegetable oil
  1/4 cup minced fresh parsley
   2 garlic cloves, minced
   1 tablespoon grated fresh gingerroot *or* 1/2
      teaspoon ground ginger
   2 teaspoons dried oregano
   2 teaspoons dried rosemary, crushed
  1/2 teaspoon paprika
  1/2 teaspoon salt, optional
  1/4 teaspoon pepper
  1/4 teaspoon ground nutmeg

Place tenderloins in an ungreased 13-in. x 9-in. x 2-in. glass baking dish. Combine remaining ingredients; rub over tenderloins. Cover and refrigerate 6 hours or overnight. Bake, un-

covered, at 425° for 25-30 minutes or until a meat thermometer reads 160°-170°. Let stand for 5 minutes before slicing. **Yield:** 8 servings. **Diabetic Exchanges:** One serving (prepared with ground ginger and without salt) equals 3-1/2 lean meat, 1/2 fat; also, 241 calories, 45 mg sodium, 68 mg cholesterol, 1 gm carbohydrate, 25 gm protein, 15 gm fat.

Breaded Pork Chops

Fern Leinweber, Longmont, Colorado
(PICTURED AT RIGHT)

These pork chops were a much-requested dish by customers in the small cafe I owned years ago. I still like to collect recipes and experiment as often as I can.

   2 tablespoons cornmeal
   2 tablespoons whole wheat flour
  1/2 teaspoon salt
  1/2 teaspoon rubbed sage
  1/2 teaspoon sugar
  1/2 teaspoon paprika
  1/4 teaspoon onion powder
   4 pork chops (1/2 to 3/4 inch thick)
  1/4 cup milk

In a shallow bowl or large resealable plastic bag, combine the first seven ingredients. Dip pork chops into milk, then into the cornmeal mixture. Place on a rack in a shallow baking pan. Bake, uncovered, at 425° for 30-35 minutes or until juices run clear. **Yield:** 4 servings.

Crunchy Baked Pork Tenderloin

Angie Price, Bradford, Tennessee

This recipe originally called for chicken breasts, but I adapted it for pork tenderloin with mouth-watering results! I like that it calls for ingredients I already have on hand.

   1 pork tenderloin (1 pound), cut crosswise
      into 1-inch medallions
  1/4 cup butter *or* margarine, melted
  1/4 cup mayonnaise
   4 to 5 teaspoons prepared mustard
1-1/4 cups crushed herb-seasoned stuffing mix

Flatten pork tenderloin pieces to 1/4-in. to 1/2-in. thickness. In a shallow bowl, combine butter, mayonnaise and mustard; dip tenderloin pieces, then roll in stuffing crumbs. Place in a greased 13-in. x 9-in. x 2-in. baking pan. Bake, uncovered, at 425° for 13-16 minutes or until juices run clear. Let stand for 5 minutes before slicing. **Yield:** 4 servings.

> **FLAVORFUL FARE.** *Pictured at right, top to bottom: Citrus Pork Roast, Breaded Pork Chops and Spicy Pork Tenderloin (all recipes on this page).*

Pork Tenderloin Florentine

Marilyn Bazant, Albuquerque, New Mexico

My husband and I came up with this recipe one day when I had a pork tenderloin and didn't know what to do with it. It was so good, we invited friends over for a sample the next weekend.

- 1 pork tenderloin (1 pound)
- 1/8 teaspoon garlic powder
- 5 to 6 medium whole fresh mushrooms
- 1 package (10 ounces) frozen chopped spinach, thawed and well drained, *divided*
- 1/2 cup corn-bread stuffing mix
- 3 tablespoons grated Parmesan cheese, *divided*
- 3 tablespoons butter *or* margarine, melted
- 1 tablespoon sliced green onion
- Browning sauce, optional
- Dash ground nutmeg

Cut a lengthwise slit down the center of the tenderloin to within 1/2 in. of bottom. Open tenderloin so it lies flat; cover with plastic wrap. Flatten with the flat side of a meat mallet or rolling pin to 1/4-in. thickness. Remove plastic and sprinkle meat with garlic powder; set aside. Separate caps from stems of three mushrooms; set caps aside. Chop stems and remaining mushrooms to measure 1/2 cup. In a bowl, combine chopped mushrooms, half the spinach, stuffing mix, 2 tablespoons Parmesan cheese, butter and onion; mix well. Spread over tenderloin. Roll up, starting with a long edge. Secure with toothpicks. Place, seam side down, in a greased 13-in. x 9-in. x 2-in. baking pan; brush lightly with browning sauce if desired. Top with remaining spinach; sprinkle with nutmeg. Arrange mushroom caps around meat; sprinkle with remaining Parmesan. Cover and bake at 350° for 30 minutes. Uncover and bake 10 minutes longer or until a meat thermometer inserted into meat layer reads 160°-170°. Cut into 1-in. slices. **Yield:** 4 servings.

Church-Supper Ham Loaf

Rosemary Smith, Fort Bragg, California

Any leftover holiday ham gets ground up and used in this special loaf for a future meal. As the name suggests, it has made more than one appearance on the potluck table.

- 1 pound fully cooked ham, ground
- 1 pound lean pork sausage
- 2 cups soft bread crumbs
- 2 eggs
- 1 cup (8 ounces) sour cream
- 1/3 cup chopped onion
- 2 tablespoons lemon juice
- 1 teaspoon curry powder
- 1 teaspoon ground ginger
- 1 teaspoon ground mustard
- 1/8 teaspoon ground nutmeg
- 1/8 teaspoon paprika
- SAUCE:
- 1 cup packed brown sugar

- 1/2 cup water
- 1/2 cup cider vinegar
- 1/4 teaspoon pepper

In a large bowl, combine ham, sausage and bread crumbs. In a small bowl, beat eggs; add sour cream, onion, lemon juice and seasonings. Mix well; blend into meat mixture. Shape into a 9-in. x 5-in. x 2-in. loaf in a greased shallow baking pan. Bake, uncovered, at 350° for 30 minutes. Meanwhile, in a small saucepan, combine sauce ingredients; bring to a boil. Pour over loaf. Bake, uncovered, 20-30 minutes longer or until a meat thermometer reads 160°-170°, basting every 10 minutes. Let stand 10 minutes before slicing. **Yield:** 6-8 servings.

Sausage Apple Roll

Marian Butt, St. Augustine, Florida

My family loves country-style cooking. But once in a while, I like to dress up down-home dishes and make them a little more special for company. A crunchy coating adds a nice touch to a traditional sausage loaf.

- 2 pounds bulk pork sausage
- 2 cups finely chopped baking apple
- 1 cup toasted wheat germ
- 1 cup soft bread crumbs
- 1/3 cup finely chopped onion

Pat sausage onto waxed paper to form a 14-in. x 9-in. rectangle. Combine apple, wheat germ, bread crumbs and onion; mix well. Spoon and gently press onto sausage; beginning at the narrow end and using the waxed paper as an aid, roll up jelly-roll style. Place in an ungreased 13-in. x 9-in. x 2-in. baking pan. Bake at 350° for 1 hour or until a meat thermometer inserted into the center of the roll reads 160°-170°. **Yield:** 8-10 servings.

Cranberry-Stuffed Pork Chops

Marian Platt, Sequim, Washington

This has been a family favorite for years and is one that I especially enjoy serving to family and friends during the holidays. Cranberries really capture the flavor of the season.

- 2 teaspoons dried rosemary, crushed
- 1/2 teaspoon rubbed sage
- 1/2 teaspoon dried tarragon
- 1/2 teaspoon salt
- 1/2 teaspoon pepper
- 1/4 cup butter *or* margarine, melted
- 5 slices day-old bread, cut into 1/2-inch cubes
- 3/4 cup whole-berry cranberry sauce
- 2 tablespoons water
- 6 pork chops (1 inch thick)
- 1 tablespoon cooking oil

Combine the rosemary, sage, tarragon, salt and pepper; set half aside. In a large bowl, combine remaining seasonings and butter. Add bread cubes, cranberry sauce and water; toss to coat. Cut a pocket in each chop by slicing from the fat side almost to the bone. Spoon 1/4 cup stuffing into each pocket. Rub reserved seasonings over chops. In a large skillet, brown chops in oil. Transfer to a 13-in. x 9-in. x 2-in. baking pan. Bake, uncovered, at 325° for 1 to 1-1/4 hours or until pork juices run clear. **Yield:** 6 servings.

Scalloped Pork Chops

Joann Gildenmeister, Willard, Ohio

I think you'll agree this delightful meat-and-potatoes dish makes a wonderful winter meal. Every time I prepare it, the whole family showers me with compliments, especially the men.

- 4 pork chops (1/2 inch thick)
- 1 tablespoon cooking oil
- 1/4 cup chopped onion
- 1 can (10-3/4 ounces) condensed cream of mushroom soup, undiluted
- 1/2 cup milk
- 3 cups thinly sliced peeled potatoes (about 1/2 pound)
- 6 cups shredded cabbage (about 1 pound)
- 1/4 teaspoon salt
- 1/4 teaspoon pepper

In a skillet over medium heat, brown pork chops in oil; set aside. Reserve 1 teaspoon drippings; saute onion in drippings until tender. Blend in soup and milk; set aside. In a greased 2-1/2-qt. casserole, layer half of the potatoes, cabbage, salt and pepper. Pour 3/4 cup soup mixture on top. Repeat layers of potatoes, cabbage, salt and pepper. Top with pork chops. Pour remaining soup mixture over chops. Cover and bake at 350° for 50-60 minutes or until pork and vegetables are tender. **Yield:** 4 servings.

Perfect Pork Chop Bake

Jan Lutz, Stevens Point, Wisconsin

This recipe is especially useful on busy days during fall harvest or spring planting when we're short on time. It's packed with pork and produce for a filling meal.

✓ This tasty dish uses less sugar, salt and fat. Recipe includes *Diabetic Exchanges.*

- 6 pork chops (5 ounces *each*), trimmed
- 1/2 teaspoon salt, optional, *divided*
- 1 medium onion, thinly sliced into rings
- 3 medium potatoes, peeled and thinly sliced
- 6 medium carrots, thinly sliced
- 1 teaspoon dried marjoram
- 3/4 cup milk
- 3 tablespoons all-purpose flour
- 1 can (10-3/4 ounces) condensed cream of mushroom soup, undiluted

Coat a skillet with nonstick cooking spray; brown pork chops on both sides. Place in an ungreased 13-in. x 9-in. x 2-in. baking pan; sprinkle with 1/4 teaspoon salt if desired. Layer onion, potatoes and carrots over chops. Sprinkle with mar-

joram and remaining salt if desired. In a small bowl, stir milk and flour until smooth; add soup. Pour over vegetables. Cover and bake at 350° for 1 hour. Uncover and bake 15 minutes longer or until pork and vegetables are tender. **Yield:** 6 servings. **Diabetic Exchanges:** One serving (prepared with skim milk and low-fat soup and without salt) equals 2-1/2 lean meat, 2 vegetable, 1-1/2 starch; also, 280 calories, 321 mg sodium, 63 mg cholesterol, 31 gm carbohydrate, 25 gm protein, 6 gm fat.

Mustard Baked Ham with Gravy

Jean Martin, Drayton, Ontario

My mom made this dish often when I was young—and my husband's mother did the same in her kitchen! It's remained an all-time favorite in our home.

- 2 tablespoons all-purpose flour
- 1 tablespoon brown sugar
- 1 tablespoon ground mustard
- 4 teaspoons water
- 1 teaspoon vinegar
- 4 fully cooked ham steaks (1/2 inch thick)
- 1-1/4 cups milk

Combine flour, brown sugar and mustard; mix well. Stir in water and vinegar to form a paste; spread 1 teaspoon on each side of ham steaks. Place in an ungreased 13-in. x 9-in. x 2-in. baking dish. Pour milk over ham. Bake, uncovered, at 325° for 35 minutes. Serve immediately. If milk gravy is desired, transfer ham to a serving platter and keep warm. Pour pan juices into a blender; process until smooth. Transfer to a small saucepan; bring to a boil, stirring constantly. Serve immediately with ham. **Yield:** 4 servings.

Cajun Pork Roast

Mrs. Robert Krusen, Niles, Illinois

My husband and I just love New Orleans-style foods, so any time I come across a Cajun recipe, I just have to try it. This is one of our favorite ways to prepare pork.

- 1 boneless pork shoulder roast (3 to 3-1/2 pounds)
- 1/2 cup minced onion
- 1 tablespoon hot pepper sauce
- 1 tablespoon Worcestershire sauce
- 1 tablespoon steak sauce
- 4 teaspoons prepared mustard
- 3 garlic cloves, minced
- 1 teaspoon seasoned salt

Place roast in a shallow baking pan; cut 8-10 small slits in roast. Combine remaining ingredients and mix well; press into slits and over top of roast. Bake, uncovered, at 350° for 45 minutes. Cover and bake 1-3/4 hours longer or until a meat thermometer reads 160°-170°. Let stand 10 minutes before slicing. **Yield:** 8-10 servings.

Comforting Casseroles

Shepherd's Pie

Mary Arthurs, Etobicoke, Ontario

(PICTURED AT LEFT)

Of all the shepherd's pie recipes I've tried through the years, this version is my favorite. Although I live alone, I enjoy cooking and baking for friends and family.

PORK LAYER:
- 1 pound ground pork
- 1 small onion, chopped
- 2 garlic cloves, minced
- 1 cup cooked rice
- 1/2 cup pork gravy *or* 1/4 cup chicken broth
- 1/2 teaspoon salt
- 1/2 teaspoon dried thyme

CABBAGE LAYER:
- 1 medium carrot, diced
- 1 small onion, chopped
- 2 tablespoons butter *or* margarine
- 6 cups chopped cabbage
- 1 cup chicken broth
- 1/2 teaspoon salt
- 1/4 teaspoon pepper

POTATO LAYER:
- 2 cups mashed potatoes
- 1/4 cup shredded cheddar cheese

In a skillet over medium heat, brown pork until no longer pink. Add onion and garlic. Cook until vegetables are tender; drain. Stir in rice, gravy, salt and thyme. Spoon into a greased 11-in. x 7-in. x 2-in. baking dish. In the same skillet, saute carrot and onion in butter over medium heat for 5 minutes. Stir in cabbage; cook for 1 minute. Add broth, salt and pepper; cover and cook for 10 minutes. Spoon over pork layer. Spoon or pipe mashed potatoes on top; sprinkle with cheese. Bake, uncovered, at 350° for 45 minutes or until browned. **Yield:** 6 servings.

Pantry Pork Dish

Julia Trachsel, Victoria, British Columbia

(PICTURED AT LEFT)

I put this dish together one day when we had unexpected company for dinner. I used ingredients from my pantry and tossed in some ground pork. Our guests raved about the flavor.

- 1 pound ground pork
- 1 small onion, chopped, *divided*

> **GARDEN HARVEST.** *Pictured at left, clockwise from top: Shepherd's Pie, Pantry Pork Dish and Potluck Casserole (all recipes on this page).*

- 1/2 teaspoon ground allspice
- 1/2 teaspoon dried oregano
- 1/2 teaspoon salt, *divided*
- 1/2 teaspoon pepper, *divided*
- 3 medium potatoes, peeled and sliced 1/4 inch thick
- 2 tablespoons all-purpose flour
- 2-1/2 cups julienned peeled butternut squash
- 1/4 teaspoon ground nutmeg
- 1-1/2 cups frozen green beans
- 1/4 cup sliced almonds, toasted

Combine pork, half of the onion, allspice, oregano, 1/4 teaspoon salt and 1/4 teaspoon pepper. Press into the bottom of a greased 9-in. square baking dish. Top with potatoes and remaining onion. Combine flour and remaining salt; sprinkle over potatoes. Cover with foil. Bake at 350° for 40 minutes; drain. Layer squash, nutmeg, remaining pepper and beans on top of potatoes. Cover and bake 30 minutes longer or until vegetables are tender. Sprinkle with almonds; return to the oven for 5 minutes. **Yield:** 4 servings.

Potluck Casserole

Janet Wielhouwer, Grand Rapids, Michigan

(PICTURED AT LEFT)

Whenever I take this dish to picnics and potlucks—which is quite often—everyone compares it to tuna noodle casserole. It reminds folks of Mom.

✓ This tasty dish uses less sugar, salt and fat. Recipe includes *Diabetic Exchanges.*

- 1/2 pound lean boneless pork, trimmed and cut into 3/4-inch cubes
- 1 cup sliced celery
- 1/4 cup chopped onion
- 2 tablespoons water
- 2 cups cooked noodles
- 1 can (10-3/4 ounces) condensed cream of mushroom soup, undiluted
- 1 cup frozen peas
- 1/4 teaspoon salt, optional
- 1/8 teaspoon pepper
- 3 tablespoons seasoned *or* plain dry bread crumbs

In a skillet coated with nonstick cooking spray, brown the pork. Add celery, onion and water; cover and simmer for 1 hour or until pork is tender. Remove from the heat; add noodles, soup, peas, salt if desired and pepper. Transfer to an ungreased 11-in. x 7-in. x 2-in. baking dish; sprinkle with crumbs. Bake, uncovered, at 350° for 20 minutes or until bubbly. **Yield:** 4 servings. **Diabetic Exchanges:** One 1-cup serving (prepared with yolk-free noodles, low-fat soup and plain bread crumbs and without salt) equals 2 lean meat, 1-1/2 starch, 1 vegetable; also, 244 calories, 440 mg sodium, 51 mg cholesterol, 26 gm carbohydrate, 22 gm protein, 5 gm fat.

Sausage and Potato Pie

Deborah Hockman, Lansdale, Pennsylvania

When I was first married a few years back, I could barely make scrambled eggs with a recipe! This is the first recipe I've ever created. Its success encouraged my interest in cooking.

    1 pound bulk pork sausage
    3/4 cup shredded mozzarella cheese, *divided*
    1/2 cup finely chopped onion, *divided*
    1/4 cup dry bread crumbs
    1/4 cup water
      4 bacon strips
      1 cup shredded raw potato
    1/4 cup finely chopped green pepper
      4 eggs
    1/4 cup milk
    1/8 teaspoon salt
Dash pepper
    1/4 cup shredded cheddar cheese

Combine sausage, 1/2 cup mozzarella cheese, 1/4 cup onion, bread crumbs and water. Press onto the bottom and up the sides of an ungreased 9-in. pie pan, forming a rim along edge of pan. Bake at 375° for 20 minutes or until juices run clear; drain. Meanwhile, in a skillet, cook bacon until crisp; remove to paper towels to drain. Reserve 1 tablespoon of drippings. Add potato; cook over medium-high heat for 10 minutes or until browned, stirring occasionally. Add green pepper and the remaining onion. Reduce heat to medium; cook for 5 minutes or until vegetables are tender, stirring occasionally. In bowl, whisk together eggs, milk, salt and pepper; stir in cheddar cheese. Add to skillet; reduce heat and cook for 2-3 minutes or until eggs are slightly moist. Spoon into sausage shell. Sprinkle with remaining mozzarella; crumble bacon over top. Return to the oven for 5 minutes or until cheese melts. **Yield:** 6 servings.

Ham Rolls Continental

Anita Rogers, Poplar Grove, Illinois

A neighbor shared many recipes with me when I was a newlywed. This is one I still use on a regular basis. With ham, broccoli and a creamy sauce, it's a pretty dish to serve to guests.

      6 thin slices fully cooked ham (about 5-inch square)
      6 thin slices Swiss cheese (about 4-inch square)
      6 thin slices cheddar cheese (about 4-inch square)
    12 frozen broccoli spears, thawed
      1 small onion, thinly sliced into rings
      2 tablespoons butter *or* margarine
      2 tablespoons all-purpose flour
    1/2 teaspoon salt
Dash white pepper
1-1/4 cups milk

Top each ham slice with a slice of Swiss cheese, a slice of cheddar and two broccoli spears (floret ends out); roll up jelly-roll style. Place, seam side down, in an ungreased 11-in.

x 7-in. x 2-in. baking dish. Arrange onion rings on top. In a small saucepan, melt butter. Stir in flour, salt and pepper until smooth. Gradually stir in milk. Bring to a boil; boil and stir for 2 minutes. Pour over center of ham rolls. Bake, uncovered, at 350° for 25-30 minutes or until the broccoli is tender. **Yield:** 6 servings.

Apple Pork Pie

Patti Pagett, Kitchener, Ontario

While looking through my aunt's old recipes a few years ago, I came across this interesting pork pie. Now whenever my brother comes to visit, this is the meal he requests.

CRUST:
      1 cup all-purpose flour
    1/4 teaspoon salt
    2/3 cup shredded cheddar cheese
    1/3 cup shortening
      3 tablespoons cold water
FILLING:
1-1/2 pounds boneless pork, cut into 1/2-inch cubes
      1 cup water
    1/4 cup finely chopped onion
    3/4 teaspoon dried sage
    3/4 teaspoon salt
    1/4 cup all-purpose flour
    3/4 cup milk
1-1/2 cups thinly sliced peeled apples
      1 tablespoon sugar

In a bowl, combine flour and salt; mix well. Add cheese; toss to coat. Cut in shortening until mixture resembles coarse crumbs. Stir in water only until moistened. Form into a ball. Roll two-thirds of the ball into an 11-in. circle; place in a 9-in. pie pan, lining the bottom and sides. Roll remaining pastry into an 8-in. circle; cut into eight wedges. Chill pastry shell and wedges while preparing filling. Brown pork in a skillet over medium-high heat. Add water, onion, sage and salt. Reduce heat; cover and simmer for 30-40 minutes or until meat is tender. Combine flour and milk to form a smooth paste; gradually add to pork mixture. Bring to a boil; boil and stir for 2 minutes. Spoon half into prepared shell. Top with apples and sprinkle with sugar. Spoon remaining pork mixture over apples. Arrange pastry wedges on top. Bake, uncovered, at 450° for 10 minutes. Reduce heat to 350°; bake 30-40 minutes longer or until pastry is lightly browned and crisp. **Yield:** 6 servings.

Sausage-Corn Bake

Bernice Morris, Marshfield, Missouri

Corn gives this dish a mildly sweet flavor that folks find appealing. When cooking for two, I divide the ingredients into smaller dishes for fast meals in the future.

1-1/2 pounds bulk pork sausage
      1 green pepper, chopped
      1 medium onion, chopped

4 tablespoons butter *or* margarine, *divided*
3 tablespoons all-purpose flour
1/2 teaspoon salt
1/2 teaspoon white pepper
1-1/2 cups milk
1 can (14-3/4 ounces) cream-style corn
3-1/2 cups (10 ounces) egg noodles, cooked and drained
1/4 cup shredded cheddar cheese
1/2 cup dry bread crumbs

In a skillet, cook sausage, green pepper and onion until sausage is no longer pink; drain and set aside. In a saucepan, melt 3 tablespoons butter over medium heat. Stir in flour, salt and pepper. Add milk, stirring until smooth. Bring to a boil; boil and stir for 2 minutes. Stir in corn. Add corn mixture and noodles to sausage mixture; mix gently. Fold in the cheese. Transfer to a greased 13-in. x 9-in. x 2-in. baking dish. Melt remaining butter; add bread crumbs. Sprinkle over casserole. Bake, uncovered, at 325° for 30-40 minutes or until crumbs are lightly browned and casserole is heated through. **Yield:** 6-8 servings.

Cheesy Zucchini Medley

Anne Stevenson, Sidney, Ohio

My family can hardly wait for zucchini to ripen in summer so I can make this casserole. With rice, sausage and vegetables, it's a hearty meal-in-one.

1/2 cup uncooked long grain rice
1 pound bulk pork sausage
1/2 cup chopped onion
3-1/2 cups sliced zucchini
1 cup chopped fresh tomato
2 cans (4 ounces *each*) mushroom stems and pieces, drained
1/4 teaspoon salt
1/4 teaspoon pepper
8 ounces process American cheese, cubed, *divided*

Cook rice according to package directions; set aside. In a large skillet, cook sausage and onion until sausage is no longer pink and onion is tender; drain. Stir in zucchini, tomato, mushrooms, salt, pepper, 6 ounces of cheese and rice. Spoon into a greased 11-in. x 7-in. x 2-in. baking dish. Bake, uncovered, at 325° for 50-60 minutes, stirring every 20 minutes, or until vegetables are tender. Top with remaining cheese; return to the oven until cheese melts. **Yield:** 6-8 servings.

Mexican Manicotti

Lisa Bloss, Pawnee City, Nebraska

My family loves both pasta dishes and Mexican food, so I came up with this recipe that combines the best of both worlds. You'll find this irresistible on cool evenings.

1-1/2 pounds bulk pork sausage
1/2 cup chopped onion
1 can (16 ounces) refried beans

1/2 teaspoon chili powder
1/2 teaspoon ground cumin
1 package (8 ounces) manicotti, cooked and drained
1 can (15 ounces) tomato sauce
1 can (4 ounces) chopped green chilies, optional
2 cups (8 ounces) shredded cheddar cheese

In a skillet, cook sausage and onion until sausage is no longer pink and onion is tender; drain. Stir in beans, chili powder and cumin. Stuff into manicotti shells; place in a greased 13-in. x 9-in. x 2-in. baking dish. Combine tomato sauce and chilies if desired; pour over manicotti. Sprinkle with cheese. Bake, uncovered, at 350° for 45 minutes or until heated through. **Yield:** 6 servings.

Simple Sausage Ring

Jean Wilkins, Cabot, Arkansas

I received this recipe from our son, who fixed it for the family one Saturday morning. We were all pleased—and surprised—with his culinary skills. Now he and I often swap recipes.

1 pound bulk pork sausage
2 tubes (12 ounces *each*) refrigerator biscuits
2 cups (8 ounces) shredded Monterey Jack cheese

In a skillet, cook sausage until no longer pink; drain and set aside. Flatten each biscuit to a 3-in. diameter. Press half of the biscuits onto the bottom and 2 in. up the sides of a greased 10-in. fluted tube pan. Spoon sausage into pan; sprinkle with cheese. Top with remaining biscuits. Bake at 350° for 20-25 minutes or until golden brown. Let stand 10 minutes before inverting onto a serving plate. **Yield:** 8-10 servings.

Ham-Noodle Bake

Mary Richards, Ellendale, Minnesota

My husband and I build up an appetite after a long day doing chores on the farm. So I've come to rely on this creamy, comforting casserole. Horseradish and mustard add a little zip.

1/4 cup butter *or* margarine
1/4 cup all-purpose flour
1/2 teaspoon salt
1/8 teaspoon pepper
2-1/2 cups milk
3 to 4 teaspoons prepared horseradish
1 tablespoon prepared mustard
6 cups cooked wide egg noodles
2 cups cubed fully cooked ham
1 cup cubed cheddar cheese
1/2 cup bread crumbs, toasted

In a saucepan over medium heat, melt butter. Stir in flour, salt and pepper until smooth. Gradually add milk, stirring constantly. Bring to a boil; boil and stir for 2 minutes. Add horseradish and mustard; mix well. Stir in noodles, ham and cheese. Pour into a greased 2-1/2-qt. baking dish. Cover and bake at 350° for 20 minutes. Uncover; sprinkle with bread crumbs. Bake 10-15 minutes longer or until bubbly and heated through. **Yield:** 4-6 servings.

Southwestern Eggs

Shirley Seitz, Affton, Missouri
(PICTURED AT RIGHT)

Cooking is a hobby I've enjoyed for as long as I can remember. I love experimenting with new recipes and trying them out on my willing family of taste-testers.

    1 pound bulk pork sausage
    1 medium onion, chopped
    1/2 pound fresh mushrooms, sliced
    1/4 teaspoon salt
    1/4 teaspoon pepper
    6 eggs
    3 tablespoons milk *or* whipping cream
    1 can (10 ounces) diced tomatoes with green chilies, drained
    1/2 cup *each* shredded cheddar, mozzarella and Monterey Jack cheeses

In a skillet, cook sausage, onion, mushrooms, salt and pepper until meat is no longer pink; drain and set aside. In a blender, process eggs and milk for 1 minute or until smooth. Pour into a greased shallow 1-1/2-qt. baking dish; bake at 400° for 5 minutes. Cover with tomatoes and the sausage mixture. Sprinkle with cheeses. Reduce heat to 350°; bake 20 minutes more or until heated through. **Yield:** 6-8 servings.

MAKE ROOM FOR 'SHROOMS! To keep mushrooms fresher longer, keep them in their original packaging and store in the refrigerator. Mushrooms need air circulation, so don't put them in the crisper compartment.

Sausage-Broccoli Puff Pancake

Kathy Steppler, Brockton, Montana
(PICTURED AT RIGHT)

This pretty pancake looks so fancy but is actually quite easy to prepare. It's packed with lots of flavors and is especially fun to serve to overnight guests.

    1/4 cup butter *or* margarine
    3/4 cup milk
    2/3 cup all-purpose flour
    2 eggs
    1/2 teaspoon salt
FILLING:
    2 cups sliced fresh mushrooms
    1 small onion, sliced into rings
    2 tablespoons butter *or* margarine
    1 pound bulk pork sausage
    1 package (10 ounces) frozen chopped broccoli
    1/3 cup uncooked instant rice
    1 cup (4 ounces) shredded cheddar cheese

Place butter in a glass 9-in. pie plate; place in a 400° oven for 2-3 minutes or until butter is melted. Remove from the oven. In a bowl, whisk milk, flour, eggs and salt until smooth; pour into hot pie plate. Bake at 400° for 25 minutes or until puffed and golden. Meanwhile, in a skillet, saute mushrooms and onion in butter until tender; remove and set aside. In the same skillet, cook sausage over medium heat until no longer pink; drain. Stir in broccoli and rice. Cover and cook for 6-7 minutes or until broccoli and rice are tender. Stir in mushroom mixture and cheese. Cover and keep warm. When pancake is removed from oven, immediately spoon filling into center and serve. **Yield:** 6 servings.

Spinach and Sausage Pie

Nancy Brown, Janesville, Wisconsin

A flaky homemade crust holds up well in this pleasing pie brimming with sausage, cheese and vegetables. Serve it for breakfast, lunch or dinner along with a fruit cup or garden salad.

CRUST:
    2 cups all-purpose flour
    1/2 cup white cornmeal
    1/4 cup grated Parmesan cheese
    1/2 teaspoon salt
    3/4 cup cold butter *or* margarine
    7 to 9 tablespoons water
FILLING:
    3/4 pound bulk pork sausage
    1/2 cup chopped onion
    1/2 cup chopped fresh mushrooms
    2 garlic cloves, minced
    2 cups ricotta cheese
    3 eggs, *divided*
    1 package (10 ounces) frozen chopped spinach, thawed and well drained
1-1/2 cups shredded mozzarella cheese
    1/3 cup Parmesan cheese
    2 tablespoons all-purpose flour

In a bowl, combine flour, cornmeal, Parmesan cheese and salt. Cut in butter until mixture resembles coarse crumbs. Stir in water, 1 tablespoon at a time, until mixture can be formed into a ball. Wrap tightly with plastic wrap and chill for at least 30 minutes. Meanwhile, cook sausage and onion in a skillet until sausage is no longer pink; drain. Add mushrooms and garlic. Saute for 5 minutes or until mushrooms are tender; drain and set aside. In a large bowl, combine ricotta and 2 eggs; mix well. Add spinach, mozzarella, Parmesan, flour and sausage mixture; mix well. Divide dough in half; roll one half to fit a 9-in. pie plate. Spoon filling into crust. Roll remaining pastry for top crust; place over filling. Flute edges and cut slits in top crust. Beat remaining egg and brush over top crust. Place on lower rack in oven. Bake at 425° for 15 minutes. Reduce heat to 350° and bake 25-30 minutes longer or until golden brown. If necessary, cover edges of crust with foil to prevent overbrowning. Let stand for 10 minutes before cutting. **Yield:** 6-8 servings.

FARM-STYLE BREAKFASTS. *Pictured at right, top to bottom: Southwestern Eggs and Sausage-Broccoli Puff Pancake (both recipes on this page).*

Ham Hot Dish

Judy Babeck, Bismarck, North Dakota

Parmesan cheese makes this a rich and tasty variation of traditional macaroni and cheese. My family has come to expect this meal whenever I have leftover ham.

    1/4 cup chopped onion
    1/4 cup butter *or* margarine
      3 tablespoons all-purpose flour
    1/2 teaspoon salt
    Dash ground nutmeg
    Dash pepper
    2-3/4 cups milk
    1/4 cup chopped green pepper
      1 can (4 ounces) mushroom stems and pieces,
        drained
      1 jar (4 ounces) diced pimientos, drained
      1 package (7 ounces) macaroni, cooked and
        drained
    1-1/2 cups cubed fully cooked ham
    1/2 cup plus 2 tablespoons grated Parmesan cheese,
        divided

In a saucepan, saute onion in butter for 3 minutes or until tender. Stir in flour, salt, nutmeg and pepper. Gradually add milk, stirring constantly. Add the green pepper, mushrooms and pimientos. Bring to a boil; boil and stir for 2 minutes. Remove from the heat; add macaroni and mix well. Spoon half into a greased 13-in. x 9-in. x 2-in. baking pan. Sprinkle with ham and 1/2 cup Parmesan cheese. Top with the remaining macaroni mixture. Sprinkle with remaining cheese. Bake, uncovered, at 375° for 20-30 minutes or until bubbly. **Yield:** 6-8 servings.

Sausage, Hominy and Egg Brunch

Mary Ellen Andrews, Newville, Alabama

This casserole spotlights hominy, which is a basic ingredient in Southern cooking. It's especially nice to serve on cold winter days for a hearty brunch or supper.

      1 pound bulk hot pork sausage
      6 hard-cooked eggs, sliced
      2 cans (15-1/2 ounces *each*) yellow hominy, drained
      1 can (10-3/4 ounces) condensed cream of
        mushroom soup, undiluted
      1 cup (8 ounces) sour cream
    1/4 teaspoon Worcestershire sauce
      1 cup (4 ounces) shredded cheddar cheese
      1 cup soft bread crumbs
      3 tablespoons butter *or* margarine, melted

In a skillet, cook sausage until no longer pink; drain. Spoon into a 2-1/2-qt. ungreased baking dish. Cover with layers of eggs and hominy. Combine soup, sour cream and Worcestershire sauce; spread over hominy. Sprinkle with cheese.

Combine bread crumbs and butter; sprinkle over top. Bake, uncovered, at 325° for 30-35 minutes or until bubbly and golden brown. **Yield:** 6-8 servings.

Individual Brunch Casseroles

Peggy Meador, Kell, Illinois

I created this recipe one Sunday morning when I needed to use up some potatoes. Our two daughters especially look forward to sitting down to these individual casseroles.

      3 cups shredded raw potatoes
    3/4 cup diced onion
    1/2 cup diced celery
    1/2 cup diced green pepper
      2 to 4 tablespoons cooking oil
      4 eggs
    1/2 teaspoon salt
    1/4 teaspoon pepper
      1 cup (4 ounces) shredded cheddar cheese
    1/2 pound sliced bacon, cooked and crumbled
      1 can (4 ounces) mushroom stems and pieces,
        drained

In a large skillet, saute potatoes, onion, celery and green pepper in 2 tablespoons oil until vegetables are just tender. If necessary, add additional oil to prevent sticking. Remove from the heat. In a large bowl, beat eggs, salt and pepper. Add cheese, bacon and mushrooms; mix well. Stir in potato mixture. Pour into four greased individual baking dishes. Bake, uncovered, at 350° for 25-35 minutes or until a knife inserted near the center comes out clean. Let stand for 5 minutes before serving. **Yield:** 4 servings.

Tex-Mex Eggs

Mary Ellen Abel, Welcome, Minnesota

Every biteful of this egg dish is loaded with crusty bread, hearty sausage, rich cheeses and outstanding flavor! Whenever I make this, the men ask for seconds and the women ask for the recipe.

     10 slices English muffin toasting bread, cut into
        1-inch cubes
    3/4 pound bulk pork sausage
      1 medium onion, chopped
      1 can (4 ounces) chopped green chilies
      2 cups (8 ounces) shredded Monterey Jack cheese
      4 ounces process American cheese, cubed
      5 eggs
      2 cups milk
      1 cup salsa

Place half the bread cubes in a greased 13-in. x 9-in. x 2-in. baking dish; set remaining bread aside. In a skillet over medium heat, cook sausage and onion until meat is no longer pink and onion is tender; drain. Stir in chilies. Spoon half of the sausage mixture over bread; top with half of each cheese. Repeat layers of bread, sausage mixture and cheese. In a bowl, lightly beat eggs. Stir in milk and salsa. Pour over cheese; cover and refrigerate 8 hours or overnight. Remove from refrigerator 1 hour before baking. Bake, uncovered, at 325° for 50-55 minutes or until a knife inserted in the center comes out clean. Let stand for 5 minutes before cutting. **Yield:** 6-8 servings.

Dilly Ham and Eggs

Pat Yielding, North Little Rock, Arizona

I created this recipe as a way to combine ham and eggs in one dish. Everyone agrees the results are mouth-watering. They especially like the blend of seasonings.

1-1/2 cups diced fully cooked ham
   1 large onion, chopped
   1 cup chopped green pepper
   2 tablespoons butter *or* margarine
1-1/4 cups shredded cheddar cheese, *divided*
  10 eggs
 1/2 cup sour cream
 1/4 cup milk
 1/2 cup chopped green onions
   1 jar (2 ounces) diced pimientos, drained
   2 tablespoons picante sauce
   1 tablespoon chopped fresh parsley
   1 teaspoon dill weed
 1/2 teaspoon dried basil
 1/2 teaspoon pepper
 1/2 teaspoon salt

In a skillet, saute ham, onion and green pepper in butter until vegetables are crisp-tender. Transfer to a greased 13-in. x 9-in. x 2-in. baking dish. Sprinkle with 3/4 cup cheese. In a bowl, beat eggs, sour cream and milk; mix in the next eight ingredients. Pour into the baking dish. Bake, uncovered, at 350° for 25-30 minutes or until eggs are set. Top with remaining cheese. **Yield:** 8-10 servings.

Upside-Down Breakfast

Tracy McDowell, Moose Jaw, Saskatchewan

I first sampled this casserole at my mother-in-law's and knew immediately I wanted the recipe. Pineapple and brown sugar add a touch of sweetness to the rice and ham.

   3 tablespoons butter *or* margarine, melted
   3 tablespoons brown sugar
   1 can (8 ounces) sliced pineapple, drained
   2 slices fully cooked ham (6-1/4 inches x 4-1/2 inches x 1/2 inch)
1-1/2 cups uncooked instant rice
   1 cup milk
   1 cup water
   2 tablespoons plus 1-1/2 teaspoons all-purpose flour
1-1/2 teaspoons dried minced onion
 1/2 teaspoon salt
 1/8 teaspoon pepper

In an ungreased 11-in. x 7-in. x 2-in. baking dish, combine

butter and brown sugar. Arrange pineapple slices and ham on top. In a saucepan over medium heat, combine the remaining ingredients; bring to a boil. Reduce heat; cover and simmer, stirring occasionally, for 5 minutes or until rice is tender. Spread over ham. Bake, uncovered, at 400° for 10 minutes. Let stand for 3 minutes. Invert onto a serving platter and let stand for 1 minute before removing baking dish. **Yield:** 4 servings.

Ham 'n' Cheese Strata

Elizabeth Randolph, North Ridgeville, Ohio

Two young boys keep me busy, so I often prepare this casserole the night before for dinner the next day. I'm a happy homemaker who loves to share family-favorite recipes with others.

   3 cups soft rye bread cubes, crusts removed
   2 cups diced fully cooked ham
 3/4 cup diced green pepper
   2 cups (8 ounces) shredded cheddar cheese
   6 eggs
   2 cups milk
   1 teaspoon prepared horseradish
   1 teaspoon prepared mustard

Place bread cubes in a greased 13-in. x 9-in. x 2-in. baking dish. Layer with ham, green pepper and cheese. Beat eggs, milk, horseradish and mustard; pour over all. Cover and chill 8 hours or overnight. Remove from the refrigerator 30 minutes before baking. Bake, uncovered, at 350° for 30-35 minutes or until a knife inserted near the center comes out clean. Let stand 5 minutes before cutting. **Yield:** 8 servings.

Sausage Cabbage Bake

Marilyn Callahahan, Mt. Morris, Michigan

This recipe is like stuffed cabbage rolls in casserole form. It always goes over well at potlucks. Stirring before serving nicely blends the light, tasty tomato flavor throughout.

 1/2 pound bulk Italian sausage
 1/2 pound bulk hot Italian sausage
   1 medium onion, chopped
   2 cups cooked long grain rice
   4 cups shredded cabbage
   1 can (15 ounces) tomato sauce
   1 tablespoon brown sugar
   1 tablespoon lemon juice
   1 teaspoon Worcestershire sauce
 1/2 teaspoon pepper
 1/2 teaspoon seasoned salt

In a skillet, cook sausage and onion until meat is no longer pink and onion is tender; drain. Stir in rice and cabbage; pour into a greased 3-qt. baking dish. Combine remaining ingredients; pour over sausage mixture. Bake, uncovered, at 350° for 1 hour or until cabbage is tender. Stir before serving. **Yield:** 6 servings.

Pork Potpie

Linda Flor, Marmarth, North Dakota

(PICTURED AT LEFT)

Although I determine what foods will appear on our table each night, the whole family decides if the new dishes I try are winners or losers. This hearty potpie was a hands-down keeper!

CRUST:
- 3 cups all-purpose flour
- 1/2 teaspoon salt
- 1 cup shortening
- 5 to 6 tablespoons cold water
- 1 egg
- 1 tablespoon vinegar

FILLING:
- 1-1/2 cups cubed peeled potatoes
- 1/2 cup thinly sliced carrots
- 1/4 cup thinly sliced celery
- 1/4 cup chopped onion
- 1 cup water
- 2 cups diced cooked pork
- 3/4 cup pork gravy
- 1/2 teaspoon dried rosemary, crushed, optional
- 1/4 teaspoon salt
- 1/8 teaspoon pepper

Half-and-half cream, optional

In a bowl, combine flour and salt; cut in shortening until the mixture resembles coarse crumbs. Combine 5 tablespoons water, egg and vinegar; sprinkle over dry ingredients, 1 tablespoon at a time. Toss lightly with a fork until dough forms a ball; add additional water if necessary. Divide into two balls; chill while preparing filling. In a saucepan, cook potatoes, carrots, celery and onion in water for 10 minutes or until crisp-tender; drain well. Add pork, gravy, rosemary if desired, salt and pepper; set aside. On a floured surface, roll one ball of dough to fit a 9-in. pie plate. Fill with meat mixture. Roll remaining pastry to fit top of pie. Cut slits in top crust and place over filling; seal and flute edges. Brush pastry with cream if desired. Bake at 375° for 50-55 minutes or until golden brown. **Yield:** 6 servings.

Italian Potato Casserole

Jackie Jacoby, Gettysburg, Pennsylvania

(PICTURED AT LEFT)

After one taste, you'll see why this delicious dish won grand prize in a local newspaper cooking contest. It's a great variation on traditional shepherd's pie.

- 1 pound bulk Italian sausage
- 3 cups mashed potatoes

DISH-TO-PASS PARTY. *Pictured at left, top to bottom: Pork Potpie, Italian Potato Casserole and Meaty Corn-Bread Squares (all recipes on this page).*

- 1 cup chopped onion
- 3/4 cup chopped green pepper
- 2 garlic cloves, minced
- 1 tablespoon cooking oil
- 2 cups sliced fresh mushrooms
- 2 cups chopped fresh tomatoes
- 1 can (2-1/4 ounces) sliced ripe olives, drained
- 1 teaspoon dried basil
- 1/4 teaspoon salt
- 1/8 teaspoon pepper
- 1/4 cup grated Parmesan cheese
- 1 tablespoon chopped fresh parsley *or* 2 teaspoons dried parsley flakes

In a skillet, cook sausage until no longer pink; drain. Place in a greased 9-in. square baking dish. Top with potatoes. In the same skillet, saute onion, green pepper and garlic in oil for 5 minutes or until vegetables are crisp-tender. Stir in the mushrooms, tomatoes, olives, basil, salt and pepper. Spoon over potatoes to within 1 in. of edge of dish. Sprinkle Parmesan cheese and parsley on top. Bake, uncovered, at 350° for 30-35 minutes or until top is lightly browned. **Yield:** 4-6 servings.

Meaty Corn-Bread Squares

Rebecca Meyerkorth, Wamego, Kansas

(PICTURED AT LEFT)

Working full-time outside of the home doesn't allow me to cook as often as I'd like. So when I get a spare moment, I create plenty of delicious foods for my family. This is an all-time favorite I'm asked to make often.

- 1 can (10 ounces) diced tomatoes with green chilies, undrained
- 1 tablespoon cornstarch
- 1 pound diced fully cooked ham
- 1/4 cup chopped onion
- 2 teaspoons chili powder
- 1 garlic clove, minced
- 1 cup all-purpose flour
- 1/2 cup cornmeal
- 2 teaspoons baking powder
- 2 eggs
- 1 can (16 ounces) whole kernel corn, drained
- 3/4 cup milk
- 3 tablespoons vegetable oil

1-1/2 cups (6 ounces) shredded Monterey Jack cheese

Salsa, optional

Drain tomatoes, reserving juice in a skillet; set tomatoes aside. Add cornstarch to juice; mix well. Add ham, onion, chili powder, garlic and tomatoes. Bring to a boil over medium heat; boil and stir for 2 minutes. Set aside. In a bowl, combine flour, cornmeal and baking powder. In another bowl, combine eggs, corn, milk and oil; stir into dry ingredients just until moistened. Spread half the batter into a greased 9-in. square baking dish. Spoon meat mixture over batter. Sprinkle with cheese. Spoon remaining batter on top. Bake, uncovered, at 350° for 35-40 minutes or until golden brown. Let stand for 5 minutes before cutting. Serve with salsa if desired. **Yield:** 6 servings.

Ham and Broccoli Supper

Angela Liette, Piqua, Ohio

I found this recipe in an old Amish cookbook a while back. It combines lots of my family's favorite foods, like ham, broccoli and rice, and it makes a very tasty meal.

1-1/2 cups chopped broccoli
  1/2 cup finely chopped onion
1-1/2 cups cooked rice
1-1/2 cups diced fully cooked ham
  1 can (10-3/4 ounces) condensed cream of
    mushroom soup, undiluted
1-1/2 cups (6 ounces) shredded cheddar cheese
  1/4 cup milk
  2 slices bread, crusts removed
  2 tablespoons butter *or* margarine

In a saucepan, cook broccoli and onion in a small amount of water until crisp-tender; drain. In a greased 1-1/2-qt. baking dish, layer rice, ham and broccoli mixture. Combine soup, cheese and milk; spoon over broccoli. Bake, uncovered, at 350° for 20 minutes. Meanwhile, coarsely crumble bread. In a skillet, cook crumbs in butter over medium-high heat until lightly browned. Sprinkle over casserole. Bake an additional 15 minutes. **Yield:** 4 servings.

Macaroni and Cheese Deluxe

Deborah Johnson, Woodbridge, Virginia

This recipe is hearty, flavorful and simple to prepare. My husband loves it and has even made it himself several times. It appeals to the kid in all of us.

  1 package (7-1/2 ounces) macaroni and cheese
  1 pound diced fully cooked ham
  1 package (10 ounces) frozen chopped broccoli,
    thawed and drained
  1 can (10-3/4 ounces) condensed cream of celery
    soup, undiluted

Prepare macaroni and cheese according to package directions. Stir in ham, broccoli and soup; pour into a greased 2-qt. baking dish. Cover and bake at 350° for 30-45 minutes or until bubbly. **Yield:** 6 servings.

South-of-the-Border Quiche

Marjorie Hennig, Seymour, Indiana

This dish is deliciously different from traditional quiches with a pastry crust. The corn bread base gives a nice country-style texture, while green chilies add a subtle zest.

  1 package (8-1/2 ounces) corn bread/muffin mix
  2 tablespoons butter *or* margarine, melted
  1 tablespoon water

13 eggs, *divided*
  1 cup (4 ounces) shredded Monterey Jack cheese,
    divided
  1 pound bulk pork sausage, cooked and drained
  1 cup milk
  1 can (14-3/4 ounces) cream-style corn
  2 cans (4 ounces *each*) chopped green chilies
  2 tablespoons finely chopped onion
  1 cup salsa

In a bowl, combine muffin mix, butter, water and 1 egg; stir just until moistened. Spread over the bottom of a greased 13-in. x 9-in. x 2-in. baking pan. Sprinkle with 1/2 cup cheese. In a large bowl, beat remaining eggs. Add sausage, milk, corn, chilies and onion; pour over batter. Bake, uncovered, at 350° for 60-70 minutes or until a knife inserted near the center comes out clean. Top with salsa and sprinkle with remaining cheese. Return to the oven for 10 minutes or until cheese is melted. Let stand for 5 minutes before cutting. **Yield:** 12-14 servings.

Sausage Apple Squares

Eylene Struble, Marshall, Minnesota

Our family and four others used to camp together every summer. These squares were our traditional dinner the first night out. They sure disappeared in a hurry!

  1 package (8 ounces) fully cooked breakfast
    sausage links
  3 cups sliced peeled baking apples
  1 package (8-1/2 ounces) corn bread/muffin mix
Applesauce, warmed

In a skillet, brown sausages. Meanwhile, arrange apples in a greased 8-in. square baking pan; top with sausages. Prepare corn bread batter according to package directions; spoon over sausages. Bake at 350° for 30-35 minutes or until a toothpick inserted into the corn bread comes out clean. Cut into squares; top with warm applesauce. **Yield:** 4-6 servings.

Oven-Baked Chop Suey

Nadine Dahling, Elkader, Iowa

Whenever I take this casserole to a potluck, I come home with an empty dish...and with many recipe requests! Macaroni makes it a nice switch from other chop suey recipes.

  2 pounds boneless pork steak, cut into 1-inch
    pieces
  1 package (7 ounces) shell macaroni, cooked and
    drained
  2 cups diced celery
  2 medium onions, diced
  1 cup chopped green pepper
  1 can (10-3/4 ounces) condensed cream of
    mushroom soup, undiluted
  1 can (10-3/4 ounces) condensed cream of chicken
    soup, undiluted

1 can (4 ounces) mushroom stems and pieces, drained
1/4 cup soy sauce
1 jar (2 ounces) diced pimientos, drained
2 cups chow mein noodles

In a large skillet over medium-high heat, brown the pork; drain. Add the next nine ingredients; mix well. Pour into a greased 13-in. x 9-in. x 2-in. baking dish. Top with chow mein noodles. Bake, uncovered, at 350° for 1 to 1-1/4 hours or until pork is tender. **Yield:** 8 servings.

Ham Souffle

Joyce Carlsen, Endicott, New York

This is an old-time recipe that has made numerous appearances at potlucks and family get-togethers. The tater tots are a fun and easy way to add potatoes to a tasty dish.

1 package (1 pound) frozen tater tot potatoes, *divided*
1-1/4 cups frozen peas
1-1/2 cups diced fully cooked ham
1 cup (4 ounces) shredded Swiss cheese, *divided*
1/3 cup sliced green onions
1-1/4 cups milk
3 eggs
3/4 teaspoon salt
1/2 to 3/4 teaspoon dried tarragon
1/2 teaspoon pepper

Place half of the potatoes in a greased 11-in. x 7-in. x 2-in. baking dish. Layer with peas, ham, 3/4 cup cheese, onions and remaining potatoes. In a bowl, whisk milk, eggs and seasonings; pour over potatoes. Sprinkle with remaining cheese. Bake, uncovered, at 350° for 1 hour. **Yield:** 6 servings.

Saucy Sausage and Veggies

Janice Rose, Abilene, Kansas

This recipe calls for a broccoli-carrot-water chestnut blend, but feel free to use whatever mixed vegetables you like.

2 packages (1 pound *each*) frozen mixed broccoli, carrots and water chestnuts, thawed
1 pound fully cooked smoked sausage, cut into 1/2-inch pieces
1 can (10-3/4 ounces) condensed golden corn soup, undiluted
3/4 cup milk
3/4 cup cubed process American cheese
1/2 teaspoon pepper
1/2 cup sour cream
1/2 cup seasoned dry bread crumbs
2 tablespoons butter *or* margarine, melted

Place vegetables in a greased 11-in. x 7-in. x 2-in. baking dish. In a skillet, brown sausage; drain. Layer over the vegetables. In a saucepan, combine soup, milk, cheese and pepper. Cook over low heat until cheese is melted; remove from the heat. Stir in sour cream; pour over the vegetables and sausage. Combine bread crumbs and butter; sprinkle over casserole. Bake, uncovered, at 350° for 45 minutes or until browned and bubbly. **Yield:** 6-8 servings.

Hot Pork Salad Supreme

Dawn Eason, Carmichael, California

The original recipe for this dish called for chicken, but I decided to use "the other white meat". It's a nice dish to pass at a luncheon or shower.

2 cups diced cooked pork
2 cups cooked rice
1 can (10-3/4 ounces) condensed cream of chicken soup, undiluted
1 cup diced celery
1/2 cup mayonnaise
1 can (4 ounces) mushroom stems and pieces, drained
1 tablespoon lemon juice
1 tablespoon finely chopped onion
1/4 teaspoon salt
1 cup cornflake crumbs
1/2 cup sliced almonds
2 tablespoons butter *or* margarine, melted

Combine the first nine ingredients; mix well. Spoon into an ungreased 11-in. x 7-in. x 2-in. baking dish. Combine crumbs, almonds and butter; sprinkle on top. Bake, uncovered, at 350° for 30-40 minutes or until lightly browned. **Yield:** 4-6 servings.

Easy Ham Hash

Esther Johnson Danielson, Greenville, Texas

As the oldest of six children, I learned to cook early in life. Now my files are bulging with a variety of recipes. This delicious casserole remains an old standby.

1 pound fully cooked ham, finely ground
1 large onion, finely chopped
3 medium potatoes, peeled and cooked
2 tablespoons butter *or* margarine, melted
2 tablespoons grated Parmesan cheese
1 tablespoon prepared mustard
2 teaspoons Worcestershire sauce
1 teaspoon prepared horseradish
1/4 teaspoon pepper
1 cup (4 ounces) shredded cheddar cheese
1/2 cup shredded Monterey Jack cheese

In a bowl, combine ham and onion. Shred potatoes and add to ham mixture. Stir in butter, Parmesan cheese, mustard, Worcestershire sauce, horseradish and pepper. Spoon into a greased 11-in. x 7-in. x 2-in. baking dish, pressing down firmly. Combine cheddar and Monterey Jack; sprinkle over top. Bake, uncovered, at 350° for 35 minutes. **Yield:** 6 servings.

Ribs & Grilled Favorites

Hawaiian Ribs

Sheryl VanderWagen, Coopersville, Michigan

(PICTURED AT LEFT)

My husband doesn't usually request pork for dinner, but these ribs are the exception. He enjoys the slightly sweet sauce.

- 1 large onion, sliced
- 3 to 3-1/2 pounds country-style pork ribs
- 3 garlic cloves, minced
- 1/4 teaspoon salt
- 1/4 teaspoon pepper
- 1/2 cup water, *divided*
- 1 can (20 ounces) crushed pineapple in juice, undrained
- 1 bottle (12 ounces) chili sauce
- 1/2 cup packed brown sugar
- 1 teaspoon ground ginger
- 1/2 teaspoon ground mustard

Place onion in a 13-in. x 9-in. x 2-in. baking pan. Rub ribs with garlic and sprinkle with salt and pepper; place over onion. Pour 1/4 cup water around ribs. Cover and bake at 350° for 30 minutes. Meanwhile, combine pineapple, chili sauce, brown sugar, ginger, mustard and remaining water. Drain fat from pan; pour pineapple mixture over ribs. Bake, uncovered, 1-1/2 hours longer or until meat is tender. **Yield:** 6 servings.

Herbed Pork Chops

Dianne Esposite, New Middletown, Ohio

(PICTURED AT LEFT)

Herbs are a fast and flavorful way to dress up pork. Plus, they make the chops look so pretty on a platter. I prepare these year-round as a way to capture the taste of summer.

✓ This tasty dish uses less sugar, salt and fat. Recipe includes *Diabetic Exchanges.*

- 4 boneless butterfly pork chops (4 ounces *each*)
- 2 teaspoons lemon juice
- 2 tablespoons chopped fresh parsley
- 1/2 teaspoon dried rosemary, crushed
- 1/2 teaspoon dried thyme, crushed
- 1/4 teaspoon pepper

Brush pork chops with lemon juice. Combine seasonings; rub over chops. Grill, covered, over medium coals, turning occasionally, for 16-20 minutes or until juices run clear. **Yield:** 4 servings. **Diabetic Exchanges:** One serving equals 3 lean meat; also, 148 calories, 44 mg sodium, 59 mg cholesterol, 1 gm carbohydrate, 22 gm protein, 6 gm fat.

> **FINGER-LICKIN' GOOD.** *Pictured at left, top to bottom: Hawaiian Ribs, Herbed Pork Chops and Mandarin Pork (all recipes on this page).*

Mandarin Pork

Flo Weiss, Seaside, Oregon

(PICTURED AT LEFT)

I often serve this pork with fried rice and Chinese-style vegetables. It also makes a great appetizer by itself. Folks have fun dipping the nuggets into the two homemade sauces.

- 1 cup soy sauce
- 1/2 cup vegetable oil
- 3 tablespoons honey
- 1 tablespoon ground ginger
- 1 tablespoon ground mustard
- 1 garlic clove, minced
- 2 pork tenderloins (3/4 to 1 pound *each*)

SWEET-AND-SOUR SAUCE:
- 1/2 cup orange marmalade
- 2 tablespoons vinegar
- 1 tablespoon diced pimientos
- 1/8 teaspoon paprika

Dash salt

FIRE-HOT MUSTARD:
- 1/4 cup boiling water
- 1/4 cup ground mustard
- 1/2 teaspoon salt

Combine the first six ingredients in a large resealable plastic bag or shallow glass container; add pork and turn to coat. Seal bag or cover container; refrigerate overnight, turning meat several times. Meanwhile, combine sauce ingredients in a bowl; cover and chill. In another bowl, stir boiling water into mustard; add salt and stir until smooth. Cover and let stand at room temperature for 1 hour; chill. Drain meat and discard marinade. Grill, covered, over medium coals, turning occasionally, for 18-20 minutes or until a meat thermometer reads 160°-170°. Let stand for 5 minutes before slicing. Serve with sauce and mustard for dipping. **Yield:** 6-8 servings.

Honey Citrus Chops

Cheryl Stawicki, Joliet, Illinois

With just three marinade ingredients that you likely have on hand, this dish is one you'll prepare often.

- 2/3 cup lemon-lime soda
- 1/2 cup soy sauce
- 1/4 cup honey
- 6 boneless pork chops (3/4 inch thick)

In a large resealable plastic bag or glass container, combine soda, soy sauce and honey; mix well. Add pork and turn to coat. Seal bag or cover container; refrigerate overnight, turning occasionally. Drain and discard marinade. Grill, covered, over medium coals, turning several times, for 12-16 minutes or until juices run clear. **Yield:** 6 servings.

Grilled Stuffed Pork Chops

Dianne Gates, Cypress, Texas

Living in Texas, where summers get quite warm, I do a lot of cooking on the grill. I think you'll enjoy the one-of-a-kind combination of stuffing and sauce in these zesty chops.

- 1 cup medium picante sauce
- 2 tablespoons honey
- 1 teaspoon Worcestershire sauce
- 4 pork chops (1 inch thick)
- 1/2 pound bulk hot pork sausage
- 1/2 teaspoon garlic powder
- 1/4 teaspoon pepper
- 1/4 cup prepared zesty Italian salad dressing

Combine picante sauce, honey and Worcestershire sauce; stir until honey is dissolved. Divide the sauce into two small bowls; set aside. Cut a deep slit in each chop, forming a pocket. Stuff with sausage; secure with toothpicks. Sprinkle chops with garlic powder and pepper. Brush each side with Italian dressing. Grill, covered, over medium coals for 5 minutes on each side. Grill 10-15 minutes longer or until meat juices run clear, basting twice with sauce from one bowl. Remove toothpicks. Serve with sauce from the second bowl. **Yield:** 4 servings.

Pork Ribs and Chilies

Jayne Yount, Aurora, Colorado

This recipe comes from my mother-in-law, but my husband—who has a knack for spicy creations—perfected the flavor. When we invite friends for dinner, they ask if this is on the menu!

- 2-1/2 to 3 pounds boneless country-style pork ribs
- 2 cans (14-1/2 ounces *each*) diced tomatoes, undrained
- 2 cans (14-1/2 ounces *each*) chicken broth
- 1 jar (16 ounces) salsa
- 1 can (4 ounces) chopped green chilies
- 2 to 3 garlic cloves, minced
- 2 teaspoons ground cumin
- 1 teaspoon crushed red pepper flakes
- 1/2 teaspoon ground coriander, optional
- 1/4 teaspoon salt
- 1/8 teaspoon pepper
- 2 tablespoons cornstarch
- 1/4 cup cold water
- Hot cooked rice
- Shredded cheddar *or* Monterey Jack cheese, optional
- Sour cream and guacamole, optional

Place ribs in a deep roasting pan. Cover and bake at 450° for 30 minutes; drain. Reduce temperature to 350° and bake, uncovered, 45 minutes longer; drain. Allow to cool; cut meat into 1-in. cubes and return to pan. Combine tomatoes, broth, salsa, chilies and seasonings; pour over ribs. Cover and bake for 2 hours. Combine cornstarch in water until smooth; stir into rib mixture. Bake, uncovered, 15 minutes longer. Serve over rice. Top with cheese, sour cream and guacamole if desired. **Yield:** 8 servings.

Lemon Pork Steaks

Sue Reber, Rudolph, Wisconsin

This is an unusual recipe that you'll find irresistible. The lemonade acts as a tenderizer, so the pork steaks stay nice and juicy.

- 1 can (12 ounces) frozen lemonade concentrate, thawed
- 2/3 cup soy sauce
- 1 teaspoon seasoned salt
- 1 teaspoon celery salt
- 2 garlic cloves, minced
- 6 pork steaks (1/2 inch thick)

In a large resealable plastic bag or shallow glass container, combine the first five ingredients; mix well. Reserve 1/2 cup for basting and refrigerate. Add pork to remaining marinade and turn to coat. Seal bag or cover container; refrigerate overnight, turning meat several times. Drain and discard marinade. Grill, covered, over medium coals for 5 minutes. Turn; baste with reserved marinade. Cook 15-20 minutes longer, basting occasionally, or until juices run clear. **Yield:** 6 servings.

Cordon Bleu Pork Chops

Marcia Obenhaus, Princeton, Illinois

This recipe is a variation of one I found in a church cookbook. I prepare these cheesy chops year-round...on vacation, at tailgate parties or at home.

- 4 pork chops (1 inch thick)
- 1/2 cup ketchup
- 1/2 cup water
- 1/4 cup vinegar
- 2 tablespoons Worcestershire sauce
- 2 tablespoons brown sugar
- 2 tablespoons dried minced onion
- 1 tablespoon soy sauce
- 1 tablespoon lemon juice
- 1 teaspoon garlic powder
- 1 teaspoon ground mustard
- 4 thin slices fully cooked ham
- 4 thin slices mozzarella cheese

Cut a pocket in each chop. Combine the next 10 ingredients. Reserve 1/2 cup for basting and refrigerate. Pour remaining marinade into a large resealable plastic bag or shallow glass container. Add pork and turn to coat. Seal bag or cover container; refrigerate overnight, turning meat occasionally. Place a slice of cheese on each slice of ham; roll up jelly-roll style. Drain pork and discard marinade. Insert a ham/cheese roll in each pocket; fasten with toothpicks. Grill, covered, over medium coals, turning and basting occasionally with reserved marinade, for 25-35 minutes or until juices run clear. Remove toothpicks. **Yield:** 4 servings.

Tropical Pork Kabobs

Lisa Eddins, Durham, North Carolina

My dad created the sauce in this recipe years ago, and I began using it on these kabobs. With three children, I grill often because it's a no-fuss way to put good food on the table.

1-1/2 pounds boneless pork, cut into 3/4-inch cubes
   1 medium sweet yellow pepper, cut into 1-inch pieces
   1 medium sweet red pepper, cut into 1-inch pieces
   1 medium zucchini, cut into 1-inch slices
  12 large fresh mushrooms
   1 can (20 ounces) pineapple chunks in juice, undrained
   1 cup molasses
 2/3 cup soy sauce

Place pork, peppers, zucchini and mushrooms in a large resealable plastic bag or shallow glass container. Drain the pineapple, reserving 1/2 cup juice. Add pineapple chunks to pork mixture. Combine molasses, soy sauce and pineapple juice; mix well. Reserve 1/2 cup for basting and refrigerate. Pour remaining sauce over meat and vegetables. Seal bag or cover container; refrigerate several hours. Drain and discard marinade. On 12 metal or soaked bamboo skewers, alternate pork, vegetables and pineapple. Grill, uncovered, over medium coals, turning and basting with reserved marinade, for 12-15 minutes or until the pork juices run clear. **Yield:** 6 servings (12 kabobs).

Hot 'n' Spicy Spareribs

Myra Innes, Auburn, Kansas

I always keep this dry rub in a shaker on my shelf so I have it ready to use in an instant. It's a deliciously different way to prepare barbecued ribs.

   1 tablespoon brown sugar
   1 tablespoon pepper
   1 tablespoon paprika
1-1/2 teaspoons chili powder
 3/4 teaspoon crushed red pepper flakes
 3/4 teaspoon salt
 1/2 teaspoon garlic powder
   3 pounds pork spareribs
   3 sheets (40 inches x 18 inches) heavy-duty foil

Combine the first seven ingredients; mix well. Rub all of it onto both sides of ribs. Stack the three sheets of foil and place ribs in the center. Bring opposite long edges of foil together; fold down several times. Fold the short edges toward the food and crimp tightly to prevent leaks. Refrigerate overnight. Remove from refrigerator 30 minutes before grilling. Grill, covered, over indirect heat and medium-low coals with meat side down, for 45 minutes. Turn and cook 45 minutes longer or until meat is fork-tender. Remove ribs from foil and

place on grill rack. Grill, uncovered, for 10-15 minutes or until crispy, turning once. **Yield:** 4 servings.

Quick & Easy

Carry-Along Hot Dogs

Lorraine Priebe, Noonan, North Dakota

These versatile sandwiches can be made over the grill or in the oven, so they're great anytime of year. We especially like them when camping.

1/3 cup ketchup
  2 tablespoons sweet pickle relish
  1 tablespoon finely chopped onion
  1 teaspoon prepared mustard
  8 hot dog buns, split
  8 slices American cheese
  8 hot dogs

In a small bowl, combine the first four ingredients. Place a slice of cheese on the bottom half of each bun. Slice hot dogs in half lengthwise; place two halves on each bun. Spoon 1 tablespoon of sauce over each hot dog. Replace top of bun and wrap each sandwich in foil. Grill, uncovered, over medium coals, turning often, for 10-15 minutes; or place on a baking sheet and bake at 350° for 10 minutes. **Yield:** 8 servings.

BARBECUE BASICS. A traditional charcoal fire takes about 30-40 minutes to get hot enough for cooking, so add that time to your meal prepartion plan. The coals are ready when covered with a fine gray ash.

Paradise Pork Chops

Nancy Johnson, Goshen, Indiana

I'm the only one in the family who really loves pork. But one day when these chops were on the grill, the wonderful aroma drew everyone to the dinner table!

1/2 cup soy sauce
  1 teaspoon *each* dried marjoram, thyme, sage, oregano, tarragon, basil and rosemary, crushed
1/4 teaspoon garlic powder
  4 boneless pork sirloin chops (1 inch thick)

Combine soy sauce and seasonings; reserve half for basting and refrigerate. Pour remaining marinade into a large resealable plastic bag or shallow glass container. With a fork, pierce both sides of the pork several times; place in the marinade and press marinade into both sides of meat. Seal bag or cover container; refrigerate overnight. Drain and discard marinade. Grill, uncovered, over medium coals for 3 minutes. Turn and baste with reserved marinade. Continue turning and basting 7-10 minutes longer or until juices run clear. **Yield:** 4 servings.

Mom's Best Ribs

Kathryn Prust, Marshfield, Wisconsin
(PICTURED AT RIGHT AND ON THE BACK COVER)

My mom shared this recipe with me several years ago. Family and friends agree these are the best ribs they've ever tasted!

    4 pounds baby back pork ribs
  3/4 cup chicken broth
  1/2 cup packed brown sugar
  1/4 cup spicy brown mustard
  1/4 cup Dijon mustard
    3 tablespoons steak sauce
    3 tablespoons soy sauce
  3/4 teaspoon hot pepper sauce
  1/4 teaspoon ground cloves

Cut ribs into serving-size pieces. Place ribs, meat side up, in a roasting pan. Bake, uncovered, at 325° for 2 hours; drain. Combine remaining ingredients; pour over ribs. Reduce temperature to 300°; bake, uncovered, basting occasionally, 1 to 1-1/4 hours longer or until ribs are tender and a small amount of sauce remains in the bottom of the pan. **Yield:** 6-8 servings.

Grilled Pork Chops with Maple Butter

Anita Alford, Madisonville, Kentucky
(PICTURED AT RIGHT AND ON THE BACK COVER)

This recipe takes some time to prepare. But after one taste, you'll agree it's worth the extra effort. These chops get rave reviews.

MAPLE BUTTER:
    1 teaspoon minced green onion
    8 tablespoons butter (no substitutes), *divided*
  1/4 cup apple juice
  1/2 cup whipping cream
  1/2 cup maple syrup
  1/2 teaspoon salt
  1/2 teaspoon pepper
GLAZED APPLES AND ONIONS:
    2 large cooking apples, peeled, cored and sliced
  1/2 cup sliced onion
    2 tablespoons butter *or* margarine
    2 tablespoons brown sugar
CHOPS:
    8 pork chops (1/2 inch thick)
  1/2 teaspoon pepper
    2 teaspoons vegetable oil
  1/4 cup coarsely chopped pecans, toasted

In a saucepan, saute green onion in 1 tablespoon butter. Add apple juice; cook until reduced by half. Add cream, syrup, salt and pepper; again, cook until reduced by half and mixture is caramel-like. Add remaining butter, 1 tablespoon at a time, stirring until melted. In a skillet, cook apples, onion, butter and brown sugar over medium heat for 3 minutes or until onion is crisp-tender and apples are softened; set aside.

Sprinkle chops with pepper. Brush each side with oil. Grill, uncovered, over medium coals for 7 minutes per side or until juices run clear. Rewarm maple butter and glazed apples. Divide apples between four plates; top each with two chops and a fourth of the maple butter. Sprinkle with pecans. **Yield:** 4 servings.

Dijon Pork Chops

Vivian Kelby, Crown Point, Indiana
(PICTURED AT RIGHT AND ON THE BACK COVER)

I have four children, 16 grandchildren and four great-grand-children...so it's a good thing I like to cook! My family has enjoyed these simply delicious chops for years.

✓ **This tasty dish uses less sugar, salt and fat. Recipe includes** *Diabetic Exchanges.*

  1/4 cup red wine vinegar
    2 tablespoons vegetable oil
    2 tablespoons Dijon mustard
    2 teaspoons chopped fresh parsley
  1/2 teaspoon chopped fresh chives
  1/4 teaspoon dried tarragon
    4 butterfly pork chops (4 ounces *each*), trimmed
Additional chives, optional

In a small bowl, combine the first six ingredients; mix well and set aside. Grill chops, uncovered, over medium coals for 4 minutes per side for 1/2-in. chops (6 minutes per side for 1-in. chops). Brush with mustard mixture and grill 2 minutes more. Turn; baste and grill 2 minutes longer or until juices run clear. Sprinkle with chives if desired. **Yield:** 4 servings. **Diabetic Exchanges:** One serving equals 3 lean meat, 1 fat; also, 236 calories, 236 mg sodium, 59 mg cholesterol, 1 gm carbohydrate, 22 gm protein, 13 gm fat.

Western Ribs

Eloise Neeley, Norton, Ohio

I reach for this recipe whenever I crave ribs. Everyday ingredients really perk up store-bought barbecue sauce.

    3 pounds pork spareribs
    1 cup barbecue sauce
  1/2 cup tomato juice
    2 tablespoons Italian salad dressing
    1 tablespoon dried parsley flakes
    1 small onion, diced

Place the ribs in an ungreased 13-in. x 9-in. x 2-in. baking pan. Cover with foil. Bake at 325° for 1-1/2 hours or until just tender; drain. Combine remaining ingredients; spoon over ribs. Bake, uncovered, 45 minutes longer, basting occasionally. Cut into serving-size pieces. **Yield:** 4 servings.

> **PLENTIFUL PLATES.** *Pictured at right, top to bottom: Mom's Best Ribs, Grilled Pork Chops with Maple Butter and Dijon Pork Chops (all recipes on this page).*

Peanut Butter Pork with Spicy Dipping Sauce

Dennis Gilroy, Stover, Missouri

I love to cook, and these skewers are one of my favorite things to prepare. They have a wonderfully different flavor and go great with rice.

- 1/4 cup creamy peanut butter
- 2 tablespoons soy sauce
- 2 tablespoons ground coriander
- 1 tablespoon lemon juice
- 1 tablespoon vegetable oil
- 2 teaspoons ground cumin
- 1/2 teaspoon chili powder
- 1 garlic clove, minced
- 1 pork tenderloin (1 pound), cut into 1-inch cubes

SPICY DIPPING SAUCE:
- 1/4 cup soy sauce
- 1/4 cup vinegar
- 2 tablespoons water
- 1 garlic clove, minced
- 1 tablespoon molasses
- 1/2 teaspoon crushed red pepper flakes

In a large resealable plastic bag, combine the first eight ingredients; mix well. Add pork; seal bag and turn meat several times. Refrigerate several hours or overnight. Meanwhile, combine all sauce ingredients; cover and chill at least 1 hour. Thread meat on skewers, leaving a small space between pieces. Grill, uncovered, over hot coals, turning often, for 10-15 minutes or until meat is no longer pink. Serve with sauce. **Yield:** 4 servings.

Plum-Barbecued Spareribs

Eva Doucet, Bathurst, New Brunswick

I worked in a restaurant for 18 years and still enjoy cooking meals for my husband. Our children and grandchildren love these finger-licking-good ribs in a unique plum sauce.

- 4 pounds spareribs *or* baby back pork ribs
- 1 tablespoon salt
- 1 can (16-1/2 ounces) purple plums in heavy syrup, undrained
- 1 tablespoon chopped onion
- 2 teaspoons soy sauce
- 1/4 teaspoon grated lemon peel
- 1/4 teaspoon ground cinnamon

Dash *each* ground cloves and nutmeg

Cut ribs into serving-size pieces; place in a Dutch oven or large kettle. Sprinkle with salt and cover with water. Bring to a boil. Reduce heat, cover and simmer for 20 minutes. Drain. Drain plums, reserving syrup. Remove and discard pits from plums. In a blender, combine plums, syrup, onion, soy sauce, lemon peel, cinnamon, cloves and nutmeg; process until smooth. Pour into a saucepan; bring to a boil.

Cook, stirring constantly, for 3 minutes. Remove from the heat. Place ribs, meat side up, in a 13-in. x 9-in. x 2-in. baking pan; spread 2/3 cup plum sauce over ribs. Cover and bake at 375° for 25 minutes. Uncover and bake 30 minutes longer or until ribs are tender, basting three times with remaining sauce. **Yield:** 6 servings.

Ribs with Caraway Kraut And Stuffing Balls

Patricia Johnson, Santa Paula , California

I live alone but like entertaining often and offering hearty meals to guests. Everyone compliments me on these ribs and their old-world flavor.

- 3 pounds boneless country-style pork ribs
- 1 can (14 ounces) sauerkraut, drained
- 1-1/2 cups tomato juice
- 1/2 cup chicken broth
- 1 medium apple, diced
- 1 tablespoon brown sugar
- 2 to 3 teaspoons caraway seed
- 1/8 teaspoon salt
- 1/8 teaspoon pepper

STUFFING BALLS:
- 1 package (8 ounces) herb-seasoned stuffing mix
- 1-1/3 cups hot water
- 1/2 cup butter *or* margarine, melted
- 2 eggs

In a large skillet, brown ribs; drain. Combine the sauerkraut, tomato juice, broth, apple, brown sugar, caraway, salt and pepper; pour over ribs. Cover and simmer 1-1/2 hours or until meat is very tender. For stuffing balls, combine stuffing mix, water and butter; mix lightly and let stand for 5 minutes. Stir in eggs; mix well. Shape into 2-in. balls; place over ribs and sauerkraut. Cover and simmer for 20 minutes. **Yield:** 6 servings.

Sesame Pork Kabobs

Mildred Sherrer, Bay City, Texas

My son and daughter-in-law discovered this recipe while living in Japan. Folks always comment on the wonderful marinade and crunchy sesame seeds.

✓ **This tasty dish uses less sugar, salt and fat. Recipe includes** *Diabetic Exchanges.*

- 3/4 cup finely chopped onion
- 1/2 cup soy sauce
- 1/4 cup sesame seeds, toasted
- 1/4 cup water
- 3 tablespoons sugar
- 4-1/2 teaspoons minced garlic
- 1-1/2 teaspoons ground ginger
- 1/8 teaspoon cayenne pepper
- 2 pork tenderloins (3/4 pound *each*), trimmed

In a large resealable plastic bag or shallow glass container, combine the first eight ingredients. Cut pork across the grain into 1/4-in.-thick medallions; add to marinade and turn to coat. Seal bag or cover container; refrigerate for at least 1 hour. Drain and discard marinade. Accordion-fold each medallion, threading about 10 pieces each onto long skewers. Grill, uncovered, over medium coals, turning often, for 9-12 minutes or until meat is no longer pink. **Yield:** 6 servings. **Diabetic Exchanges:** One serving (prepared with light soy sauce) equals 4 very lean meat; also, 156 calories, 385 mg sodium, 67 mg cholesterol, 3 gm carbohydrate, 25 gm protein, 4 gm fat.

Peppered Pork Chops
Bob Brandel, Brookfield, Wisconsin

These chops are easy to prepare, which makes them just right for dinner on busy weeknights. My wife and I have shared this recipe with family and friends and now we pass it on to you!

    3 tablespoons soy sauce
    2 teaspoons coarsely ground pepper
    1 to 1-1/2 teaspoons ground coriander
    1 teaspoon brown sugar
    2 garlic cloves, minced
    4 boneless pork chops (1-1/2 inches thick)

Combine the first five ingredients in a large resealable plastic bag or shallow glass container; add pork and turn to coat. Seal bag or cover container; refrigerate 1 to 1-1/2 hours. Drain and discard marinade. Grill, covered, over indirect heat for 20-30 minutes or until a meat thermometer reads 160°-170°. **Yield:** 4-6 servings.

Slow-Cooked Country Ribs in Gravy
Tammi Visser, Uxbridge, Massachusetts

This is a very easy recipe (just the kind I like!) that I got from my sister-in-law. I like to make it in winter as a way to capture the barbecues of summer.

    3 pounds country-style pork ribs
    1 cup water
1/2 cup ketchup
    1 medium onion, chopped
    2 tablespoons vinegar
    1 tablespoon sugar
    4 teaspoons Worcestershire sauce
    1 teaspoon salt
    1 teaspoon ground mustard
    1 beef bouillon cube
1/4 teaspoon paprika
1/4 teaspoon pepper

Place ribs in a slow cooker. Combine remaining ingredients and pour over ribs. Cover and cook on high for 1 hour; reduce heat to low and cook 3-4 hours longer. Remove ribs to serving platter and keep warm. Thicken cooking liquid for gravy. **Yield:** 6 servings.

Cilantro Pork Tenderloin
Elaine Comstock, Edmond, Oklahoma

I found this recipe in a magazine, then added extra cumin and mustard to satisfy my family's taste for spicy foods. I like to serve pork frequently.

1-1/2 cups chopped fresh cilantro
    1/2 cup packed brown sugar
    1/2 cup soy sauce
      3 tablespoons honey
      6 garlic cloves, minced
      2 teaspoons ground cumin
      2 teaspoons ground mustard
      1 pork tenderloin (1 to 1-1/4 pounds)

Combine the first seven ingredients in a large resealable plastic bag or shallow glass container; add pork and turn to coat. Seal bag or cover container; refrigerate overnight, turning meat occasionally. Drain and discard marinade. Grill, covered, over indirect heat, for 10-14 minutes or until a meat thermometer reads 160°-170°. Let stand for 5 minutes before slicing. **Yield:** 4-6 servings.

Jalapeno Ribs
Shirley Manthey, Omaha, Nebraska

These ribs are unique because of the spicy rub and the combination of sweet brown sugar and spicy jalapeno peppers in the sauce. I always make them for my husband's birthday.

      4 teaspoons light brown sugar
      2 teaspoons chili powder
      1 teaspoon paprika
      1 teaspoon salt
      1 teaspoon pepper
    1/8 teaspoon garlic powder
3-1/2 to 4 pounds pork spareribs
JALAPENO BARBECUE SAUCE:
      2 cans (8 ounces *each*) tomato sauce
    2/3 cup packed light brown sugar
    1/3 cup lemon juice
    1/4 cup Worcestershire sauce
      1 small onion, finely chopped
      2 jalapeno peppers, seeded and finely chopped
      2 beef bouillon cubes

Combine the first six ingredients; mix well. Rub all of the mixture onto both sides of ribs. Place ribs, meat side up, on a rack in a foil-lined roasting pan. Bake at 325° for 1-1/2 to 1-3/4 hours or until tender. Meanwhile, combine sauce ingredients in a saucepan; simmer, uncovered, for 30-40 minutes or until thickened. Transfer ribs to grill. Grill, uncovered, over medium coals, basting with sauce and turning several times, for 10-15 minutes. Reheat remaining sauce and serve with ribs. **Yield:** 4 servings. **Editor's Note:** Ribs may be baked and sauce may be prepared a day ahead and refrigerated. Then grill and baste for 15 minutes or until heated through and nicely glazed.

OUTDOOR EATING. *Clockwise from upper right: Honey-Lime Ham, Grilled Pork Tenderloin, Barbecued Baby Back Ribs, Maple-Glazed Kabobs and Marinated Pork Chops (all recipes on pages 106 and 107).*

Honey-Lime Ham

Dorothy Layman, Waynesboro, Pennsylvania
(PICTURED ON PAGE 105)

When I first made this recipe for my husband and our boys, there weren't any leftovers. I immediately knew it was a winner!

1/2 cup butter *or* margarine
1/4 cup honey
1/4 cup lime juice
2 teaspoons seasoned salt
1 fully cooked ham center slice (1-1/2 pounds)

In a small saucepan, heat the first four ingredients until butter is melted. Place ham in a resealable plastic bag or shallow baking dish; pour honey mixture over ham. Seal bag or cover container; refrigerate overnight. Bring to room temperature. Drain and discard marinade. Grill, uncovered, over hot coals, turning several times, for 5-10 minutes or until heated through. **Yield:** 4-6 servings.

Grilled Pork Tenderloin

Steve Ehrhart, Villa Park, Illinois
(PICTURED ON PAGE 105)

Folks can find me grilling...no matter what the weather. This moist, flavorful pork is everyone's favorite. My wife especially likes the fact that she doesn't have to do the cooking!

1 teaspoon salt
1 teaspoon seasoned salt
1 teaspoon poultry seasoning
1 teaspoon onion powder
1 teaspoon garlic powder
1 teaspoon chili powder
1/4 teaspoon cayenne pepper
2 pork tenderloins (3/4 to 1 pound *each*)

Combine the first seven ingredients; sprinkle 4 to 5 teaspoons on all sides of pork (reserve remaining seasoning blend for future use). Grill, covered, over indirect heat for 20-30 minutes or until a meat thermometer reads 160°-170°. Let stand for 5 minutes before slicing. **Yield:** 6-8 servings. **Editor's Note:** Leftover sliced tenderloin, simmered in barbecue sauce and seasoned to taste with reserved seasoning blend, makes great sandwiches.

Barbecued Baby Back Ribs

Jamie Barnett, Syracuse, Missouri
(PICTURED ON PAGE 105)

This recipe came about by accident when I was making ribs for company and discovered I didn't have enough sauce. I combined the ingredients on hand and came up with this special sauce.

4 pounds baby back pork ribs
1/2 teaspoon salt
1/4 teaspoon pepper

1-1/2 teaspoons liquid smoke, *divided*, optional
3/4 cup barbecue sauce
1/3 cup honey-Dijon barbecue sauce
1/3 cup ketchup
1/4 cup honey

Cut ribs into serving size pieces; place in a Dutch oven and cover with water. Add salt, pepper and 1 teaspoon liquid smoke if desired; bring to a boil. Reduce heat; cover and simmer for 1-1/4 hours or until ribs are just tender. Do not overcook. Meanwhile, combine barbecue sauces, ketchup, honey and remaining liquid smoke if desired. Drain ribs and transfer to grill. Grill, uncovered, over medium coals, basting both sides several times with sauce, for 8-10 minutes or until ribs are tender and well-glazed. **Yield:** 6 servings.

Marinated Pork Chops

Jean Neitzel, Beloit, Wisconsin
(PICTURED ON PAGE 104)

I make these tasty chops all the time and my family never tires of them. The secret to these tender chops is overnight marinating.

3/4 cup vegetable oil
1/3 cup soy sauce
1/4 cup vinegar
2 tablespoons Worcestershire sauce
1 tablespoon lemon juice
1 tablespoon prepared mustard
1 teaspoon salt
1 teaspoon pepper
1 teaspoon dried parsley flakes
1 garlic clove, minced
6 pork chops (1 inch thick)

Combine the first 10 ingredients in a large resealable plastic bag or shallow glass container; add pork and turn to coat. Seal bag or cover container; refrigerate overnight. Drain and discard marinade. Grill, covered, over medium coals, turning occasionally, for 20-25 minutes or until juices run clear. **Yield:** 6 servings.

Maple-Glazed Kabobs

Sue Gronholz, Columbus, Wisconsin
(PICTURED ON PAGE 104)

I recently received this recipe from a friend who makes his own maple syrup. My family often requests these slightly sweet kabobs for our summer Sunday dinner cookout.

8 small new potatoes *or* 1 large potato, cut into 8 chunks
3 carrots, cut into 8 pieces (2 inches each)
1 pork tenderloin (1 pound)
1 large green *or* sweet red pepper
8 large mushrooms
1/4 cup butter *or* margarine
1/4 cup maple syrup
1-1/2 teaspoons grated orange peel

Cook potatoes and carrots in boiling water for 7-10 minutes or until barely tender. Cut pork into 12 equal pieces and pepper into eight chunks. Thread meat and vegetables alternately onto four long skewers; set aside. Combine butter, syrup and orange peel in a small saucepan; cook and stir over low heat until butter is melted. Grill kabobs, uncovered, over medium heat for 5 minutes; turn and brush with butter mixture. Continue cooking, turning and basting frequently, for 14-17 minutes or until meat juices run clear. **Yield:** 4 servings.

Country-Style Pork Ribs

Heidi Mellon, Waukesha, Wisconsin

Neither my husband nor myself are big pork eaters, but we absolutely love these ribs. My mom has been preparing them for as long as I can remember.

- 3/4 cup soy sauce
- 1/2 cup sugar
- 1/2 cup water
- 1 garlic clove, minced
- 4 pounds country-style pork ribs

Combine the first four ingredients; stir to dissolve sugar. Pour into a large resealable plastic bag or shallow glass container; add ribs and turn to coat. Seal bag or cover container; refrigerate overnight, turning occasionally. Drain and discard marinade. Grill, covered, over medium coals, turning occasionally, for 30-40 minutes or until juices run clear. **Yield:** 6-8 servings.

Sweet Mustard Chops

DeAnn Alleva, Columbus, Ohio

These pork chops are perfect for company because they marinate overnight in a special barbecue sauce. Then just pop them on the grill when you're ready to eat. They're fast and flavorful.

- 1/2 cup mayonnaise
- 1/4 cup packed brown sugar
- 1/4 cup prepared mustard
- 2 teaspoons seasoned salt
- 1/3 cup red wine vinegar
- 4 pork chops (1 inch thick)

Combine mayonnaise, brown sugar, mustard and seasoned salt; mix well. Blend in vinegar. Pour into a large resealable plastic bag or shallow glass container; add pork. Seal bag or cover container; refrigerate overnight. Drain and discard marinade. Grill, covered, over medium coals, turning occasionally, for 20-25 minutes or until juices run clear. **Yield:** 4 servings.

Slow Cooker Ribs

Alpha Wilson, Roswell, New Mexico

These simple-to-prepare ribs call for everyday ingredients. So I never complain when my family asks me to make them. Everyone enjoys their down-home goodness.

- 3 pounds pork spareribs
- 1/2 teaspoon salt
- 1/4 teaspoon pepper
- 1-3/4 cups sliced onion
- 1 bottle (18 ounces) barbecue sauce

Place ribs, meat side up, on a broiling pan. Sprinkle with salt and pepper. Broil 6 in. from the heat for 15-20 minutes or until browned. Cool; cut into serving-size pieces. Place onion in a slow cooker; top with ribs. Pour barbecue sauce over all. Cover and cook on high for 1 hour; reduce heat to low and cook 3-4 hours or until ribs are tender. **Yield:** 4 servings.

Teriyaki Tangerine Ribs

Diane Hixon, Niceville, Florida

We usually prepare ribs on the grill. But this recipe is so good, you won't miss that smoky flavor if you bake these in the oven instead. Tangerines are a favorite of mine, but oranges work just as well.

- 4 pounds country-style pork ribs
- 2/3 cup fresh tangerine *or* orange juice
- 1/3 cup light corn syrup
- 2 tablespoons soy sauce
- 1 teaspoon grated tangerine *or* orange peel
- 1/2 teaspoon ground ginger
- 1 garlic clove, minced

Place ribs, meat side down, on a rack in a foil-lined shallow roasting pan. Bake at 425° for 30 minutes. Drain; turn ribs. Reduce temperature to 350° and bake 30 minutes longer. Meanwhile, combine remaining ingredients in a saucepan; bring to a boil. Remove from the heat and set aside. Remove ribs from rack; discard drippings and foil. Return ribs to pan; pour tangerine mixture over ribs. Bake, uncovered, turning ribs often, for 30-40 minutes or until tender. **Yield:** 8 servings.

Pork Souvlakia

Linda Brossoit, Huntingdon, Quebec

I'm a cook in a senior citizens' home where I don't get much of an opportunity to experiment with cooking. So whenever I get a chance, I head to my own kitchen and create new dishes like this.

- 1/4 cup olive *or* vegetable oil
- 2 tablespoons lemon juice
- 1 garlic clove, minced
- 1 teaspoon dried oregano
- 1/2 teaspoon chicken bouillon granules
- 1/4 teaspoon pepper
- 1/8 teaspoon cayenne pepper
- 1 pound boneless pork, cut into 1-1/4-inch cubes

In a large resealable plastic bag or shallow glass container, combine the first seven ingredients; add pork. Seal bag or cover container; refrigerate overnight. Drain and discard marinade. Thread meat on skewers, leaving a small space between pieces. Grill, covered, over medium coals for 15-20 minutes or until meat is no longer pink. **Yield:** 4 servings.

Spareribs Cantonese

Gail Millman, Dollard des Ormeaux, Quebec

My aunt gave me this recipe more than 20 years ago. The thing we like most about it is that there isn't an overabundance of sauce, so the fabulous flavor of pork can shine through.

- **4 pounds pork spareribs**
- **1 cup orange marmalade**
- **3/4 cup water**
- **1/2 cup soy sauce**
- **1/2 teaspoon garlic powder**
- **1/2 teaspoon ground ginger** *or* **2 teaspoons grated fresh gingerroot**
- **1/4 teaspoon salt, optional**
- **Dash pepper**
- **Lemon wedges, optional**

Cut the ribs into serving-size pieces; place with meat side down in a shallow roasting pan. Cover with foil; bake at 450° for 45 minutes. Drain; turn ribs. Combine marmalade, water, soy sauce and seasonings; spoon over ribs. Bake, uncovered, 1 hour longer or until tender, basting occasionally with sauce. Garnish with lemon wedges if desired. **Yield:** 4-6 servings.

Dazzling Marinated Pork Chops

Mrs. Mark Graber, Archbold, Ohio

My family enjoys these pork chops year-round, which is fine with me since they're so simple to prepare. Whenever I present these to company, they're met with rave reviews.

- **1 cup water**
- **1/2 cup soy sauce**
- **1 tablespoon frozen orange juice concentrate**
- **1 tablespoon honey**
- **6 boneless pork chops (3/4 inch thick)**

Combine the first four ingredients in a large resealable plastic bag or shallow glass container; add pork and turn to coat. Seal bag or cover container; refrigerate at least 6 hours, turning occasionally. Drain and discard marinade. Grill, uncovered, over hot coals, or broil 6 in. from the heat, for 10-14 minutes or until juices run clear. **Yield:** 6 servings.

Oven-Baked Ribs

Eric Spencer, Frankfort, Indiana

This recipe was developed by a college buddy of mine. Now I make it often for family and friends. The sweet-hot sauce has a unique subtle orange flavor.

- **4 pounds pork spareribs**
- **2 medium oranges**

- **1 bottle (28 ounces) barbecue sauce**
- **1 cup coarsely chopped onion**
- **2/3 to 1 cup packed brown sugar**
- **1 tablespoon Worcestershire sauce**
- **1-1/2 teaspoons chili powder**
- **1 to 1-1/2 teaspoons hot pepper sauce**
- **1/4 to 1/2 teaspoon cayenne pepper**

Cut ribs into serving-size pieces; place in a large kettle or Dutch oven. Cover with water; bring to a boil. Reduce heat and simmer for 10 minutes; drain. Place ribs in an ungreased 13-in. x 9-in. x 2-in. baking dish. Squeeze oranges, reserving 1/2 cup juice and the peel. Combine juice, barbecue sauce, onion, brown sugar, Worcestershire sauce, chili powder, hot pepper sauce and cayenne; mix well. Cut orange peel into large chunks and add to sauce; pour sauce over ribs. Cover and bake at 350° for 1-1/2 hours. Uncover and bake 30-45 minutes longer or until ribs are tender and sauce is thickened, turning ribs several times to coat with sauce. Remove orange peel. **Yield:** 4-6 servings.

Busy-Day Barbecued Ribs

Sherry Smalley, South Milwaukee, Wisconsin

I don't have a lot of time on weekends to spend in the kitchen. That's when this recipe comes in handy. I put all the ingredients in the slow cooker, and before I know it, dinner is ready!

- **3-1/2 to 4 pounds country-style pork ribs**
- **1 can (10-3/4 ounces) condensed tomato soup, undiluted**
- **1/2 cup packed brown sugar**
- **1/3 cup cider vinegar**
- **1 tablespoon soy sauce**
- **1 teaspoon celery seed**
- **1 teaspoon chili powder**

Place ribs in a slow cooker. Combine remaining ingredients; pour over ribs. Cover and cook on high for 1 hour. Reduce heat to low and cook 4-5 hours longer. Thicken sauce for gravy if desired. **Yield:** 6-8 servings.

Herb-Marinated Pork Loin

Jean Ham Evenson, Osage, Iowa

I use pork quite often in many recipes, but this pork loin is a real favorite. The mildly seasoned marinade appeals to everyone who's ever sampled this tender meat.

- **1/2 cup tomato juice**
- **1/2 cup vegetable oil**
- **1/2 cup finely chopped onion**
- **1/4 cup lemon juice**
- **1/4 cup chopped fresh parsley**
- **1 garlic clove, minced**
- **1 teaspoon salt**
- **1 teaspoon dried marjoram**
- **1 teaspoon dried thyme**

1/2 teaspoon pepper
1 boneless pork loin roast (3 pounds)

In a large resealable plastic bag or shallow glass container, combine the first 10 ingredients; add pork and turn to coat. Seal bag or cover container; refrigerate overnight, turning meat occasionally. Drain and discard marinade. Grill, covered, over indirect heat, turning occasionally, for 1-1/4 to 1-3/4 hours or until a meat thermometer reads 160°-170°. Let stand for 5 minutes before slicing. **Yield:** 10-12 servings.

Chinese Ribs

Rosemarie Balowas, New Port Richey, Florida

Folks who sample these are surprised to hear honey isn't one of the ingredients! These ribs are crisp on the outside and tender inside. I've also used the marinade for chicken wings.

1-1/2 pounds pork spareribs
3/4 cup sugar
1/2 cup vinegar
1/3 cup soy sauce
3 tablespoons apple juice
Cooking oil for deep-fat frying

Cut the ribs between the bones into single pieces; place in an 8-in. square baking dish. Bring the sugar, vinegar, soy sauce and apple juice to a boil; pour over the ribs. Cover and refrigerate at least 1 hour. Heat at least 1 in. of oil in an electric skillet or deep-fat fryer to 350°. Drain and pat ribs dry with paper towel. Fry, turning frequently, for 7-8 minutes or until meat is tender and no longer pink when cut with a knife and shrinks slightly from the bone. Drain on paper towels. **Yield:** 2 servings.

Cranberry-Glazed Spareribs

H.G. Frazer, Maple Ridge, British Columbia

My mother would agree that coming up with foods that a husband and 13 children all liked could be a real challenge. Each and every one of us thought these ribs were delicious. Now my own family loves them, too!

3 pounds pork spareribs
1/4 cup packed brown sugar
3 tablespoons all-purpose flour
1/2 teaspoon salt
1/4 teaspoon ground mustard
1/4 teaspoon ground cloves
1-3/4 cups cranberry juice
1 cup water
2 tablespoons vinegar
1 tablespoon lemon juice

Place ribs on a rack in a foil-lined shallow roasting pan. Broil 6 in. from the heat for 12-20 minutes per side or until browned. Remove ribs from rack; drain drippings. Return ribs to pan. Combine brown sugar, flour, salt, mustard and cloves in a saucepan; gradually add cranberry juice, stirring until smooth. Add water, vinegar and lemon juice. Bring to a boil; boil and stir for 2 minutes. Pour over ribs. Cover and bake at 350° for 45 minutes. Uncover and bake 20-30 minutes longer or until ribs are tender. **Yield:** 4 servings.

Applesauce-Sauerkraut Spareribs

LaDonna Lieberth, Port Washington, Ohio

All seasons are beautiful here, but I especially like fall so I can serve more hearty fare like this. Served with mashed potatoes and pumpkin pie, these ribs soothe the soul.

3 to 3-1/2 pounds country-style pork ribs
1 teaspoon oil
1 can (32 ounces) sauerkraut
2 cups applesauce
2 cups thinly sliced onion
3/4 cup chicken broth
3/4 cup apple juice

In a large skillet over medium-high heat, brown ribs in oil. Arrange ribs in an ungreased 13-in. x 9-in. x 2-in. baking dish. Rinse and squeeze sauerkraut; layer sauerkraut, applesauce and onion over ribs. Combine broth and apple juice; pour over all. Cover and bake at 350° for 1-3/4 hours; uncover and bake 15 minutes longer or until onion just begins to brown. **Yield:** 6 servings.

Honey-and-Herb Grilled Pork Roast

Cathy Irwin, Ontario, New York

I learned to cook from my grandmother and fondly recall canning fruits and vegetables with her each summer. Her memory lives on whenever I make satisfying meals such as this.

3/4 cup ginger ale
1/3 cup Dijon mustard
1/3 cup honey
2 tablespoons vegetable oil
2 tablespoons chopped onion
3/4 teaspoon dried rosemary, crushed
1/2 teaspoon salt
1/4 teaspoon garlic powder
1/8 teaspoon pepper
1 boneless pork loin roast (2-1/2 to 3 pounds)

In a large resealable plastic bag or shallow glass container, combine the first nine ingredients; add pork and turn to coat. Seal bag or cover container; refrigerate overnight, turning meat occasionally. Drain and discard marinade. Place roast in a disposable foil pan. Grill, covered, over indirect heat for 1-1/2 hours or until a meat thermometer reads 160°-170°. Let stand for 10 minutes before slicing. **Yield:** 8-10 servings.

Index

APPETIZERS & SNACKS
Bacon-Wrapped Water Chestnuts, 8
Braunschweiger Vegetable Dip, 9
Cajun Pork Sandwiches, 7
Deviled Ham and Egg Appetizer, 9
Ham 'n' Cheese Puffs, 9
Ham Balls, 7
Party Pitas, 9
Sausage Dip, 8
Sausage-Stuffed Mushrooms, 9
Smokehouse Quesadillas, 8
Super Ham Spread, 7
Tasty Pork Nuggets, 8

APPLE
Apple Pork Pie, 86
Apple Scrapple, 60
Apple-Topped Ham Steak, 46
Applesauce-Sauerkraut Spareribs, 109
Baked Pork Chops and Apples, 78
Curried Pork Chops, 56
Grilled Pork Chops with Maple Butter, 100
Nutty Ham and Apple Sandwiches, 21
Old-Fashioned Pork Roast, 77
Pork Roast with Apple-Mushroom Sauce, 67
Sausage 'n' Apple Baked Squash, 17
Sausage Apple Roll, 82
Sausage Apple Squares, 94
Sausage-Stuffed Baked Apples, 18

BACON (also see Canadian Bacon)
Bacon and Macaroni, 61
Bacon Breakfast Sandwiches, 29
Bacon Broccoli Salad, 12
Bacon, Cabbage and Noodles, 17
Bacon-Wrapped Water Chestnuts, 8
Barbecued Beans, 65
BLT Tortillas, 21
Creamy Pork Tenderloin, 79
Fantastic Potatoes, 17
Ham and Chicken Gumbo, 34
Individual Brunch Casseroles, 90
Italian Cabbage and Rice, 60
Liverwurst Deluxe, 26
Mom's Chinese Dish, 46
Peasant Skillet, 54
Potato Bacon Chowder, 41
Quick Wild Rice Soup, 35
Sweet-and-Sour Baked Beans, 17
Tomato-Bacon Rarebit, 31

BEANS
Barbecued Beans, 65
Chalupa, 63
Company's Coming Soup, 38
Country Cassoulet, 64
Lima Bean Casserole, 16
Lima Bean Sunshine Stew, 35
Navy Bean Soup, 38
Pork Chili, 63
Sausage Bean Delight, 11
Sweet 'n' Snappy Chili, 34
Sweet-and-Sour Baked Beans, 17

BROCCOLI
Bacon Broccoli Salad, 12
Ham and Broccoli Divan, 45
Ham and Broccoli Supper, 94
Ham Rolls Continental, 86
Macaroni and Cheese Deluxe, 94
Mushroom-Broccoli Stuffed Crown Roast, 76
Sausage-Broccoli Puff Pancake, 88

CABBAGE & SAUERKRAUT
Applesauce-Sauerkraut Spareribs, 109
Bacon, Cabbage and Noodles, 17
Bologna and Sauerkraut Stew, 41
Brat Hoagies with Coleslaw, 30
Hearty Ham and Cabbage Chowder, 35
Italian Cabbage and Rice, 60
Italian Sausage and Sauerkraut, 78
Old-Fashioned Kraut Dinner, 57
Pork and Cabbage Pockets, 23
Pork and Cabbage Rolls, 72
Pork and Sauerkraut with Potatoes, 64
Ribs with Caraway Kraut and Stuffing
    Balls, 102
Rosemary's Ham Reubens, 24
Sauerbraten Stew, 33
Sausage Cabbage Bake, 91
Sesame Pork with Cabbage, 19

CANADIAN BACON
Canadian Bacon and Cheese Biscuits, 22
Canadian Cheese Soup, 33
Spicy Southern-Style Tomato Cups, 13

CHEESE
Canadian Bacon and Cheese Biscuits, 22
Canadian Cheese Soup, 33
Cheesy Bratwurst, 45
Cheesy Zucchini Medley, 87
Cordon Bleu Pork Chops, 98
Curry Cheddar Grill, 30
Ham 'n' Cheese Melts, 24
Ham 'n' Cheese Puffs, 9
Ham 'n' Cheese Strata, 91
Ham 'n' Swiss Muffins, 23
Ham 'n' Swiss Ring, 67
Italian Ham and Cheese Salad, 17
Macaroni and Cheese Deluxe, 94
Pork Chops Parmesan, 53
Rosemary's Ham Reubens, 24

CHILI
Chalupa, 63
Pork Chili, 63
Sweet 'n' Snappy Chili, 34

CHOWDER
Confetti Chowder, 43
Hearty Ham and Cabbage Chowder, 35
Potato Bacon Chowder, 41
Surprise Clam Chowder, 39
Wild Rice and Ham Chowder, 36

CORN
Corn and Ham Stew, 35
Pork and Corn Barbecue, 31
Sausage and Creamed Corn Casserole, 19
Sausage Corn Bake, 86

CORN BREAD & CORNMEAL
Breaded Pork Chops, 80
Creamed Ham 'n' Cornmeal Cakes, 59
Inside-Out Pork Chops, 61
Meaty Corn-Bread Squares, 93
Pork Stew with Corn-Bread Dumplings, 42
Sausage Apple Squares, 94

CRANBERRIES
Cranberry-Glazed Spareribs, 109
Cranberry-Stuffed Pork Chops, 82
Stuffed Crown Roast of Pork, 69

DIABETIC EXCHANGE RECIPES
(Lower in salt, sugar and fat, and
evaluated for diabetics)
Main Dishes
Apple-Topped Ham Steak, 46
Basil Baked Chops for Two, 72
Citrus Pork Roast, 80
Citrus Pork Skillet, 56
Dijon Pork Chops, 100
Fruited Pork Picante, 53
Garden Pork Skillet, 52
Hawaiian Pizza, 68
Herbed Pork Chops, 97
Perfect Pork Chop Bake, 83
Pork Chop Potato Bake, 67
Pork Chops Deluxe, 45
Potluck Casserole, 85
Rosemary Pork Roast with Vegetables, 68
Sesame Pork Kabobs, 102
Spicy Pork Tenderloin, 80
Sandwiches
Basil Pasta and Ham Salad, 11
BLT Tortillas, 21
Cajun Pork Sandwiches, 7
Curried Ham and Fruit Salad, 12
Luncheon Pasta Salad, 18
Maple Ham Peaches, 19
Party Pitas, 9
Pork 'n' Sweet Potato Salad, 16
Smoked Tenderloin Salad, 11
Smokehouse Quesadillas, 8
Stuffed Ham Slices, 26
Sweet 'n' Sour Pockets, 27
Tasty Pork Nuggets, 8
Tender Pork Sandwiches, 22
Turnips, Taters and Ham, 13
Warm Fajita Salad, 16
Soups & Stews
Canadian Cheese Soup, 33
Hot Pot Stew, 43
Lima Bean Sunshine Stew, 35
Pork and Pasta Stew, 34
Split Pea and Ham Soup, 42
Surprise Clam Chowder, 39

DUMPLINGS
Dublin Dumpling Stew, 36
Paprika Pork with Dumplings, 51
Pork Stew with Corn-Bread Dumplings, 42

EGG DISHES
Bacon Breakfast Sandwiches, 29
Deviled Ham and Egg Appetizer, 9
Dilly Ham and Eggs, 91
Ham 'n' Cheese Strata, 91
Ham 'n' Onion Frittata, 79
Ham Fried Rice, 61
Ham Souffle, 95
Humpty-Dumpty Sandwich Loaf, 27
Individual Brunch Casseroles, 90
Sausage and Potato Pie, 86
Sausage, Hominy and Egg Brunch, 90
South-of-the-Border Quiche, 94
Southwestern Eggs, 88
Spinach and Sausage Pie, 88

Tex-Mex Eggs, 90
Zesty Breakfast Burritos, 59

FRUITS (also see specific kinds)
Apricot Pork Loin, 76
Citrus Pork Roast, 80
Curried Ham and Fruit Salad, 12
Honey-Lime Ham, 106
Lemon Pork Steaks, 98
Okanagan Pork Stew, 38
Plum-Barbecued Spareribs, 102
Pork Chops with Sauteed Plums, 57

GROUND PORK
Appetizers
Ham Balls, 7
Sandwiches
Meaty Mexican Sandwiches, 26
South-of-the-Border Submarine, 24
Chili & Stew
Cauliflower Pork Stew, 39
Sweet 'n' Snappy Chili, 34
Main Dishes
Barbecued Meatballs, 70
Ham Balls with Mustard Dill Sauce, 47
Holiday Ham Ring, 69
Homemade Pork Sausage, 59
Hungarian Pork Loaf, 70
Italian Cabbage and Rice, 60
Pantry Pork Dish, 85
Pork and Cabbage Rolls, 72
Pork Lo Mein, 60
Pork Patties Oriental, 54
Pork-Stuffed Eggplant, 73
Shepherd's Pie, 85
Zesty Breakfast Burritos, 59

HAM
Appetizers
Deviled Ham and Egg Appetizer, 9
Ham 'n' Cheese Puffs, 9
Ham Balls, 7
Party Pitas, 9
Smokehouse Quesadillas, 8
Super Ham Spread, 7
Main Dishes
Apple-Topped Ham Steak, 46
Church-Supper Ham Loaf, 82
Cordon Bleu Pork Chops, 98
Creamed Ham 'n' Cornmeal Cakes, 59
Creamy Ham Fettucini, 50
Dilly Ham and Eggs, 91
Easy Ham Hash, 95
Ham and Broccoli Divan, 45
Ham and Broccoli Supper, 94
Ham 'n' Cheese Strata, 91
Ham 'n' Onion Frittata, 79
Ham and Spinach Rolls, 77
Ham 'n' Swiss Ring, 67
Ham Balls with Mustard Dill Sauce, 47
Ham Fried Rice, 61
Ham Hot Dish, 90
Ham Loaf Pie, 73
Ham Rolls Continental, 86
Ham Souffle, 95
Ham Steak with Potatoes and Onions, 54
Ham-Noodle Bake, 87
Hawaiian Pizza, 68
Holiday Ham Ring, 69

Honey-Lime Ham, 106
Jambalaya, 57
Macaroni and Cheese Deluxe, 94
Meaty Corn-Bread Squares, 93
Mom's Paella, 50
Mustard-Baked Ham with Gravy, 83
Saucy Ham and Rice, 57
Scalloped Potatoes 'n' Ham, 52
Stuffed Easter Ham, 78
Stuffed Ham Slices, 72
Tangy Glazed Ham, 76
Upside-Down Breakfast, 91
Salads
Basil Pasta and Ham Salad, 11
Crunchy Ham Salad, 11
Curried Ham and Fruit Salad, 12
Ham and Spaghetti Salad, 12
Italian Ham and Cheese Salad, 17
Luncheon Pasta Salad, 18
Side Dishes
Maple Ham Peaches, 19
Potluck Potatoes, 16
Spicy Southern-Style Tomato Cups, 13
Turnips, Taters and Ham, 13
Sandwiches
Coffee House Sandwiches, 27
Curry Cheddar Grill, 30
Ham 'n' Cheese Melts, 24
Ham 'n' Swiss Muffins, 23
Ham and Onion Squares, 26
Ham Wafflewiches, 29
Humpty-Dumpty Sandwich Loaf, 27
Mock Monte Cristos, 23
Nutty Ham and Apple Sandwiches, 21
Pineapple Ham Sandwiches, 21
Rosemary's Ham Reubens, 24
Stuffed Ham Slices, 26
Sweet 'n' Sour Pockets, 27
Tortilla Roll-Ups, 23
Soups
Company's Coming Soup, 38
Confetti Chowder, 43
Creamy Ham and Asparagus Soup, 36
Ham and Chicken Gumbo, 34
Ham and Vegetable Soup, 33
Hearty Ham and Cabbage Chowder, 35
Hearty Ham Borscht, 39
Navy Bean Soup, 38
Split Pea and Ham Soup, 42
Surprise Clam Chowder, 39
Wild Rice and Ham Chowder, 36
Stews
Corn and Ham Stew, 35
Country Ham Stew, 42
Hot Pot Stew, 43
Lima Bean Sunshine Stew, 35

HOMINY
Pork Sausage Hominy, 18
Sausage, Hominy and Egg Brunch, 90

HONEY
Honey-and-Herb Grilled Pork Roast, 109
Honey Citrus Chops, 97
Honey-Lime Ham, 106

MUSHROOMS
Pork Roast with Apple-Mushroom Sauce, 67
Mushroom-Broccoli Stuffed Crown Roast, 76
Sausage-Stuffed Mushrooms, 9

MUSTARD
Dijon Pork Chops, 100
Ham Balls with Mustard Dill Sauce, 47
Mustard-Baked Ham with Gravy, 83
Orange Dijon Pork, 79
Sweet Mustard Chops, 107

NUTS
Nutty Ham and Apple Sandwiches, 21
Pork with Peanuts, 56
Walnut Pork Chops, 69

ONIONS
Ginger Pork Chops with Caramelized Onions, 47
Ham 'n' Onion Frittata, 79
Ham and Onion Squares, 26
Ham Steak with Potatoes and Onions, 54
Roast Pork with Onion Stuffing, 77

ORANGES
Dazzling Marinated Pork Chops, 108
One-Pan Pork a la Orange, 52
Orange Dijon Pork, 79
Orange Pork Roast, 65
Oven-Baked Ribs, 108
Smoked Tenderloin Salad, 11
Spareribs Cantonese, 108
Teriyaki Tangerine Ribs, 107

PASTA & NOODLES
Bacon and Macaroni, 61
Bacon, Cabbage and Noodles, 17
Basil Pasta and Ham Salad, 11
Creamy Ham Fettucini, 50
Ham and Spaghetti Salad, 12
Ham Hot Dish, 90
Ham-Noodle Bake, 87
Italian Ham and Cheese Salad, 17
Luncheon Pasta Salad, 18
Macaroni and Cheese Deluxe, 94
Mexican Manicotti, 87
Mexican Pork and Pasta, 53
Oven-Baked Chop Suey, 94
Pork and Pasta Stew, 34
Pork Lo Mein, 60
Potluck Casserole, 85
Slow-Cooked Spaghetti Sauce, 65

PEACHES
Fruited Pork Picante, 53
Maple Ham Peaches, 19
Peachy Pork Steaks, 65

PEARS
Pork Chops with Pear Stuffing, 69
Pork Tenderloin Sandwiches, 29

PEPPERS
Pork Fajitas, 47
Stuffed Banana Peppers, 73
Warm Fajita Salad, 16

PINEAPPLE
Hawaiian Pizza, 68
Hawaiian Ribs, 97
Pineapple Ham Sandwiches, 21
Sweet 'n' Sour Pockets, 27
Sweet-and-Sour Pork, 51
Upside-Down Breakfast, 91

PORK CHOPS

Baked Pork Chops and Apples, 78
Basil Baked Chops for Two, 72
Braised Pork Chops, 51
Breaded Pork Chops, 80
Cajun Chops, 50
Cordon Bleu Pork Chops, 98
Cranberry-Stuffed Pork Chops, 82
Curried Pork Chops, 56
Dazzling Marinated Pork Chops, 108
Dijon Pork Chops, 100
Ginger Pork Chops with Caramelized
 Onions, 47
Grilled Pork Chops with Maple Butter, 100
Grilled Stuffed Pork Chops, 98
Herbed Pork Chops, 97
Honey Citrus Chops, 97
Inside-Out Pork Chops, 61
Marinated Pork Chops, 106
Old-Fashioned Kraut Dinner, 57
Orange Dijon Pork, 79
Paradise Pork Chops, 99
Peppered Pork Chops, 103
Perfect Pork Chop Bake, 83
Pork and Sauerkraut with Potatoes, 64
Pork Chop and Rice Dinner, 79
Pork Chop Potato Bake, 67
Pork Chops and Sweet Potatoes, 73
Pork Chops Deluxe, 45
Pork Chops Parmesan, 53
Pork Chops with Pear Stuffing, 69
Pork Chops with Sauteed Plums, 57
Scalloped Pork Chops, 83
Stuffed Pork Chops, 77
Sweet Mustard Chops, 107
Vegetable Pork Chop Dinner, 76
Walnut Pork Chops, 69

PORK CUBES & STRIPS

Appetizers
 Tasty Pork Nuggets, 8
Main Dishes
 Apple Pork Pie, 86
 Curried Pork and Green Tomatoes, 61
 Garden Pork Skillet, 52
 Greek Pitas, 21
 Green Chili Burritos, 60
 Hot Pork Salad Supreme, 95
 Pork 'n' Potato Skillet, 46
 Pork Chop Suey, 56
 Pork Fajitas, 47
 Pork Potpie, 93
 Pork Souvlakia, 107
 Potluck Casserole, 85
 Tropical Pork Kabobs, 99
Salads & Side Dishes
 Baked Chimichanga Salad, 12
 Pork 'n' Sweet Potato Salad, 16
 Salsa Potatoes and Pork, 18
 Sesame Pork with Cabbage, 19
Soups & Stews
 Country Cassoulet, 64
 Dublin Dumpling Stew, 36
 Hot Pot Stew, 43
 Lumberjack Stew, 41
 Okanagan Pork Stew, 38
 Pork and Pasta Stew, 34
 Pork Chili, 63
 Pork Stew with Corn-Bread
  Dumplings, 42
 Sauerbraten Stew, 33

Southwestern Pork Stew, 43
Southwestern Stew, 64
Sweet Potato Pork Stew, 38

PORK CUTLETS

One-Pan Pork a la Orange, 52
Pork Schnitzel, 50
Pork with Peanuts, 56
Tender Pork Sandwiches, 22

PORK LOIN

Fruited Pork Picante, 53
Sweet-and-Sour Pork, 51
Warm Fajita Salad, 16

PORK STEAKS

Lemon Pork Steaks, 98
Oven-Baked Chop Suey, 94
Paprika Pork with Dumplings, 51
Peachy Pork Steaks, 65
Spanish Pork Steaks, 68
Stovetop Pork Dinner, 54

PORK TENDERLOIN

Cajun Pork Sandwiches, 7
Cilantro Pork Tenderloin, 103
Citrus Pork Skillet, 56
Creamy Pork Tenderloin, 79
Crunchy Baked Pork Tenderloin, 80
Grilled Pork Tenderloin, 106
Mandarin Pork, 97
Maple-Glazed Kabobs, 106
Marinated Spiedis, 22
Mom's Chinese Dish, 46
Peanut Butter Pork with Spicy Dipping
 Sauce, 102
Pork Tenderloin Florentine, 82
Pork Tenderloin Sandwiches, 29
Pork Tenderloin with Raspberry Sauce, 59
Sesame Pork Kabobs, 102
Smoked Tenderloin Salad, 11
Southwestern Stir-Fry, 52
Spicy Pork Tenderloin, 80

POTATOES

Easy Ham Hash, 95
Fantastic Potatoes, 17
Ham Steak with Potatoes and Onions, 54
Italian Potato Casserole, 93
Paprika Pork with Dumplings, 51
Pork 'n' Potato Skillet, 46
Pork and Sauerkraut with Potatoes, 64
Pork Chop Potato Bake, 67
Potato Bacon Chowder, 41
Potluck Potatoes, 16
Salsa Potatoes and Pork, 18
Sausage and Potato Pie, 86
Scalloped Potatoes 'n' Ham, 52
Turnips, Taters and Ham, 13

QUICK & EASY RECIPES

Appetizers
 Braunschweiger Vegetable Dip, 9
 Deviled Ham and Egg Appetizer, 9
 Party Pitas, 9
Main Dishes
 Citrus Pork Skillet, 56
 Creamy Ham Fettucini, 50
 Ham and Broccoli Divan, 45
 Pork 'n' Potato Skillet, 46
 Pork Chops Parmesan, 53

Sausage Stroganoff, 46
Scalloped Potatoes 'n' Ham, 52
Southwestern Stir-Fry, 52
Sweet-and-Sour Pork, 51
Salads & Side Dishes
 Lima Bean Casserole, 16
 Maple Ham Peaches, 19
 Pork Sausage Hominy, 18
 Sausage Bean Delight, 11
 Sesame Pork with Cabbage, 19
 Spicy Southern-Style Tomato Cups, 13
 Spinach Salad with Avocado Dressing, 12
Sandwiches
 Bacon Breakfast Sandwiches, 29
 BLT Tortillas, 21
 Coffee House Sandwiches, 27
 Curry Cheddar Grill, 30
 Ham 'n' Cheese Melts, 24
 Ham and Onion Squares, 26
 Humpty-Dumpty Sandwich Loaf, 27
 Liverwurst Deluxe, 26
 Pork Tenderloin Sandwiches, 29
 Tender Pork Sandwiches, 22
 Tomato-Bacon Rarebit, 31
Soups & Stews
 Ham and Chicken Gumbo, 34
 Country Ham Stew, 42
 Quick Wild Rice Soup, 35

RIBS

Baby Back Ribs
 Barbecued Baby Back Ribs, 106
 Mom's Best Ribs, 100
Country-Style Ribs
 Applesauce-Sauerkraut Spareribs, 109
 Busy-Day Barbecued Ribs, 108
 Country-Style Pork Ribs, 107
 Hawaiian Ribs, 97
 Pork Ribs and Chilies, 98
 Ribs with Caraway Kraut and
  Stuffing Balls, 102
 Slow-Cooked Country Ribs in
  Gravy, 103
 Teriyaki Tangerine Ribs, 107
Spareribs
 Chinese Ribs, 109
 Cranberry-Glazed Spareribs, 109
 Hot 'n' Spicy Spareribs, 99
 Jalapeno Ribs, 103
 Oven-Baked Ribs, 108
 Plum-Barbecued Spareribs, 102
 Slow-Cooker Ribs, 107
 Spareribs Cantonese, 108
 Western Ribs, 100

RICE

Dirty Rice, 18
Ham Fried Rice, 61
Italian Cabbage and Rice, 60
Jambalaya, 57
Mom's Paella, 50
Pork Chop and Rice Dinner, 79
Quick Wild Rice Soup, 35
Saucy Ham and Rice, 57
Sausage Pilaf, 19
Wild Rice and Ham Chowder, 36

ROASTS

Crown Roasts
 Mushroom-Broccoli Stuffed Crown
  Roast, 76

Stuffed Crown Roast of Pork, 69

Loin Roasts
Apricot Pork Loin, 76
Citrus Pork Roast, 80
Herb-Marinated Pork Loin, 108
Herbed Pork Roast, 68
Honey-and-Herb Grilled Pork Roast, 109
Marinated Pork Loin Roast, 72
Old-Fashioned Pork Roast, 77
Pork Roast Provencale, 70
Pork Roast with Apple-Mushroom Sauce, 67
Pork Wellington, 70
Roast Pork with Onion Stuffing, 77
Rosemary Pork Roast with Vegetables, 68
Sunday Pot Roast, 63

Shoulder Roasts
Cajun Pork Roast, 83
Chalupa, 63
Creole-Style Pork Roast, 78
Maltese Stew, 42
Orange Pork Roast, 65
Pork and Corn Barbecue, 31
Pork Carnitas, 64
Porkettas, 24

SALADS
Bacon Broccoli Salad, 12
Baked Chimichanga Salad, 12
Basil Pasta and Ham Salad, 11
Crunchy Ham Salad, 11
Curried Ham and Fruit Salad, 12
Ham and Spaghetti Salad, 12
Italian Ham and Cheese Salad, 17
Luncheon Pasta Salad, 18
Smoked Tenderloin Salad, 11
Spinach Salad with Avocado Dressing, 12
Warm Fajita Salad, 16

SAUSAGE

Appetizers
Braunschweiger Vegetable Dip, 9
Sausage Dip, 8
Sausage-Stuffed Mushrooms, 9

Main Dishes
Apple Scrapple, 60
Apricot Pork Loin, 76
Carry-Along Hot Dogs, 99
Cheesy Bratwurst, 45
Cheesy Zucchini Medley, 87
Church-Supper Ham Loaf, 82
Country Cassoulet, 64
Grilled Stuffed Pork Chops, 98
Italian Potato Casserole, 93
Italian Sausage and Sauerkraut, 78
Jambalaya, 57
Mexican Manicotti, 87
Mexican Pork and Pasta, 53
Mom's Paella, 50
Old-Fashioned Kraut Dinner, 57
Peasant Skillet, 53
Saucy Sausage and Veggies, 95
Sausage and Potato Pie, 86
Sausage and Zucchini, 53
Sausage Apple Roll, 82
Sausage Apple Squares, 94
Sausage-Broccoli Puff Pancake, 88
Sausage Cabbage Bake, 91
Sausage Corn Bake, 86
Sausage Gravy, 45

Sausage, Hominy and Egg Brunch, 90
Sausage Stroganoff, 46
Simple Sausage Ring, 87
Slow-Cooked Spaghetti Sauce, 65
South-of-the-Border Quiche, 94
Southwestern Eggs, 88
Spinach and Sausage Pie, 88
Stuffed Banana Peppers, 73
Tex-Mex Eggs, 90

Side Dishes
Dirty Rice, 18
Lima Bean Casserole, 16
Pork Sausage Hominy, 18
Sausage 'n' Apple Baked Squash, 17
Sausage and Creamed Corn Casserole, 19
Sausage Bean Delight, 11
Sausage Pilaf, 19
Sausage-Stuffed Baked Apples, 18

Sandwiches
Brat Hoagies with Coleslaw, 30
Liverwurst Deluxe, 26
Meat Loaf Sandwiches, 27
Pork and Cabbage Pockets, 23
Pork Pocket Pasties, 29
Saucy Italian Sausage Sandwiches, 31
Sausage 'n' Spinach Pockets, 30
Wiener Wraps, 22
Zesty Italian Loaf, 30

Soups & Stews
Bologna and Sauerkraut Stew, 41
Corn and Ham Stew, 35
Smoked Sausage Stew, 34
Woodcutter's Stew, 39
Zucchini Soup, 41

SOUPS *(also see Chili and Chowder)*
Canadian Cheese Soup, 33
Company's Coming Soup, 38
Creamy Ham and Asparagus Soup, 36
Ham and Chicken Gumbo, 34
Ham and Vegetable Soup, 33
Hearty Ham Borscht, 39
Navy Bean Soup, 38
Quick Wild Rice Soup, 35
Split Pea and Ham Soup, 42
Zucchini Soup, 41

SPINACH
Ham and Spinach Rolls, 77
Pork Tenderloin Florentine, 82
Pork Wellington, 70
Sausage 'n' Spinach Pockets, 30
Spinach and Sausage Pie, 88
Spinach Salad with Avocado Dressing, 12

SQUASH & ZUCCHINI
Cheesy Zucchini Medley, 87
Sausage 'n' Apple Baked Squash, 17
Sausage and Zucchini, 53
Zucchini Soup, 41

STEWS
Bologna and Sauerkraut Stew, 41
Cauliflower Pork Stew, 39
Corn and Ham Stew, 35
Country Ham Stew, 42
Dublin Dumpling Stew, 36
Hot Pot Stew, 43
Lima Bean Sunshine Stew, 35
Lumberjack Stew, 41
Maltese Stew, 42

Okanagan Pork Stew, 38
Pork and Pasta Stew, 34
Pork Stew with Corn-Bread Dumplings, 42
Sauerbraten Stew, 33
Smoked Sausage Stew, 34
Southwestern Pork Stew, 43
Southwestern Stew, 64
Sweet Potato Pork Stew, 38
Woodcutter's Stew, 39

SWEET POTATOES
Pork 'n' Sweet Potato Salad, 16
Pork Chops and Sweet Potatoes, 73
Sweet Potato Pork Stew, 38

TOMATOES
BLT Tortillas, 21
Curried Pork and Green Tomatoes, 61
Salsa Potatoes and Pork, 18
Spicy Southern-Style Tomato Cups, 13
Tomato-Bacon Rarebit, 31

VEGETABLES *(also see specific kinds)*
Basil Baked Chops for Two, 72
Cauliflower Pork Stew, 39
Confetti Chowder, 43
Country Ham Stew, 42
Creamy Ham and Asparagus Soup, 36
Creole-Style Pork Roast, 78
Dublin Dumpling Stew, 36
Garden Pork Skillet, 52
Green Chili Burritos, 60
Ham and Chicken Gumbo, 34
Ham and Vegetable Soup, 33
Hearty Ham Borscht, 39
Herbed Pork Roast, 68
Hot Pot Stew, 43
Lumberjack Stew, 41
Maltese Stew, 42
Maple-Glazed Kabobs, 106
Oven-Baked Chop Suey, 94
Pantry Pork Dish, 85
Peasant Skillet, 53
Perfect Pork Chop Bake, 83
Pork and Pasta Stew, 34
Pork Chop Suey, 56
Pork Lo Mein, 60
Pork Patties Oriental, 54
Pork Pocket Pasties, 29
Pork Potpie, 93
Pork Ribs and Chilies, 98
Pork-Stuffed Eggplant, 73
Rosemary Pork Roast with Vegetables, 68
Saucy Sausage and Veggies, 95
Scalloped Pork Chops, 83
Shepherd's Pie, 85
Smoked Sausage Stew, 34
Southwestern Pork Stew, 43
Southwestern Stew, 64
Southwestern Stir-Fry, 52
Spanish Pork Steaks, 68
Spinach Salad with Avocado Dressing, 12
Split Pea and Ham Soup, 42
Stovetop Pork Dinner, 54
Stuffed Ham Slices, 72
Tortilla Roll-Ups, 23
Tropical Pork Kabobs, 99
Turnips, Taters and Ham, 13
Vegetable Pork Chop Dinner, 76
Woodcutter's Stew, 39

If You Like *Country Pork*, You'll *Love* Our Other Best-Selling Cookbooks!

Every single one offers up easy-to-make, family-pleasing dishes from hundreds of recipes shared by good country cooks just like you.

Country Ground Beef is stuffed with some 300 never-before-published recipes for the country's favorite meat that are big on taste, short on effort and economical besides. Many of the dishes are shown in full color so you can see what they'll look like before you make them. Hardcover, 100 pages, 8-3/8" x 11-1/8". **24157**

Grandma's Great Desserts gathers some 300 desserts for such recipes as "Apple Fritters", "Date Nut Torte", "Eggnog Pound Cake" and "Chocolate Shoppe Pie". If you've ever wondered why Grandma's desserts were so unbelievably delicious, this cookbook shows you! Hardcover, 100 pages, full color, 8-3/8" x 11-1/8". **24226**

Cookin' Up Country Breakfasts includes some 300 new breakfast ideas with such chapters as Oven Dishes... Skillet Specialties...Pancakes, Waffles & French Toast...Breads & Spreads... Magnificent Muffins...Satisfying Cereals...Fruits & Beverages...even Breakfasts for Kids. Hardcover, 100 pages, full color, 8-3/8" x 11-1/8". **24159**

Bountiful Harvest puts the homegrown goodness of your garden—or the local farmer's market—to hundreds of new uses! Every chapter "stars" a different country-fresh fruit or vegetable in dozens of mouth-watering main dishes ...tempting side dishes and salads... soups—you name it. Hardcover, 100 pages, full color, 8-3/8" x 11-1/8". **24158**

Home-Style Soups, Salads and Sandwiches contains a wide assortment of meals (some 300!) on the lighter side, including mouth-watering hot and cold sandwiches...main-dish and side salads ...and the tastiest assortment of soups, chowders and chilis you'll likely ever eat. Hardcover, 116 pages, full color, 8-3/8" x 11-1/8". **20382**

Country Chicken is guaranteed to bring delight to your family's dinner table—especially if your family loves chicken, but not the monotony of "the same old thing" prepared "the same old ways". This book overflows with some 300 of the best family-favorite recipes you'll ever try. Hardcover, 100 pages, 8-3/8" x 11-1/8". **24227**